My First *Word*

My First Word

By Kathryn McLane

XULON PRESS

Xulon Press
2301 Lucien Way #415
Maitland, FL 32751
407.339.4217

www.xulonpress.com

Unless otherwise indicated, Scripture quotations taken from the King
James Version (KJV) – *public domain.*

Printed in the United States of America

Paperback ISBN-13: 978-1-6322-1384-6
Ebook ISBN-13: 978-1-6322-1385-3

To my Grandmother
Mary Agnes Wilson
September 10, 1892–January 30, 1932

A Climb Up Mt. Wilson

FATHER, AS THOU DOST LEAD ME ALONG THIS STRANGE small path whose end I cannot see, whose sudden turns bewilder, whose steep ascents seem sometimes rough and hard, I know that ever and again when my strength seems failing, you will lead me upward to a sharp curve and some lovely distant vision will burst into view. Looking backward, I will understand more deeply the path I treaded and see the real proportion of the hills that seemed so great.

Lord, if I lose my path and stray by ways cooler or fairer, lead me back onto the narrow dusty trail where you have led others. They have followed you wisely and with devotion up to the great mountain peak rising in majesty.

Father, I thank thee that I do not go alone, that there are others on the trail. Sometimes they call from further on and one is sure the hidden path is there beyond. Sometimes it is only holding to each other that we can bridge the narrow pass, sometimes it is only the friend's hand that keeps our feet from slipping.

The path I keep treads along a precipice, but with the Lord as my guide I do not fear falling. Now and again wider, less rocky trails beckon me to go different ways, some with inviting meadows and streams, but you lead me onward on your path and I follow. Looking back, I find joy for my feet have beaten the trail smoother and clearer for others to follow.

Approaching the mountain top, I see the others who have gone ahead of me. Some are stronger and traveled faster. Some were wiser and did not linger along the way, but with His help I too will reach my goal. At the top we will have a single vision and gaze together in wondering joy toward where the earth and sky unite as one. Father, I thank thee for this life. Amen.

M.A.W. 1917

Rose Dulles Wilson (left) and Mary Agnes Wilson (right), 1904

INTRODUCTION

MARY AGNES WILSON ("AGNES") WAS BORN TO Reverend Samuel Graham Wilson and Annie Rhea Wilson on September 10, 1892, at the Presbyterian Mission in Tabriz, Persia. Her father was the principal of the Boys' School at the mission and devoted his life to the education of Persian children. After living in Persia for sixteen years, Agnes was sent to live with relatives and go to college in America. *My First Word* is based on the handwritten journals she kept from 1909 to 1920 as she navigated hurdles to become a young woman in a strange land.

America in the decade from 1910-1920 was in the midst of political, social, and technological upheaval. The automobile was replacing horse-drawn transportation, silent movies became popular as a source of entertainment, and sightings of the Wright brothers in their flying machines became common. The Victorian corset with its tiny waist gave way to the Edwardian corset with more freedom of movement, and then corsets were suddenly banned due to America's involvement in World War I.

The Federation of Reconciliation, F.O.R., led by Norman Thomas called for social reform. The Student Volunteer Movement called for "Evangelization of the World in this Generation." Margaret Sanger fought for birth control. Women continued to fight, as they had for the past fifty years, for women's suffrage and eventually won.

In the summer of 1914, the "Great War" erupted in Europe. Women sought increasing representation in government and decisions on peace terms. The Women's Peace Party was founded by Crystal Eastman and led by Jane Addams. Wilson declared war on Germany in April 1918 and the government passed the Sedition Act, which made it a crime to speak against the war effort. The Act was also used to suppress socialist reform groups.

Agnes was stimulated and persuaded by many of these influences, and it made her a politically and socially conscious woman, like so many others of her time. Her story is not her own. It represents an era of civil involvement in political and social policy that is rare in American history.

Agnes's story is timely, with the 100th anniversary of World War I, the 1918 influenza pandemic, and the Congressional approval of the Nineteenth Amendment. The Armenian Genocide that occurred during World War I was only formally recognized by the United States Congress in 2019. Agnes and her family were committed to the Armenian Relief Effort and sacrificed for that cause.

After the last chapter, a list of the members of Agnes's family and short biographical information for the main characters are included.

Left: Rev. Samuel Graham Wilson, 1904
Right: Annie Rhea Wilson, 1904

Chapter 1

PRESBYTERIAN MISSION, TABRIZ, PERSIA, 1909

SITTING AT THE TOP OF THE STAIRS, I CAREFULLY removed my shoes and tiptoed down the steps, hoping none would creak. Mother was practicing hymns on the piano in the parlor and singing loudly, and I slipped past the door without her noticing me. Rose, my younger sister, was outside tending the children, and I could hear their shrill laughter in the garden as they picked flowers. Once past the dining room, I poked my head into the kitchen. Kizbus, our Persian cook, and Mousa, our doorkeeper and general factotum, were gone, likely at the bazaar, shopping for that night's supper. When I reached Father's study, the door was closed, but I could hear Father's and Howard's voices. I pressed my ear against the keyhole.

"Agnes is too young to be married," Father said. "We want her to finish her education in America, even her grandmother went to college. Besides, there is the age difference—you're twenty-four and she's only sixteen."

"Please reconsider, Reverend Wilson," Howard pleaded. "I know Agnes is also fond of me."

"How do you know that?"

"She asked me to kiss her."

"She did what?"

"I must admit her request took me by surprise."

"Good gracious. With all the unrest surrounding Tabriz, with the Persian Revolution knocking at our door, I need to focus my concern on the safety of the mission, not on a child who thinks her life is a romance novel."

"Sir?"

"Howard, my final answer is ..."

A sharp tap on my shoulder startled me, and I turned to see Mother glaring at me. I had been so absorbed by the conversation that I hadn't noticed the music stopped. I didn't hear Mother coming down the hall.

"Agnes, what do you think you are doing listening in on your Father?"

"I ..."

Mother stood stiffly with her hands on her hips. "Go up to your room and stay there until supper."

I walked slowly past her and upstairs in my stocking feet, still clenching my shoes.

I quietly closed the door to the room I shared with my sister Rose and flopped back-first on my bed.

"To think of it. Howard asked Father if he could marry me. Not my beautiful sister Rose, but me."

It gave me chills and thrills all over thinking about it. I got up from the bed and picked up a hand mirror from the dresser. A girl with long, light-brown hair in braids and blue-gray eyes stared back. She had a long, stern forehead, shallow cheekbones, and a prominent angular chin, Father's "Wilson chin."

There's nothing strikingly different about my appearance. Apparently, a marriage proposal does not make one suddenly beautiful. But what will happen next? Mother will only withdraw her affection for a few days, sufficient punishment I should think. But Father sounded so angry. Would he forgive me for asking Howard to kiss me?

A coldness spread over my face and neck; my stomach felt like a hollow pit. *What did Father finally say to Howard? I'm not ready to be married.*

Two years earlier, Howard had come to the Presbyterian Mission in Tabriz, Persia. It was a cold night in November 1907 when Father exclaimed at dinner, "There's a new teacher for the Boys' School coming. He's from Princeton and has an eighteen-month teaching assignment from the Presbyterian Board."

"News came that he arrived in Poti last week," Mother added. "We need to greet him with a traditional *peshwaz*. Agnes and Rose, please go with your Father to meet him."

(*peshwaz*, or *pehshwaaz* is Kurdish, meaning "he who receives guests." It is a tradition for a group to ride out to meet travelers.)

"A young man is coming here to be a teacher," I mused. "All of the rest of the teachers are women. This should be interesting."

Kisbuz packed lavash and Kookoo sabzi, an herb omelet, in Father's saddle bag, and we headed out on the broad plain stretching toward Julfa. The mid-November day was cold enough to require a wool jacket, and the wind in our faces turned our cheeks bright red. Rose rode with Father, sitting in the back of his saddle and hugging his waist, while I rode my own horse, RoRo. I was jealous of Rose, remembering the warm, assuring feeling of holding onto Father's strong torso. Father had literally built the mission school with his hands, and his unusually strong physique was the result of lifting bricks.

The horses were frisky, but we kept them reined in, waiting for sight of the caravan. After three hours, Father abruptly stopped and squinted at a speck on the horizon.

"I believe that would be our party," Father hooted. "The race is on."

The horses responded immediately to our prods, and we were off, galloping down the wide dirt road, kicking up a cloud of dust behind us. Father held back at the very end to let me win the race and dismounted quickly, enthusiastically extending his hand to the young man standing next to the wagon. "Reverend Samuel Wilson."

"Howard Baskerville," the young man responded.

Father helped me and my sister down from our horses, introducing us in succession, "Agnes and Rose. We are here to take you to Tabriz and the mission, after a brief snack."

As we sat on the ground and shared the Kookoo sabzi and lavash, Rose and I examined the new teacher, looking down quickly if his head turned toward us. He was medium build and about Father's height, with straight, wispy, reddish-brown hair. He had a stern face with a long forehead, thin light-brown eyebrows, and small recessed eyes that were a pleasant blue color. His nose and chin were distinctly pointed, features that may have been passed on through generations of Baskervilles like our "Wilson chin."

Father monopolized the conversation, talking to Howard about the events in Persia, about the death of the Shah and the new Constitution. He suddenly stopped and looked at the sky. "Say, we only have about four hours of good sunlight left. We're at over four thousand feet above sea level, and the air will cool quickly. Shall we be on our way, young man?"

"We shall," Howard replied smiling widely.

As we rode back toward Tabriz along the wind-swept plateau, mountain ranges surrounded us on all sides, rising one behind the other, bare treeless volcanic rocks of different colors: rusty-red to bright orange, yellow, tan, gray, and often capped with a spray of salty white. Although barren and unappealing in the glare of the midday sun, the hills took on their own mystical beauty in the less harsh light at the end of the day. Mount Sahand, Tabriz's largest mountain, loomed over the city, a mass of purple granite capped with snow.

As we entered the city gates, the roads became crowded with donkeys carrying baskets of fruits and vegetables, building materials, and little barefoot boys. An occasional camel blocked our path, carrying a white-turbaned mullah on top of a deep cushioned saddle. Little boys peeked at us from the flat roofs of one-story mud houses. Women enveloped in chaddar and veil darted through the crowds like ghosts.

"Tabriz is donkeys par excellence," Father shouted at Howard. "I love every crooked street of this city."

When we reached the mission, Father said to Howard, "Come, you will stay in our guest room for the first two months. We will need to teach you Azeri."

"You don't speak Azeri?" I exclaimed.

"Unfortunately, I don't," Howard replied. "The Mission Board made a last-minute decision to send me to Tabriz. I had applied to go to China."

"Then Agnes and I will teach you," Rose said.

"Of course," I mumbled.

Mother called the children downstairs. Bobby and Annie stood at the parlor door and stared with wide blue eyes at Howard, speechless. "Howard will be part of our mission family for the next year and a half," Mother said, then turned to Howard. "This is Annie, she's seven, and Bobby's four. Bobby has been asking for a big brother, so he's happy to see you. I'll take you on a quick tour of the house."

"Such a stunning house," Howard said. "I noticed a charming veranda on the side covered with trailing vines."

"The children play out there all summer. We have beautiful summers as the mountain breezes temper the heat, but our winters are cold and snowy."

Mother led us down the hall from the parlor. "The house is built to accommodate Persian custom. Here at the front of the house is the men's entrance and Samuel's study. His male guests come in and go directly into his study, leaving their shoes at the door. After they've closed the door, I count the number of shoes to determine the number of cups of coffee to bring. Across the hall is the kitchen." As she spoke, a medium-built Armenian woman with large dark eyes came to the kitchen door, smiling widely. "This is Kizbus, our cook and nanny."

"Welcome to our house," Kizbus said, bowing her head slightly.

Mother proceeded down the hall. "The dining room is to the right and the parlor to the left. When we have large social gatherings, we fold back the partitions between the study, parlor, and dining rooms, and create one large room that is big enough for sixty. The piano in the parlor is a much-loved wedding present from Samuel's father and our primary source of entertainment.

"The door next to the stairs is the women's entrance. Upstairs are the bedrooms and washroom. The large upstairs room at the front of the house serves as a Samuel's and my bedroom at night. During the day, it's used as the classroom for the mission children. I call it the school of 'Annie Rhea Wilson' since I'm the primary teacher. More advanced lessons, such as Latin, French, German, and European Literature, are taught by the teachers from the Boys' School in the evenings."

"I could teach a geometry class," Howard offered.

"That would be particularly useful for Agnes, our oldest. She is fifteen and studying to take college entrance exams in two years."

Howard turned me. "I'd be happy to help you study for your exams." *Maybe he will be useful after all.*

"Rose and Agnes share this room, and Annie and Bobby share the one across the hall. This is the guest room. The washroom is next to the stairs."

"I sorely need to use it," Howard said, swiping a line through the dust on his cheek with a finger.

"I see that Samuel and Mousa brought your bags up while I was showing you around. Feel free to freshen up and then join us downstairs for tea." Then, turning toward Rose and me, Mother added, "You two could use some freshening up as well."

After we heard Howard leave the washroom and walk downstairs, Rose and I hurried in to clean our faces and quickly changed our clothes. We knew there would be something special for tea for the new arrival. When we ran down the stairs, we almost ran into Mousa who was carrying the samovar filled with hot tea into the parlor. Kizbus followed him, carrying a silver platter of Persian pastries filling the air with the smell of cinnamon.

"Your European furniture and Persian rugs are beautiful. I didn't know what to expect," Howard said settling into a chair.

"We are civilized, you know," Mother retorted, "but when Persians come to visit, we push the furniture to the walls and sit on the floor."

At dinner that night, the children bombarded Howard with questions.

"Where'd you come from?" Annie asked.

"I was born in North Platte, Nebraska. My family moved to South Dakota before I left for Princeton."

"Father and most of our uncles went to Princeton," Rose said.

"And that's why I accepted this corn husker," Father exclaimed.

"You're a corn husker?" Bobby exclaimed, "I thought you were a teacher."

"We don't have corn in Persia, Bobby, so I decided that Mr. Baskerville would be more useful as a teacher instead," Father said, grinning.

"What will you teach?" I said blandly, tired of the silliness.

"I was a history major at Princeton, so I thought I would teach history to the boys."

Father interjected, "We need to make the most of your brief stay here. You'll teach English and geometry—English, being your language, and math, because it is easier to teach with a weak command of Azeri."

"How many students are there?" Howard asked.

"There are eighty Muslims and one hundred and thirty-five Christian Armenians enrolled in the Boys' School," Father said. "It is curious to call roll, because half of the students have the title Khan followed by the father's title—'Glory of the Court,' 'Pride of the Army' et cetera, et cetera."

"Sam takes a personal interest in each of his students and their development," Mother commented.

"It's hard to explain the incredible degree of satisfaction one receives educating these little Khans," Father said, his eyes tearing up with emotion. "Persian fathers send me letters, pleading to have their sons accepted to my school. They offer to pay me, and I decline, as a missionary."

"Is there a Girls' School?" Howard asked.

"A girls' school was built by the Presbyterian Church a mile away," Mother replied. "Our women teachers give lessons to the Persian girls."

"A school for girls was quite controversial at the time," Father added.

"There has always been resistance to our schools," Mother continued. "The Persian community watched with great interest as Sam dug clay in the yard, baked bricks, and heaved them to build the Boys' School. He sweated with the other Persian workers, shoulder to shoulder. In the end, he won the hearts of the men and women of Tabriz of all faiths—Muslims, Christians, and Jews."

Howard gasped. "I had no idea."

"She gives me too much credit," Father said, "This is what I chose to do with my life. It's my mission to teach Persian boys to be future leaders of their people and teachers of their schools."

"After over twenty years at the Tabriz mission, neither of us would ever choose to have done anything different with our lives," Mother said as she placed her hand on Father's.

"I never want to live anywhere else either," I said.

Father laughed. "Keep in mind that I intend for all of my children to go to college. Since there are no colleges in Persia, you will need to live in America or Europe when that time comes."

"But I'll return," I said, sticking my lower lip out in determination.

"Persia really is our home," Father said to Howard. "Every eight to ten years of service, missionaries are granted a year's furlough in America. After a month there I'm aching to return here. This is my life."

After dinner we retired to the parlor, where Father read verses from the Bible. After about a half hour, Mother nudged Father gently. He looked up and Mother pointed toward the chair where Howard sat, slumped over and sound asleep. "Samuel, could you take the young man upstairs? I would say that we are finished for the night."

As we ate breakfast in the dining room the next morning, we could hear Father bellowing and knocking loudly on Howard's door. "Up young man. We've a full day today."

"How old is Howard?" I asked.

"I think he's twenty-three from the birthdate I remember on his application," Mother replied.

"But how is he to get along here, let alone teach the students, if he cannot speak Azeri?"

"You learned Azeri before English from your nanny, Kizbus. When your father and I came here we also needed to quickly learn Azeri out of necessity."

As we spoke, Howard descended the stairs wearing the same clothes he had traveled in the day before. His straight, reddish-brown hair was disheveled, with a few clumps sticking up in the back. He looked quite bewildered. "I was not sure where I was when I awoke."

"After you eat your breakfast, I'll take you for a tour of the mission," Father said.

Rose and I tagged along behind Father and Howard as they walked outside.

"The importance of education was drilled into me by my father when I was growing up in Indiana, Pennsylvania," Father said. "When

I came to Tabriz in 1880, there was only a two-room Boys' School. We built the new mission in 1890 with the donation of ten thousand dollars Annie's mother worked to secure. Providing schools for Persian boys and girls has been my top priority as a missionary."

"Yesterday, when we arrived at sunset, I didn't realize how expansive the mission compound was," Howard said.

"The mission was once a large abandoned Muslim estate, with several houses, stables, a large garden filled with roses, and an orchard with apricot, citrus, and walnuts trees. The building that is now the dormitory was a distillery for manufacturing spirits from raisins that was never used. First, we built the new Boys' School and the large house where the family lives. Then we built the hospital, church, and cemetery to the west."

Howard pointed to a long, single-story building with several doors. "What's that building?"

"It was the secluded residence of the harem. It was remodeled for lodging for the teachers and their families. There are four mission families here, the Pittmans, the Wrights, the Vannemans, and our family. We also have four single teachers, all women, and our medical doctor, Dr. Mary Bradford."

As we walked toward the Boys' School, a young boy ran up to Father and tugged at his sleeve. "Reverend Wilson," he shouted, "a boy has stolen my books."

"Which boy stole your books, Mizra?" Father asked.

"Hedar. He took my books to the bazaar and sold them to a merchant."

"Wait here." Father turned abruptly and marched into the Boys' dormitory. When he emerged, he was pulling a boy alongside him by the arm and walking so swiftly that the boy was being dragged off his feet.

"So what do you have to say, Hedar?" Father shouted at the boy, releasing his arm as though throwing it in disdain.

"I need money for my mother," Hedar said. "She is sleeping in the streets. She has no money and nothing to eat."

"Why didn't you send her to the mission? You know we would care for her."

"I don't know where Mother is. Her sister came to me secretly, asking me to find something to sell so she could give Mother money for food."

"And why is your mother living on the streets and not at home?"

"My father became angry and said he divorced her."

"I'll send for your father and meet with him today. Rose, run and tell Mousa to find Hedar's mother and bring her here. Mrs. Wilson will counsel her."

After Rose ran to the house, Father said to Hedar, "Go to the chapel and pray for forgiveness for stealing." Father shook his head as we continued toward the school. "A man can annul his marriage by simply saying 'divorce' three times. We'll go to the bazaar and look for the books after I show you the Boys' School."

Father whispered as we walked down the halls with classes in session. "The school has six classrooms, one for each grade. In addition, there's a chapel and a library on the first floor."

"Do you require the students to attend chapel?" Howard asked.

"Yes, but I emphasize the passages in the Bible that have ethical significance and apply to real life. Since Muslims are quite accepting of Jesus as a prophet, I refrain from referring to Christ as the son of God."

"Who comes to the regular church services?"

"Christian Armenians, Jews, and Muslims. Whoever is interested is welcome. Reverend Pittman and I deliver sermons in church, one in English for the Europeans and one in Azeri for the Persians. I also offer private religious counsel to men of all faiths. Annie is also sought after for religious and social counsel. She's saved many from divorce. Persian women come to the house escorted by Mousa, or Annie goes to their home. She is so busy that she can rarely attend Sunday church service at the mission."

"Do you get along with the Muslims?"

"The mission provides medical care and education to whoever wants to come, regardless of faith. For this reason, most Muslims respect missionaries. Annie and I have a number of close Muslim friends. One of the mullahs comes to visit me every week to debate verses in the Bible. For instance, last week he asked me, 'And at the wedding of Cana, when Jesus turned the water to wine, what type of wine was it?' and I answered, 'Oh, I suppose the same wine as the one Mohammed says flows like a river through the streets of Paradise.' He was quite amused. I thoroughly enjoy religious debate of this sort."

The central bazaar was a huge brick structure with vaulted ceilings and halls lined with thousands of store fronts ten feet wide on either side. The merchants were selling jewelry, clothes, textiles, prints, glass, china, vases, rugs, leather, and maps. Father headed toward the section of the bazaar where they sold maps and books. "Whoever spots the stolen books first wins the hunt," he said.

I darted about, looking between people crowded around the merchandise and spotted a sign saying 'English books' in Azeri.

I tugged on Father's shirtsleeve and whispered, "Over here, Father."

As Father approached the shop, the vendor's eyes grew large and he put his hand on the handle of a sword he wore in his belt. "I only want to take the schoolbooks," Father said to him in Azeri and held a toman in his outstretched hand. The merchant smiled and took it.

As Father tucked the books under one arm, he turned to me, smiling. "Agnes, you won the hunt for the books. What would you like as a reward?"

"To go up the Arg," I answered.

Father led the way to the Arg, a set of one-hundred-foot-tall stone arches in the middle of Tabriz. "You've likely seen this from the mission, Howard, and wondered what it was," Father said. "The Arg is the remnants of a citadel built in the early 1300s but was never completed after the roof of the mausoleum collapsed during construction."

As we climbed the stairs to the top of the Arg, Howard was breathing heavily.

"The view is our reward," I said as I twirled around on my toes, taking in the three-hundred-and-sixty-degree view of the city and the mountains to the east and the west. "It's so beautiful here, I never want to leave."

"Far to the west are the Zagoros Mountains that separate Persia from Turkey," Father said. "That shining silver streak on the horizon is Lake Urmia. Closer to us is Mount Sahand where we take the children camping." Father turned to the north and pointed down toward the city. "The bridge over the large river, Aji Chay, was part of the Silk Road connecting the Orient with Turkey and Russia. Biblical clues place Tabriz at the gates of Paradise, and the Aji Chay flowed out of the Garden of Eden." Father then turned to the southeast. "There you can see the mission compound nestled between the Armenian and Muslim sections."

We descended the steps and proceeded down the street, passing the American Consulate building, with its American flag waving in the breeze. "The American consulate is William Doty. We often invite him for dinner. I disapprove of his drinking publicly, but otherwise we are good friends."

"Drinking publicly is frowned on?" Howard asked.

"Of course, it is. The population of Tabriz is primarily Muslim and to deserve their respect, the entire mission abstains. I should let you know that my brother, Robert Wilson, is a professor at Princeton, and he told me your classmates nicknamed you 'Baccus.' So behave yourself."

"I will, sir."

"And you'll want to. They have a retched spirit called arak that they distill from raisins, a veritable fire water."

As we walked back, Howard asked, "Who is the ruler of Persia? You were speaking of the Shah's death yesterday."

"Mohammed Ali Shah," Father retorted. "Muzaffar-ad-Din, his father, died last year right after signing Persia's new Constitution. It allowed the people to have a representative Parliament. As the new ruler, his son swore on the Qur'an that he would preserve the Constitution and the newly formed Parliament, but the rumor is that he seeks to do away with both. He enlisted Russian officers to drill his troops and purchased cannons from them."

"Why would Russia want to be involved with Persia?"

"For many years, Russia and England have competed for influence over Persia. Last year they officially divided Persia into 'regions of influence.' England took the southern Persian provinces and Russia took the north. A cartoon in the October issue of *Punch, The London Chariavri,* satirized it, showing a British lion and a Russian bear playing with the tail and head of a terrified Persian cat. The cat was saying, 'I don't remember being consulted about this.' The Shah wasn't consulted about the 'regions of influence' either."

"Politics have never interested me," Howard said.

"Young man, not having a political bent is an asset here. All of us at the mission need to stay neutral regarding Persian political affairs. We must obey the Persian-American Friendship Treaty of 1856 or the government can tell us to leave."

"You needn't worry. I'm already confused by Persian politics."

Later that afternoon, when we came to the parlor for tea, Mother looked up from her knitting and whispered, "Hedar's father came to speak with Father. They've been talking in Father's study for over an hour. It's a good sign."

And it was, for a few minutes later Father entered the room with a smile on his face and said, "Annie, could you bring Hedar's mother here. Her husband is ready to take her home."

We looked at each other and smiled.

"Healing hearts is what you do best, Sam," Mother murmured.

After Howard moved to the Boys' School dormitory, he came to the house two evenings a week and held a special geometry class, which Aimee and Dorothy Vanneman, and Rose and I attended. Howard was an energetic teacher and tried to inject some humor into the subject. One evening when he told a bad joke and smiled, I realized that I suddenly found him attractive.

After that revelation, I carefully prepared difficult questions to ask Howard during class, and as he answered, I looked deep into his eyes, pretending to be enthralled by his explanation. If I wasn't mistaken, his cheeks became pink as he spoke.

Rose caught on to my flirtations and while preparing for bed one night she said, "Your flirting with Howard is becoming quite annoying. If you don't stop, I'll tell Mother and Father." Reluctantly, I ceased my flirtatious game with Howard during our geometry class, but I was determined to find another way to continue to get his attention. For the next days, I watched Howard's comings and goings from the Boys' School and soon learned his schedule. Every day when there was a good chance of seeing him, I found a reason to walk across the mission compound. More frequently than not we 'accidently' met. I smiled sweetly and said, "Good day, Mr. Baskerville," looking admiringly into his eyes.

"Good day, Miss Wilson," Howard would respond and smile. "Out for a stroll?"

"Out on an errand for Mother."

"How sweet you are to help her."

And so our 'romance' continued, but in my eye, quite unsatisfactorily.

One summer evening over dinner, Howard asked Father, "Reverend Wilson, could I take Rose and Agnes horseback riding in the hills beyond the city?"

"That's a fine idea," Father replied. "I'm often too busy. They should go riding more often."

That summer and fall, Rose and I went riding with Howard every weekend. Then one Saturday in early November, Rose was sick. "I shouldn't go with this bad cold," she said.

I smiled to myself. This was my chance to be alone with Howard.

Howard was leading his horse on a gentle cantor when I cracked my whip and my horse went racing by him. Howard quickly joined in the chase and we raced around, laughing. When we got back to the mission, I deliberately led my horse behind the Boys' School and dismounted.

Howard came up from behind, "Where are you going?"

"I wanted to ask you a question."

Howard looked at me quizzically and dismounted. "What is it?"

"Do you have a girl in America that you plan to go back to when your teaching position ends in May?"

"No. Why do you ask?"

"While we were riding it occurred to me that I'd like you to kiss me. I'm sixteen and I've never been kissed."

Howard seemed surprised and reluctant. "I'm not sure I should be the first man to kiss you."

"Please, I don't want to go to America and tell the other girls I've never been kissed."

"Very well, I'll kiss you then." Howard bent toward me and pressed his soft, wet lips on my cheek.

And that's how it happened, my "first kiss." I had expected a rush of emotion, or at least a tingling sensation, but there was nothing. Father's kisses were soft and dry, and his mustache tickled my cheek and made me laugh. Howard's kiss was mushy and wet, and it made me want to wash my face, which I did as soon as I returned home.

Yes, my first kiss was a disappointment, but I felt proud. I was sixteen and I could say that I had been kissed by a young man. My cousin Anna in America wrote me letters every week and bragged that her boyfriend Jack had kissed her. Now I could write to her about Howard and my first kiss.

Howard was so easily won over by my flirtations. He had fallen for my little game like a puppet, and I felt like a masterful puppeteer. *I'll be able to win over any man I want, won't I?*

Wilson House, Tabriz, 1908

Tabriz Arg, 1908

Chapter 2

THE PERSIAN REVOLUTION, 1908

ON JUNE 23, MOHAMMED ALI SHAH ORDERED HIS Russian-trained soldiers to fire their cannons on the Parliament building in Tehran, initiating the Persian Revolution. Fighting burst into full force between the Royalists, supporters of the Shah and his autocratic regime, and the Nationalists, supporters of the Constitution, the Parliament, and a representative government. The Shah censored newspapers that published anti-Royalist commentaries. He ordered Nationalist leaders arrested and hanged, and he brutally suppressed uprisings in the provinces.

Mizra Husayn Sharifzadeh, a teacher at the mission school, was Howard's friend and translator. As one of the Nationalist leaders, Mizra was assassinated by the Royalists and Howard was deeply affected by this unexpected loss. When I saw Howard cry for his Persian friend, I realized what a passionate man he was, and my heart softened toward him.

As I came downstairs, I overheard Father speaking to Mother in the parlor. "It would be good for Howard's spirits if I took him with me to Urmia. The four-day ride will help to clear his head."

"It's a good idea," Mother replied. "I'm happy that you aren't going alone. You never know where fighting will erupt next."

I burst in, wailing, "Please don't go, Father. What if they start fighting here?"

"I'll hear if the Shah's Royalist army is moving toward Tabriz. I can be back in two days."

Two weeks after Father and Howard left Tabriz, the Nationalists dragged a cannon to the top of the Arg and started firing toward a sector where Royalists were camped. Fortunately, it was in the opposite direction from the mission.

"The way they keep firing that thing day and night rattles my nerves," Mother complained. Annie and Bobby crawled into bed with Mother and huddled together. Mousa bravely guarded the front door all night, holding a kitchen knife.

"I'm terrified," Rose whispered from her bed next to mine. "I wish Father was here."

After two days without sleep, we were finally so tired that we slept through the sound of constant gunfire, the cannon echoing through the hills and the trumpets calling the men together. Everyone was too afraid to go out during the day and the mission yard was empty and ghostly.

Finally, word by caravan reached Father and Howard in Urmia and they hurried home. When Mousa announced their horses had arrived at the mission, I ran to hug Father.

"We were scared for your safety," Father said stroking my hair. "We came as fast as we could."

"The fighting has spread to the bazaar district in Tabriz," Howard said. "Many streets are barricaded, and merchants have closed their shops."

"The Shah's horsemen have pillaged the villages outside of the city and laid them to waste," Father added, "and the new stores at the upper bridge were looted and burnt."

"What shall we do?" Mother asked. "Should we prepare to flee to Russia?"

"Many of the Persian intellectuals and teachers have already fled there," Father responded, "but the consuls say Americans and Europeans are safe as long as they stay out of perilous districts where fighting is active."

"Children, you must stay in the compound until the fighting is over," Mother said.

"Can't we ride horses in the hills beyond Tabriz?" I asked.

"If you did that you would surely be shot," Father retorted. "Don't you understand how serious the situation is? You must stay in the compound."

"Very well," I moaned. "The Persians won't hurt foreigners. I don't understand why we have to isolate ourselves."

In August, Rose and I visited Aimee and Dorothy Vanneman while the adults in the compound attended a monthly mission meeting at the Boys' School. We were playing a card game in the parlor when we heard fierce musketry firing coming from the next district.

"That's close by," Rose said. "Maybe we should go to the cellar." As she said this, bullets started pelting the side of the house. We instinctively sunk to the floor on our bellies.

"What should we do?" Dorothy screamed.

"Let's crawl to the kitchen and hide next to the stove," Aimee whispered. As we started to crawl toward the door, a bullet came through the windowsill and lodged in the back of the chair where I had been sitting. Every muscle in my body froze and a cold chill spread down my neck and back.

"Move," Rose screamed from the hallway. "Move to the kitchen, as fast as you can." I clambered as quickly as I could, reaching the kitchen with my knees and hands scraped and bleeding. We sat silently holding onto each other, listening. After the firing ceased, we heard the front door open. Dr. Vanneman and Father found us huddled together in the kitchen.

"A bullet came through the window," I blurted out.

"One bullet came through a window at the Boys' School as well," Father said. "There are shell casings all over the mission yard. We're lucky no one at the mission was hurt."

"Where's Mother?" I asked.

"She's in the house with Annie and Bobby. I'm here to take you home. When you're ready we will run there together." Rose and I held onto Father's arms and ran, and I never felt so relieved as I did when I was in our house and in Mother's arms.

A week later the family was sitting in the parlor when William Doty, the American consul, burst through the door. "The Shah sent a message that his army will shell the city without regard to the lives or property of foreigners," he shouted. "He gave us forty-eight minutes to seek shelter."

"I'll run and tell the others in the mission," Father responded.

We sat on bags of flour in the cellar, squeezed between rounds of cheese and jugs of milk, listening anxiously to the loud blasts.

"Will our house be destroyed?" I asked.

"Let's hold hands and pray," Father said. We closed our eyes and held hands. The human touch brought us together as one, and I imagined each missionary family in the compound doing the same.

Toward nightfall, the shelling stopped. "I'll go out and check outside," Father said. "Wait here."

When he returned, he appeared bewildered. "With all the noise of the shelling I thought that there wouldn't be a house left, but by God's mercy nothing in the mission appears to have been touched."

The next day there were white flags all over the city, and Tabriz was about to surrender to the Shah's army. Suddenly, Satter Khan and his Nationalist horsemen valiantly road into the city, tore down the white flags and drove away the Royalist troops.

"The people of Tabriz stood up to the best and the strongest that the Shah could send against them and maintained the cause for liberty," Father said. "But the Shah's armies were not defeated. They will return."

"Nothing but hunger can conquer the people of Tabriz now," Mother said.

"But winter in Tabriz will be one of great poverty and suffering, with food supplies so low," Father said.

"We made it through the fighting, now will we starve?" Rose asked.

The mission and people of Tabriz made frantic efforts to lay in stores of wheat in their cellars. With roads from the east still blocked by Royalist soldiers, only a two-month supply of food reached the city. At the end of January, the Shah's cavalry returned and surrounded Tabriz again, immediately and completely cutting off outside sources of food and fuel for the winter. Incoming and outgoing mail was seized and destroyed, and telegraph lines severed. We were cut off from all communication with the outside world.

March arrived. The snows melted early, and pink and white almond blossoms covered the trees. On a Saturday morning I sat in the parlor with Mother, Father, and Howard fidgeting. "I'm anxious to go outside for a walk," I said. "Wouldn't it be safe to go to the bazaar with Mousa?"

"There haven't been any food riots in the bazaars for weeks," Mother said. "It should be alright, don't you agree, Sam?"

"You should be safe going to the bazaar with Mousa," Father said.

"I can take her," Howard interjected. "I've wanted to go to the bazaar for several months. It would be good to go outside."

"Very well," Father replied, "but come back right away if you see soldiers or if there are crowds protesting for food."

Howard and I shuffled along the cobbled road leading to the central part of Tabriz. "I want to buy a gift for my Grandmother Wilson's birthday," I said. "She will be seventy-five on May eighth. I'm looking for Kalamar."

"What's Kalamar?" Howard asked.

"It's a traditional Persian hand-printed textile with lovely geometric patterns and brilliant colors."

When I found the merchant's shop and was about to enter, Howard said, "I'll be next door at the jewelry shop."

"What? After what Father said you're leaving me in the bazaar unescorted?" I muttered under my breath. After hastily making my purchase, I was relieved to find Howard waiting outside the shop. "Let's return to the mission," I said. "I feel uncomfortable here."

Once we were on the empty dirt road leading back to the mission, I heaved a sigh of relief. "I accomplished my mission without confronting a food riot," I said.

Howard suddenly stopped and turned to me, saying, "Stop here a minute. I have something for you." He put his hand in his pocket. "Close your eyes and hold out your hand."

I obliged and felt his fingers gently touch my hand as he laid what felt like a stone in the center of my palm.

"Now open your eyes," he whispered.

When I opened my eyes, I found Howard standing close to me and a chill ran down my spine as my eyes met his. I looked down to examine what he'd placed in my hand. It was a handsome ring, obviously old, with a red-speckled green stone engraved with an animal of some sort on its face.

"It's an antique, a man's signet. The gentleman who owned it would have worn it on his little finger, but it should fit your ring finger."

I slipped it on my finger. "Yes, it fits perfectly."

"The merchant said it was the most precious piece in his collection. Do you like it?"

"Of course, I do. It's so unique. It must have belonged to a Persian prince or aristocrat."

"It's a token of my love for you. I want you to marry me."

My diaphragm spasmed, and I could barely breathe. *Did he just propose to me? Is that what I heard? He didn't say, "Would you marry me?"*

He said, "I want you to marry me." He seemed to expect me to respond but I didn't know what to say.

"You weren't expecting this were you?" he said, searching my face.

My vision seemed clouded and the sunlight suddenly blinding. "No. This is such a surprise."

"Next fall, I plan to go to the Princeton Seminary, like your Father. I'd like you to go with me as my wife."

"I don't know what to say."

"You need some time to think it over," he said, smiling, looking deep into my eyes. "Let's go home. I'll ask your Father for his permission his afternoon."

Howard held my hand as we walked. My legs felt heavy and my stomach was a tight ball. Finally approaching the mission gate, I shook my hand free and ran into the house. Howard didn't follow me in but came later for lunch at the house. He talked with Father about his students as though nothing had happened. I tried to eat but the lavash stuck to my throat and the grapes did not taste ripe. "I feel ill," I said and excused myself. Lying on my bed, I stared at the ceiling.

I did have a crush on Howard. Don't teenage girls have crushes on their male teachers? Marriage though; that had not occurred to me. How strange things had become. *Marriage? No, I simply do not love him.*

I looked at the Persian ring I had placed on my ring finger, a green stone with red specks mounted in a simple silver setting. How beautiful and precious it was. I looked closer, trying to decipher what had been carved on the face of the stone. It was a strange animal, a bull with wings of an eagle and a human face. *What does it mean?*

I startled when I heard Mousa downstairs announcing Howard's arrival. Father, as usual, was in his study, and I heard him cordially invite Howard in and close the door. *Father, please say it is out of the question. Please, say he's too old for me.*

When I came downstairs for supper, I heard Mother and Father talking in the dining room and stopped in the hallway to listen.

"Howard won't be joining us for supper," Father said, sitting down with a sigh, "I'm afraid we have had a misunderstanding."

"What is it?" Mother asked. "Tell me now before the children come in."

"Howard asked for Agnes's hand in marriage, and I told him, 'No.' "

Mother gasped. "What was Howard thinking? Of course, the poor young man has no women his age here at the mission, but Agnes? You were gentle with him though?"

"Yes, of course. I suspect things will return to normal once he gets over the rejection."

Even though I knew Father would speak to me later about Howard, I felt an unexpected release of tension in my abdomen. *I'm not being married off to Howard. Thank God.*

After dinner, the family retired to the parlor as usual and sang as Mother played the piano. After an hour, Father turned to Rose and me, and he said, "Girls, perhaps you should take Bobby and Annie upstairs and go to bed."

We kissed Mother and Father good night and started up the stairs. Halfway up I stopped and motioned for Rose and the children to continue as I sat down on the stairs. I strained my ears to hear their conversation in the parlor.

"I asked the Pittmans if Howard could take his meals at their house," Father said. "I thought it best to be forthcoming and explain that it is because he is 'paying attention' to Agnes."

"Good," Mother said. "It would be better if he did not come to meals and evening Bible reading here for a few weeks, at least until he comes to his senses."

"This has taken us totally by surprise. How were we blind to this?"

"Looking back over the past four months, I saw that he was becoming closer to Rose and Agnes, but perhaps because of the age difference it seemed that he acted as an older brother to them. I never saw him single Agnes out nor any indication of romance."

"Will you talk to Agnes more and find out what transpired between them?"

I shifted my weight and the stair I was sitting on creaked. Mother and Father stopped talking. In panic, I frantically crawled like a toddler up the stairs and down the hall. Rose, the sweet dear, had left the door to our room ajar, and it did not make a noise as I slipped in and softly closed it behind me. I was safely in bed when Mother and Father came up the stairs.

What were my feelings for Howard anyway? Did I only want to prove to myself that I could win a young man's attention? I only wanted to flirt. I never thought it would result in a proposal. When he said, "I want you to marry me," I should have said "No, it's impossible." That would have been so wonderfully dramatic, like a heroine in a romance novel would say.

The following morning, Father said, "Agnes, your Mother and I would like to speak to you in my study."

I swallowed hard as he closed the door after me.

"Howard told me you asked him to kiss you," he continued. "Why did you ask him to do that?"

"I don't know," I mumbled, looking at the floor and playing with the ring Howard had given to me.

"Well, it gave him the wrong impression," Mother said. "You shouldn't lead men on."

Father put his hand on my shoulder and gently repeated what I had overheard him tell Mother. "Howard asked for my permission to marry you and I told him, 'No.' "

"It was a decision for your best interests," Mother interjected. "You need to complete your education, see the world. Women have their own careers these days and get married later."

Father looked at me quizzically. "You don't seem to care that I said, 'No,' or am I mistaken?"

"I did not want to get married to Howard."

"Why did you ask Howard to kiss you then?" Mother asked.

"Anna wrote me that her boyfriend, Jack, had kissed her. I thought it would be all right."

"Kissing in public is not acceptable here," Father responded.

"Did you think no one would see you and Howard?" Mother asked.

"We have the responsibility to uphold a strong moral reputation as missionaries," Father added. "What your cousin Anna is able to do in America does not apply here."

"I didn't realize ..."

"You didn't realize that your behavior disgraced your Mother and me? Don't you remember the Fifth Commandment, 'Honor thy Father and thy Mother'?"

"Exodus 20:12," I said.

Father huffed with exasperation.

"We had planned on sending you to America next year with Rose and the Vannemans," Mother interjected, "but all of the missionaries have heard about you and Howard. The gossip has damaged your reputation."

"I'm sorry that I disgraced you."

"Fortunately, Mrs. Pittman kindly offered to take you to America with them when they leave for their year's furlough," Mother continued. "If the roads are open, they plan to leave May fifteenth, less than two months from now."

"But I'm not ready to go to America," I said, alarmed at the sudden change of events. "Where will I stay?"

"I wrote to Grandmother Rhea and Grandmother Wilson and arranged for you to stay with them this summer. Consul Doty assured me that my letters got through the lines."

"Let me go with Rose and the Vannemans a year from now."

"You're ready to go to college, and there are no colleges for you to attend here in Persia," Father said. "You'll go to Vassar, where my sisters went to college."

"But, I'm not ready," I protested. "I'm only sixteen."

"I was only fourteen when I went to Princeton," Father responded. "You'll have to study hard for the next four months to pass the entrance exams."

"Your cousin Anna is going to be a freshman at Vassar next fall, and you will be together with someone you know," Mother said. "You won't be alone."

"Is this my punishment for asking Howard to kiss me?"

"No, dear," Mother replied. "This is what is best for you. Tomorrow, we will start to pack your trunk so that you will be able to leave as soon as the roads are open."

On Monday, March 29, as I came downstairs to dinner, I overheard Father and Howard in the dining room talking. "I heard that you met with Satter Kahn yesterday," Father said.

"Yes, sir," Howard replied. "He has accepted me into his army."

Father's voice became loud. "Howard, you cannot be associated with the Nationalists and be a part of the Mission. You are here to act as a teacher and not as a revolutionary."

Howard responded, just as loudly, "I cannot watch calmly from my classroom window the starving inhabitants of the city fighting for their rights. I am an American citizen and proud of it, but I am also a human being and cannot help feeling deep sympathy for the people of this city. The only difference between me and them is my place of birth, and this is not a big difference."

The next day Howard's letter of resignation was delivered to Father by Khachadoor, one of the students at the Boys' school.

"It's Mr. Moore, that Irish correspondent for *The Times of London*," Father muttered. "He joined the Nationalist army a few weeks ago, and now he's convinced Howard to join him." Father immediately responded, asking Howard to reconsider, but Howard was determined to resign.

"Sam, you did what you could," Mother said, shaking her head. "He is in God's hands now."

"I trust that God will bless him and keep him from temptations and from danger seen and unseen," Father said.

"Numbers VI:24-26," I whispered.

After hearing that Howard had joined the Nationalist army, I felt guilty that Howard left the mission. Was it because of me? What will people think of me if something happens to Howard?

I approached Mother, who sat alone in the parlor, sewing. "Mother, where has Howard gone?"

"Howard moved into the house of Satter Khan, the general of the Nationalist army."

"Will we see him again?"

"Why, of course. Father asked him to stop by the house each day and give him an update."

"What will he be doing?"

Mother shook her head. "It pains me. Despite Howard's complete lack of military experience, Satter Khan assigned Howard an army of one hundred and fifty soldiers to drill, some of them his former students."

"But he doesn't speak Azeri. How can he drill soldiers, or even get along outside the mission?"

"Both Howard and Mr. Moore were assigned translators since neither speak Azeri."

"What is drilling?"

"That is a good question. With ammunition in short supply, they won't be firing guns."

"Somehow I feel responsible that he has chosen to leave the mission."

Later at dinner Father said, "I saw Howard teaching his soldiers to march in formation in the government square today. He came rushing over, quite excited to tell me he named his troop the 'Salvation Regiment.'"

"Will they have a parade?" Bobby asked.

"I think they will only be marching in the square. If you'd like to see them, I think it would be safe to have Mousa take you there tomorrow. I'm sure Howard would like to see you."

The next day, Mousa took Annie, Bobby, Rose, and me to the government square to see Howard. He looked energetic and happy to see us, waving as he in marched with his regiment.

"Left face, right face, forward march, hut," Howard called to his soldiers.

Bobby was thrilled with the military display and later used his newly acquired knowledge to lead the other mission children in a march around the mission yard.

"I don't understand how marching helps soldiers train to fight," Rose said.

Mousa returned from the market with an empty basket. "Tabriz has reached its last two-day's supply of wheat," he said. "There are bread riots in the city."

"Go to the American consulate and tell William Doty to send a telegram to the other foreign consuls demanding that they intervene and persuade the Shah to make peace," Father said.

When Mousa returned, he said, "Telegrams were sent, but I spoke with soldiers in the government square. The Nationalist army is impatient and wants to renew fighting on April nineteenth."

"The English and Russian governments will mediate with the Shah," Father replied. "Tell the Nationalists that they should wait. Convince them if you can."

Howard visited Mother and Father in the afternoon. "Mr. Moore will not lead his men," Howard said, "and my soldiers will not go without me. It would be dastardly to desert them now. The only hope for success is for me to lead them in battle."

"Don't be impatient," Father replied. "The Shah will respond to the pleas of the foreign governments."

"Mr. Moore's judgment may be right," Mother added. "You may be recklessly endangering your life and that of your men. Remember, you are not your own, you are God's."

Howard replied, "No, I'm Persia's."

At five o'clock in the morning, a commotion outside the house woke us. Father went to the door and let a weeping boy inside. It was Khachadoor, the schoolboy who took care of Howard's horses and room. I crept to the stairwell to listen. *Why is Khachadoor crying?*

"They were bringing the wounded to the rear, and I did not at first recognize the body until I saw the brown leggings," Khachadoor said. "Howard told me that if he fell, he wished the Wilsons to know at once."

No. Surely Khachadoor is mistaken.

"Take this message to Mr. Doty to send a carriage to bring the body," Father said. "If he wants to go himself, dissuade him. Foreigner's lives have been threatened."

Mother, Rose and I dressed and came downstairs. We waited, distraught with grief and shock. I was cold and numb all over, and my stomach felt as though I had swallowed a rock.

Please let this be a nightmare.

When the carriage arrived, the boys rushed to the gate and carried Howard's body in, sobbing and lamenting. Mousa took Howard up the stairs to Mother's and Father's room and laid him on their bed. "I'll bring Dr. Vanneman," he said.

Maybe he is only unconscious, and his eyes will open when Dr. Vanneman comes.

Mother and Mrs. Vanneman removed Howard's shirt and washed off the blood covering his chest and back. Dr. Vanneman examined him. "There are two bullet holes, one in front and one in back," he said. "A single bullet entered from the back and came out just above his heart, cutting a large artery. He did not suffer; it caused instant death."

Dead? Howard dead? I began to gasp, and tears streamed down my cheeks. *How could this happen?*

Later that morning, Syyed, one of the schoolboys who had followed Howard, brought news of the battle. "Only half of Howard's Salvation Regiment showed up last night. The regiment quickly dwindled to nine or ten boys by the time they decided to fight. Howard stepped away from his small army immediately prior to the fight and knelt by a wall to pray."

"His Gethsemane," Mother gasped. "Like Jesus, when he prayed at the garden wall before his crucifixion."

Syyed continued, "When Howard emerged from behind the wall, a sniper fired a shot. Howard shot back. Then it remained quiet. Howard must have assumed that it was safe. As he turned to motion the remaining soldiers ahead, the sniper shot him in the back."

Father turned toward the window to hide the tears streaming down his cheeks, and I could hear his chest heaving. I rested my head against his back, holding his waist, and let my tears fall on the floor.

Mother and Mrs. Vanneman dressed Howard in his black suit and placed a white carnation in his buttonhole. When they finished and went downstairs, I tiptoed down the hall and opened the door. Howard looked so noble, his firm mouth set in resolution. *My poor Howard.*

His hand lay by his side and I reached for it. I paused to take a breath, and then I touched it. His hand was stiff and cold, so cold. A shiver ran down my spine. I turned and ran out of the room and down the hall to the washroom and vomited.

Bent over the basin, through gasps and sobs, I prayed. "Please, God, bring Howard back. In Kings 17:17-24, Elijah brought a woman's son back to life by praying to God. In John 11:1-44, Jesus brought his friend Lazarus back to life after he was entombed for four days. In Acts 20:7-12, Paul brought Eutychus back to life after he fell out of a window. In Acts 9:36-42, Peter brought kind and generous Tabitha back to life when she became sick and died. Howard did not do this for vain glory. His motives were the pure and lofty. Please, God, let him breathe again."

After the funeral, the situation remained critical. The death of a young American was used by the foreigners in Tabriz to emphasize the gravity of the situation as they pleaded to their governments for help. Not only were their lives in danger, but food supplies in Tabriz were nearly exhausted. People began eating clover and grass to sustain themselves, some dying of starvation in the streets. Finally, the foreign governments responded, demanding that the Shah immediately allow provisions into Tabriz. The Shah responded as requested, but his orders to allow flour into the city were ignored by his soldiers.

"The Shah's army are refusing to let the flour in because they consider the people of Tabriz their rightful prey," Mousa explained. "They plan to pillage the city, murder the men, and rape the women."

"Unfortunately, our only hope is for foreign intervention," Father said.

On April 26, Consul Doty came on an urgent visit. "The Russian Cossacks have crossed the Aras River into Persia," he said. "They are coming to relieve Tabriz from the famine."

"Thank goodness for the Russians," Rose cheered.

Father glared at her. "No, you don't understand. The Russians will allow food to come in and people will be happy at first. Then they'll realize their only chance for democracy is over."

On April 29, the Russian soldiers entered, singing as they marched, and the Shah's army melted away. Not a shot was fired. The roads were opened, and provisions came in. The people of Tabriz ate and rejoiced. They hailed the Russians as saviors.

"I can hardly believe that the three-month siege is over," Mother sighed.

Father put his arm around her shoulders and said, "Annie, it is quiet now and people have food, but another siege has already begun."

Chapter 3

TABRIZ TO ODESSA, MAY 1909

MOTHER MOTIONED TO ME TO GO UPSTAIRS WITH HER. "Let's go to your room. I'd like to talk."

She closed the door behind her and took a deep breath. "I'm concerned about how you are taking Howard's death."

"The thought of that horrible morning, Howard lying dead on your bed, makes me feel sick. I can't get it out of my mind. I somehow feel guilty about Howard's death, as though I could have prevented it."

"Death is not an easy thing to confront. But you heard what Dr. Vanneman said. He died instantly. His sacrifice was not in vain. The people of Tabriz were saved from starvation."

"No, not in vain."

"My only fear is that these events have traumatized you," Mother said. "Are you confused about your romantic attachment to Howard? From what I saw, it was only a school-girl crush. Am I wrong?"

"No, Mother. It was only a school-girl crush."

"Someday you will know what love for a man is," Mother said as she gently touched my shoulder. "Howard was not that man."

"How did you know you loved Father?"

"He was a handsome young missionary, with so much energy and devotion. I admired him immediately. I knew that life with such a sincere and compassionate man would be nothing but happy."

"But how did you know he was the right one?"

"When you find that special man, you don't fall head-over-heels like in the romance novels. It's a more practical reflection on life. You say to yourself, 'Life with this man will allow me to achieve everything I want in life and make me happy.' "

"That doesn't sound very romantic."

Mother laughed. "Promise me you won't let your lofty romantic notions about what love is obscure your practical judgement on the matter."

"I'll try."

"And, are you ready to go to America?"

"When the Russian soldiers came, I realized that I was free to go. But I'll be so lonely without you, Father, Rose, and the children. I already miss this sweet home." I couldn't hold back the tears anymore. Mother came close and held my head to her breast.

"Once you arrive in America, your relatives will take care of you. For the first month you'll be staying with Grandmother Rhea, Uncle Will, and the Dulles children. Then, the rest of the summer, you'll stay with Grandmother Wilson and Father's brothers and sisters. You'll be too busy to be lonely with your four Dulles cousins and fourteen Wilson cousins. Then, in September, Uncle Andy and Aunt Bess will take you and Anna to Vassar."

"When will I see you and the family again?"

"Rose will come to America next year with Aimee and Dorothy Vanneman, and the following year the rest of the family will come on a year's furlough."

"That's a long time to be without you and Father. What if something happens to me?"

"If you ever need someone to help you, there's always my brother Foster in Chicago."

"I'll be lonely without my missionary friends, too."

"You've forgotten that you already have missionary friends in America, the Coans and the Cochrans. Both families live in a large, two-family house in Minneapolis. Joe and Andrew Cochran are going to high school there. The older children will be at college on the East Coast in the fall. Elizabeth Coan is a junior at Wellesley and Frank Coan and Harrison Cochran are juniors at Williams. You can always visit them."

"I'll write to them as soon as I arrive in America. I especially want to see Joe. I haven't seen him for over two years."

"I remember that he was very fond of you as a young boy. Whenever his father visited us from Urmia, he insisted on coming to see you."

I smiled, thinking about seeing my childhood friends from Urmia.

"America won't be so bad, will it?" Mother murmured and planted a kiss on my cheek.

My trunk was packed, and I was leaving the next day with the Pittmans. As I did every night I went to Annie's and Bobby's room and read them a story before they fell asleep. That night it was a chapter from Baum's *The Wonderful Wizard of Oz*. When I finished, they hugged my neck with their little arms. "Don't go, Aggie," Bobby said. "We'll miss you."

"I must go," I replied. "I'm going on an adventure to a different land like Dorothy in *The Wonderful Wizard of Oz*." As I closed their bedroom door behind me, the tears I had been holding back rolled down my cheeks. Rose was fast asleep, and as I lay in my bed across from her watching her rhythmic breathing, tears dripped silently down my face.

My chest heaved in spasms, and I had to try with all my might not to sob and wake her. *How I'll miss you, Rose.*

I lay awake evaluating my situation. There were so many new things to learn in college, and I wanted to go to America, but I felt so unready. My leaving came about so suddenly. I'd feel so lost without Rose, without Mother and Father. I'd miss this sweet home, Annie and Bobby, Kizbus and Mousa. But, I would be with my cousins in America and so many other relatives. I would be able to see my friends from the mission in Urmia, Elizabeth and Frank Coan, and I was anxious to see Joe Cochran again. I finally fell asleep trying to imagine what Joe would look like.

The next morning at dawn the donkey caravan arrived. The driver loaded up my trunk in the back of the wagon and strapped the Pittmans' bags on donkeys. The Pittmans sat in front and I in back with my trunk on the hard, wooden seat. My family followed us in their wagon to the edge of the city, where we said our goodbyes. Father held me close to his chest with his lips pressed on the top of his head. I hugged his strong torso, and we rocked side-to-side for several minutes. I tried to imbed the feeling of his firm hug so I could remember it when I was scared in America.

"Be strong and courageous," Father said. "Do not be frightened, and do not be dismayed, for the Lord your God is with you wherever you go."

"Joshua 1:9," I said.

"My little girl has learned her scriptures well."

I kissed Mother's soft wet cheek and then bent down to kiss the top of Annie's and Bobby's heads. They were each clinging tightly to one of my legs so I could not move.

"Three years until I'll kiss you again," I said. "I'll send you miniature Statues of Liberty when I reach America."

"When will that be?" Annie asked.

"The end of June," Mother said. "It is a long trip by caravan, troika, train, and ship."

Mother, Father, and Rose had tears in their eyes as the caravan pulled away. Annie and Bobby cried loudly and waved frantically.

It was surreal seeing the life I had known for sixteen years fade away in the distance. My family became smaller and fainter, and finally disappeared from sight. The red and orange hills surrounding Tabriz, and the city that I knew and loved so well, vanished from the horizon. Tears welled in my eyes and spilled down my cheeks. I felt so lonely.

Mrs. Pittman turned and saw me crying. "Agnes, dear, it will be all right," she said. "We have a long journey with ample time for you to contemplate the changes ahead."

It took three days to reach Julfa from Tabriz and cross the Aras River into Transcaucasia. Every ten miles we reached a camp of Russian soldiers protecting the road. Before allowing us to pass, they questioned us, pointing their bayonets at our heads. Soldiers singled me out and approached me with leering eyes. Mr. Pittman forced himself between us and said, "Leave her alone. She's only a child."

The first two nights we slept at posthouses, and I barely slept, with thoughts in my head racing. Mother and Father had never discussed when I would come back to Persia and the mission. *Would I?* I took a deep breath and pressed my lips together hard in determination. "I will come back after Vassar," I whispered. "I'll go back with Mother and Father when they return from furlough, the year I graduate."

The third day we reached the Aras River and took the Pullman ferry across, leaving Persia and our caravan behind. Mr. Pittman arranged for troikas to take us from Julfa through the mountains to Tiflis. The troika was drawn by three massive horses and moved with terrifying speed on the rocky road, slowing only as we passed through quaint mountain villages. Swaying back and forth, I held on to the rail in case a sudden jolt sent me flying out. At night, after dismounting, all my joints quivered from the constant shaking along the mountain road all day. My back and legs were sore from sitting and my skin and clothes were caked with dust.

Along our journey, we were accompanied by the ever-present view of snow-capped Mount Ararat. Noah and his ark full of animals finally found ground and landed atop Mount Ararat after drifting in the floods of the Earth for one hundred and fifty days. I didn't fully know where I would land either.

We reached Erivan on a Saturday and took Sunday as a day of rest. A rainstorm plagued us all morning and when the sun broke through the clouds, we caught sight of a double rainbow.

"When the bow is in the clouds, I will look upon it and remember the everlasting covenant between God and every living creature of all flesh that is upon the earth," Mr. Pittman said.

"God's words to Noah," I said. "Genesis 9:16."

"Your father taught you well. Did he ever take you to see Noah's tomb in Nakhejevan?"

"Yes, in 1904 on our return journey from my first furlough in America."

"Nakhejevan means 'he descended first.' It's the village where Noah lived after he came down from Ararat with all of the animals. Legend is that if a worshipper pushes a stone on the ceiling of Noah's tomb and it sticks, that their prayers will be answered. Any luck?"

"No. Mine fell to the floor."

"Most do."

"And if my stone stuck to the roof of Noah's grave now, I'd definitely pray for a bath."

Mrs. Pittman laughed. "Yes, I'd pray for one, too."

We endured three more days by bumpy troika to Tiflis over the foothills and plateau to the Transcaucasian train. As snow-capped Mount Ararat faded in the distance, I strained my eyes for one last glimpse. It brought pangs of sadness as I realized that I was far from home, my family, and my mission friends. As darkness fell, my loneliness swallowed me up, just as the whale had swallowed Jonah.

After ten long days by wagon and troika we finally reached a train, where we could move about and more easily have conversation. The train from Tiflis took all day to reach Poti, traveling through flat, unremarkable scenery.

"Beautiful Transcaucasia," Mr. Pittman muttered three hours into the journey. "I dozed off for an hour and a half, and when I awoke the scenery was the same."

"Charles," said Mrs. Pittman, "it is beautiful in its own way. We will go the bathhouse when we reach Poti. It will feel good to bathe."

"Yes, it will," I said, "My skin sticks to my clothes."

"We will all need to bathe," said Mr. Pittman. "Otherwise we will notice the others' scent. But, Lucille, you always smell like a rose." Mr. Pittman leaned over toward Mrs. Pittman and took a long, rasping inhale through his nose. I giggled.

"Agnes," said Mrs. Pittman, "I suggest that you not encourage his silliness, or it will never end."

The public bath in Poti was divided into men's and women's sections. In the women's bath were fifty or more naked women submerged to their necks in steaming water. They occasionally dunked completely under the surface to wet their hair and faces.

"The water doesn't seem very clean," I whispered to Mrs. Pittman. "I have a distaste for public bathing."

"It will be another ten days before we are in Europe," Mrs. Pittman whispered. "Then we will have real baths but make the most of this opportunity to wash off the dust and grit from our travels."

I hesitated as I waded in, but soon the sensation of removing gritty dust from my skin and hair felt rapturous.

After bathing, we went to the harbor where the ferry was anchored. The Black Sea stretched to the west, a still and foreboding sheet of glass. "The water is a beautiful deep blue. Why do they call it the Black Sea?" I asked.

"The Greeks considered the Black Sea to be inhospitable," Mr. Pittman explained. "Even now ships disappear mysteriously. They are enveloped by a black fog with green sparkles and a churning whirlpool swallows their ship, never to be seen again."

"Charles, really," Mrs. Pittman protested.

"But it's true. The captain and his mates will stay on watch night and day for what they call the 'Whirlpool of Death.'"

Hundreds of frogs were croaking away merrily in the shallow water and on the shore. As we transferred to the ferry by a flat-bottomed boat, a frog leapt onto the boat and a Russian woman started screaming.

"Cheerio, my friend," Mr. Pittman said as he swept it off the boat's gunwale with the back of his hand.

After boarding the ferry, we retired to the dining salon for tea. Mr. Pittman lifted the tablecloth to look underneath. "Just checking for rats," he said, grinning.

"Charles, you are impossible," Mrs. Pittman said, shaking her head.

"But there are rats on these euxine ferries. Agnes's father tells marvelous tales of how they hold carnival at night and nibble passengers' ears."

"Nonsense, Charles. You will scare Agnes."

"But I've heard Father's stories and I don't believe them," I responded. "Besides, I'm not afraid of rats. I've become quite used to them in Tabriz."

The ferry suddenly lurched, spilling tea into the saucers.

"The anchor has been lifted and we are off," Mr. Pittman announced. "We've finished the first leg of our journey, and we're on our way to a new land, a new adventure."

We finished what was left of our tea and joined the gamut of nationalities on the deck. On the top deck were Russians, Turks, Persians, Armenians, Poles, Germans, and Englishmen. Below, in second class, a mixture of Asians sat on their baggage, and women had babies strapped to their backs.

The bow of the boat ploughed through the water as we picked up speed. In the distance we could see the white caps of the Alborz Mountains. Mrs. Pittman squeezed my hand and whispered, "Agnes, wave goodbye. That is your last glimpse of Persia." As we waved, tears came to my eyes. I tried to remember Father's strong hands on my shoulders and Mother's gentle smile.

During the five-day voyage across the Black Sea, I sat on the deck with a book on my lap, intending to study, but more often than not I daydreamed, staring out to sea. I felt far, far away from home, and far, far away from the terrible months that preceded the start of my journey. I wanted to put out of my mind forever all the events surrounding Howard, the kiss, the proposal, his cold body on my parents' bed.

Looking forward was no less distressing. My future was so uncertain. The Vassar entrance examinations might be difficult. If I failed them, I would once more bring disgrace on my family. If I passed, Father would be proud of me and perhaps he would even find a way to forgive me for asking Howard to kiss me. Passing the exams would also be the door to my future.

When I reached America, Uncle Will and Grandmother Rhea would meet me at the dock and take me to the Dulles estate they called "Rosenvik." I had such fond memories of Grandmother and Aunt Sophea's family.

Grandmother Rhea came to Tabriz in 1900, when I was eight years old. Father and I rode out to meet her. It was my first *peshwaz*.

Although Mother said I met Grandmother when I was two, I didn't remember her. *What would she look like?*

Heading west on our horses, Father held his hand up to shade his eyes from the glare of the sun and peered into the distance at a tiny speck on the road in the distance. "It's the caravan," he said, turning to me with a mischievous smile, and began to adjust his reins.

"Peshwaz," I screamed at the top of my lungs. Father's horse took the lead, and I strained as I tried to get my horse, RoRo, to go faster, if not to win to at least get his dust out of my face. Father slowed up enough toward the end to let me pass him and win the race.

The caravan consisted of two horse-drawn wagons and a train of six mules. None of the passengers looked familiar, but Father dismounted, and effortlessly lifted a stocky, white-haired lady from the wagon and gave her a big hug.

"Peshwaz is one of my favorite Persian traditions," the lady said. "It is such a genuine welcome to be greeted as one approaches the end of their long, arduous journey."

Father then turned toward me. "Oh, my goodness. Agnes, I forgot to help you down." Once on the ground he took my hand and led me over to the lady from the wagon.

"I'm your Grandmother Rhea. At eight you're riding a horse quite well I see." She took a deep breath in. "The air smells the same, that delicate tinge of sulfur. My longing to return has been fulfilled."

"You've been here before?" I asked.

"Yes, your grandfather, Reverend Samuel Audley Rhea, and I were married in 1860. He whisked me off to Persia right after the ceremony."

"You were missionaries like Mother and Father?" I asked.

"Yes, we were missionaries at the Presbyterian Mission in Urmia. That's where your mother was born, and her brother Foster and sister Sophea."

"Why did you leave?" I asked.

"Your grandfather died of cholera in 1865 and we returned to America," Grandmother replied. A tear rolled down her cheek and she continued after a gasp. "I've always wanted to return." Grandmother took my hand and squeezed it and a deep happiness spread through my body. *This is my dear Grandmother.*

The next day, Mother held a reception at the house and led Grandmother around the room, making introductions to the other missionaries. I found my playmates, Aimee Vanneman and Mary Whipple, talking to Dr. Bradford, a medical missionary who frequently took us on outings. We were trying to convince her to take us on a camping trip to Zenjanab, when Grandmother and Mother approached our circle.

"Aimee, Mary, and Agnes were all born in the summer of 1892," Mother said. "The following summer at our Fourth of July picnic, Dr. Bradford held a Baby Contest. Each baby won a prize—Mary, the prettiest, Aimee, the plumpest, and Agnes, the most precocious."

"Why did Agnes win for being precocious?" Grandmother asked.

"Agnes was one when we moved into our new mission house. We held a party, and I dressed her in a new pink dress for the occasion. When Mousa came in to ready for the guests, Agnes stood up, holding out her dress to show him, and said 'Bakh,' which means 'look' in Azeri. It was the first word she ever spoke."

Mousa, who was busy serving coffee to the guests, overheard his name and sauntered over to our circle. "You are telling the story of how Agnes's first word was 'Bakh,'" he said. "That her tongue opened in the Persian language means she belongs to us," he added, thumping his chest "She's ours."

"And I'll never leave you, Mousa," I said, "or Persia."

The grinding of chains lowering the anchor jolted me from my reverie, and I realized we had reached Sebastopol. Passengers lined the rail, and naked boys swam up to the ferry and dove for coins the passengers threw into the water.

"Tomorrow morning, we'll finally be arriving at our destination," Mr. Pittman said. "Odessa will be our first glimpse of the West. There will be European architecture and electric trolleys. We'll emerge into a different world. Are you ready?"

Chapter 4

ODESSA TO PARIS, JUNE 1909

THE TRAIN STATION WAS ACROSS THE STREET FROM where the ferry docked in Odessa. Mr. Pittman hired a man to transport the trunks on a flatbed wagon. As I walked alongside my legs wobbled.

"Getting used to your land legs?" Mr. Pittman asked. "Take my arm."

Once on the train we proceeded to the dining car for tea.

"I'm afraid we have another five days to Rome," Mrs. Pittman told me. "This will be a good time to get your studying in. When we reach Italy, our main occupation will be sightseeing."

The scenery was quite monotonous, but it didn't help my desire to study, it only let my mind take its own direction. I wondered when I'd be able to see Joe Cochran, if he'd changed, if he still had freckles.

The first time I met Joe was in 1900 when Grandmother Rhea visited Persia. She insisted that the family spend the summer at the mission in Urmia, where she had been a missionary and raised her family. It was a four-day horse-ride from Tabriz to Urmia, and we were greeted at the city gate by Reverend Frederick Coan and Dr. Joseph Cochran, Sr.

"I knew Fred and Josie as children," Grandmother said. "They're second-generation missionaries. Dr. Cochran's wife, Catharine, died in 1895, and Mrs. Coan takes care of Joseph Jr. and Andrew Cochran, as well as her four children, Elizabeth, Frank, Howard, and Katharine."

Father rented a house next door to the Coan-Cochran house and, in addition to Rose, I had a pack of seven missionary children as playmates. Every day we had races, games of tag, hide-and-seek, hiking, and running in the hills nearby. Joseph Cochran, Jr., "Joe," and I were both eight years old and immediately became good friends.

"I think we have a next generation of Cochran missionaries in the works," Grandmother said proudly.

When we returned to Tabriz, Joe and I became regular pen pals. We wrote long letters at least once a month and saw each other whenever Joe's father came to Tabriz.

"He pleads for me to take him with me so he can visit Agnes," Dr. Cochran said.

Then, in August 1905, Dr. Cochran died of typhoid, and Joe and his brother Andrew were taken to Minneapolis to live with their grandparents and older brothers and sister. It had been two years since I'd seen Joe, and I was excited to finally see him again. *When my cousin Anna asks me if I have a boyfriend, I'll tell her my boyfriend is Joe.*

We reached Rome late in the afternoon and retired to our rooms in the hotel to take our first real baths. I filled the bath with salts and soaked for almost an hour. It felt heavenly, as if I was being lifted out of a pile of soot. My hair even looked a lighter color brown after it dried.

As I brushed out my hair, I heard a knock on the door.

"It's Mrs. Pittman. Could you let me in?"

"I'm not dressed. All that I have on are drawers and a chemise slip."

"That's just as well. I'm here to help you dress for dinner."

I opened the door ajar and Mrs. Pittman quickly entered. She turned to me with a gentle look in her eyes. "You are a young lady now, and I promised your mother that I would make sure you dressed like one when we reached Europe. Come, let me help you. Let's get out the corset and the corset cover your mother packed. Then I'll help you select a summer shirtwaist and a skirt."

"I don't know how to put on a corset."

"That's why I'm here, to help you. It's easiest to step into it and pull it over your chemise slip. The corset should come up under your breasts, pushing them up slightly. I'll come behind you and pull your corset strings tight. Now watch me in the mirror to see how it is done."

Mrs. Pittman was so gentle as she pulled the strings of the corset and tied them for me, but the corset kept getting tighter and tighter. "You start at the bottom and work to tighten all the way up," she said. "Then return to the waist and pull as tight as you can, again pulling any loose laces up to the top. There. Now put the corset cover on and secure a pair of stockings to the corset suspenders."

"I can barely breathe."

"Yes, we all feel that way at first. Now the shirtwaist and skirt."

I slowly buttoned what seemed to be an endless number of buttons on the white shirtwaist. "Finally, that pair of brown shoes with the laces I picked out for you."

When I finished dressing, I turned to look at Mrs. Pittman.

"Oh, my dear, what a transformation. Go see yourself in the full-length mirror."

"I feel like I'm in a cast for a broken back and I look as stiff."

"Oh, Agnes, your mother would have wanted to be the one to help you, the first time that you became a young lady," Mrs. Pittman said. "I shall go and write to her now. We should be going to dinner in an hour or so."

After Mrs. Pittman left, I practiced walking and sitting. Then I looked at myself in the mirror again. My waist was so much smaller, and my figure looked like an hourglass. I turned to the side. My breasts looked fuller. It made me look older, which I liked. I wanted men to find me attractive, and I wanted to fit in with the other American girls.

If only I could breathe.

The next morning, we explored the Colosseum and the Roman ruins, and in the afternoon, we visited Saint Peter's Basilica. We nearly broke our necks trying to admire the ceiling in the Sistine Chapel. When the other visitors left the room, Mr. Pittman lay down on the floor. "Charles," Mrs. Pittman exclaimed.

"You may not feel you can join me, but I'm sure Agnes won't resist the temptation," Mr. Pittman said.

Both Mrs. Pittman and I joined him on the floor, and Mr. Pittman took us for a tour through all of Michelangelo's biblical scenes.

"It is as though God led the brush of Michelangelo," I said.

The next morning, we took the train to Florence and stayed at Pension Baptiste on the Arno River, with a view of Ponte Vecchio, a bridge covered with tiny shops. I fell in love with Florence —the view of the city on top of Duomo, the Uffizi, Michelangelo's sculptures at the Medici Chapel, and, of course, Michelangelo's "David."

"I hope my husband looks like David," I whispered to Mrs. Pittman.

"Don't count on it, dear," she replied and squeezed my hand.

After Florence, we stopped for a day in Venice and Milan, then took the train directly to Paris. At the Hotel Dijon, two letters were waiting for me from Mother, my first letters from home. I simply enjoyed holding them, pretending I could feel Mother's hands as she addressed and sealed the envelopes. I found a chair on the far side of the hotel lobby and managed to open one. Even though there was nothing but cheery updates from the family, I could not help but break down and cry. I missed my family so much.

The next day, I went with Mr. Pittman to the American Church for Sunday service. The sermon was on the parable of the Wicked Husbandmen, followed by a tenor solo, Mendelsohn's "If with all your heart." To my surprise, the pastor then announced, "Reverend

Allen Macy Dulles of Auburn, New York, will speak this afternoon at two o'clock."

"That's Uncle Will's brother," I exclaimed. "I must go."

When I returned that afternoon, I immediately searched the pews for the Dulleses. I hadn't seen them for five years, but I spotted Edith, the reverend's wife. After Dr. Dulles's talk, I found the family in the crowd.

"You've never met the children," Edith said, "Margaret, John, Allen, Eleanor, and Nataline. Why don't you join us for dinner at our apartment this evening?"

The Dulles's rented a large flat from an American heiress, and it came with a full staff of servants and cooks. Everyone spoke French at the table, even the children, and I was pleased that I could follow along.

After dinner, Allen walked me back to the hotel. The Champs-Élysées was a fairyland, ablaze with hundreds of lights, with music blaring from the cafes and crowds of fashionably dressed people. It was the first time I was proud to be dressed like a young lady, corset and all.

"I'm studying for entrance exams to attend Princeton," Allen said as we walked.

"I'm studying, too, but for Vassar," I replied.

"We can study together if you'd like," he said as he took my hand. "You must stay close to me or you'll be smuggled away by gypsies."

My cheeks were burning. He was so charming and handsome. *My Aunt Sophea's husband's nephew—that should be far enough removed for romance.* I turned and smiled at him. "You should come to Englewood to visit me at Uncle Will's," I said. "I'll be spending holidays and vacations at Rosenvik."

"I'd love to visit you there."

As the hotel doorman welcomed us, Allen squeezed my hand and said, "Safely delivered. I'll take you to lunch and the Louvre tomorrow, if you'd like to go."

"That would be wonderful," I replied.

Back at my room, I shut the door and leaned against the wall. My heart was fluttering inside my chest. "Oh, my," I exclaimed. "I've fallen head-over-heels for Allen Dulles."

The next day, Allen and I spent the entire afternoon in the Louvre.

"There are so many famous works of art here that you can't hope to see them all in an afternoon," Allen said. "I'll lead you to the ones you must see to do your visit justice."

Venus di Milo, Mona Lisa, Intervention of the Sabin Women by David, *The Broken Pitcher* by Greuze, Titian's *Man with a Glove*, and many Raphael paintings, including *St. Michael, The Holy Family of Francis I, Madonna and Child with Saint John the Baptist*, as well as fine paintings by Guido, Leonardo, Millet, and others.

"My head is spinning after seeing the painting galleries," I said. "I'm surprised that entry into this famous art museum is free to the public. Perhaps they should charge something so they can afford better lighting for the paintings. The museum itself is rather dark."

"The lighting is better in the tapestry rooms where the crown jewels are displayed," Allen said.

"I've seen the crown jewels of the Shah in Tehran," I said. "The Daria-i-Noor, the 'Sea of Light,' is one of the largest cut diamonds in the world. Napoleon's crown doesn't impress me."

"When I see diamonds and jewels it concerns me. I think of the stories of the mines where they say children in Africa work so that Europeans and Americans can have their expensive jewelry."

"In Persia, women, including foreigners, do not wear their jewels in the street, for fear of being robbed. I don't think I ever want a diamond ring."

Allen smiled. "A good thing to know."

The next day, Margaret Dulles invited me to lunch, and afterward we went to see modern paintings by Eugene Delacroix at the Luxembourg Palace.

"I'll take you into the Sorbonne, where I'm taking classes," Margaret said. We walked down long marble hallways and entered the library and reading room with high ornate archways overlooking the courtyard.

"What a beautiful place to study," I said, "I intend to study at the Sorbonne like you someday."

We walked to the Panthéon, where I especially enjoyed the paintings of St. Genevieve saving the city from Attila the Hun, and the paintings and bronze statue of Joan d'Arc. We went downstairs and roamed the vaults. It was dark and eerie, and worth seeing the tombs of the many notable men—Victor Hugo, Voltaire, Emile Zola.

"There aren't any women buried here, "I commented.

"It is like the Nobel Prize," Margaret said. "No women allowed."

On the way back, we stopped in a patisserie and bought some macrons. Margaret looked at me sideways and said, "I thought I should warn you that Allen is a notorious flirt. Nataline jokes that he'll kiss a hundred women before he's eighteen."

I started coughing on my bite of cookie. "Thanks for the warning."

My last day of sightseeing with the Pittmans disappointed me. Due to the rain, we couldn't climb to the top of Notre Dame, and the sun did not shine through the windows during our visit to Sainte-Chapelle. After visiting Les Invalides and Napoleon's tomb, we walked to the Champs de Mars to see the Eiffel Tower, a tall metal structure used as a radiotelegraph tower.

"Originally, it was painted red for the World's Fair," Mrs. Pittman said. "Last time we were here it was bright yellow, and now a rather unattractive yellow-brown."

"It's a piece of junk," Mr. Pittman said. "When Eiffel gave it to the city this year, there was talk of tearing it down for scrap metal, but I guess they changed their minds. It is, after all, the tallest structure in the world."

"Too bad you can't go to the top," I said.

"The stairs only go to that first landing," Mrs. Pittman added. "The view from there isn't worth the effort."

I decided that I didn't think much of the Eiffel Tower.

That afternoon, Allen phoned the hotel to take me to lunch before we left for America. He was waiting in the lobby when I came down, sitting across from Mr. Pittman, who was reading the newspaper. When I approached, Allen stood up and took my arm.

Mr. Pittman looked up, alarmed. "Who is this mysterious looking young man you're leaving with?"

I laughed. "Oh, I thought you had met."

"Allen Dulles," Allen said and quickly extended his hand to Mr. Pittman.

"I've been watching him out of the corner of my eye for some time," replied Mr. Pittman. "He looks like a spy with that trench coat and hat."

"I'm prepared for the rain, sir."

"You could also pass for a bodyguard. So guard her with your life, as I've been entrusted with getting her to America."

"Will do, sir," Allen called back as we walked out the door.

Allen and I had fun telling stories about our different childhoods, and when it came time for me to go, he said, "We will be going back to America the week after you. Father has written to Uncle Will, and we will come to Englewood for the July Fourth celebrations. I will see you then, but I don't know how I will stand these weeks apart."

He then leaned toward me and gave me peck on my cheek, like a "seal of friendship." I sighed as I closed the room door behind me. It was a different kiss than the one that Howard gave me. It was quite pleasant, probably because Allen did not intend anything by it. *Or did he?*

Chapter 5

PARIS TO AMERICA, JUNE 1909

A LOUD KNOCK ON THE DOOR JOLTED ME FROM MY REV-erie. "Agnes, dear," Mrs. Pitman said. "Please hurry downstairs. Our car is waiting to take us to the station."

Late in the afternoon the train reached Cherbourg, where our steamer, the S.S. Philadelphia, was anchored offshore. After a short ferry ride to the steamer, stewards dressed in blue suits with red trim took our luggage and ushered us up a seemingly endless plank to the upper deck. My first-class cabin was conveniently situated next to the Pittmans' spacious stateroom. The paint was peeling around the port hole, and my trunk took up half the floor space. "One week in this cramped, dreary dungeon," I muttered. "I'll need to use my trunk as a table."

There was a knock on the door. "It's Mrs. Pittman," said the cheery voice. "Charles and I are going to dinner and would like you to join us."

"Coming," I replied. I quickly ran a brush through my hair and joined them in the corridor to proceed to the dining salon. Dinner was beef bourguignon on a bed of noodles. The pieces of meat were tender and moist, with a rich red-wine sauce.

"Our last French meal," Mr. Pittman said, with a sigh.

"Charles, do you think so?" Mrs. Pittman asked.

"Yes," Mr. Pittman replied. "Sadly, I saw the posted menu for the voyage. American fare after tonight: pork chops, beef pot roast, roast chicken and poached salmon, no sauces mentioned. Likely they're trying to get our palates accustomed. We have a year in America ahead of us."

"I'll only be eating American food after tomorrow too," I said. "That is until I go back to Persia."

Mrs. Pittman smiled sweetly and said, "Agnes dear, you should not think about going back to Persia. You'll be at Vassar for four years, and then who knows? You may take on additional studies, get a position, or even marry. It may be many years before you have a chance to return."

I stopped eating, my fork in midair, and looked hard at Mrs. Pittman. "No one has ever put it to me that way before."

"Surely your parents told you that college was for four years, and women with your aptitudes often take graduate school training afterward. I'm sure that your parents want you to have a career."

"I've been so busy studying for entrance examinations I haven't thought about the future."

"You need to let it sink in that your new home will be in America," Mrs. Pittman said. Her voice had a quiet, concerned tone. Then her attention turned to the other travelers who sat at our table for introductions and light conversation.

I don't care what Mrs. Pittman says. After I complete college in America, I'll return to Persia, where my heart is.

Dessert was served— crème brulée. I savored every bite of the creamy custard and the crisp burnt sugar. The ship shook as the anchors were raised and swayed as it set out across the Atlantic.

"A storm has moved in," Mr. Pittman said. "This may be a rough night."

Musicians assembled on the stage to play music and couples advanced to the dance floor. After the table was cleared, a server came with coffee and tea. She looked startled when she turned to me, "You're white as a ghost. Do you feel ..."

Before she could finish, I vomited on the white tablecloth and all over the front of my dress. Mrs. Pittman calmly took me down to my cabin and helped me undress. "I'll take your dress to the laundry," she said as she handed me a nightgown that she had pulled from my trunk.

I was seasick for the next two days, lying in my stuffy cabin. Finally, on the third day, I emerged for tea. When I came to the deck, Mr. and Mrs. Pittman were sitting with another couple. "Come join us," Mr. Pittman said, motioning to me enthusiastically. "Let me introduce you to the Jacksons. We were walking the deck and ran into each other. A.V. Williams Jackson visited the mission in Tabriz in 1903 and stayed at your house."

A short, energetic man with intense hazel eyes stood up and took my hand. "Agnes, do you remember me? You were a young girl when I visited. Now look at you. You've become a pretty young lady." He lifted my hand and kissed it. He nodded to a well-dressed woman next to Mrs. Pittman. "My wife, Dora."

"Why yes, I do remember," I said. "Mother nicknamed you 'Zoroaster's lost son' and you climbed the cliff at Mount Behistun in the heat of the summer to read the Old Persian alphabet."

"Yes, the famous Persian cuneiform," Mr. Jackson said. "I'm delighted that you remember."

"He's always been a fanatic of anything Zoroaster and anything Persian," Mrs. Jackson said, as she picked her satchel off the seat next to her. "Come sit next to me, dear."

I sat down on a deck chair between Mrs. Pittman and Mrs. Jackson and breathed in the ocean breeze. After lying and breathing the stale air in my cabin for days, it was such a relief.

"What an interesting ring you're wearing," Mrs. Jackson said. "Martyr's gem."

"What?" I said, quite startled.

"Martyr's gem. It's what bloodstone is called."

A chill ran down my spine. "Why is it called that?"

"Because they say it was formed when Christ's blood stained the jasper under his cross. See the red specks in the field of green?"

"Howard gave me this ring," I gasped.

"It's all right," Mrs. Pittman said and patted me on the knee. Then she turned to Mrs. Jackson. "You see, the young man who gave Agnes the ring became known as a martyr in Persia."

"His death brought the end to the famine in Tabriz," I added.

"What a touching story," Mrs. Jackson said. "Wearing bloodstone is said to have benefits to the wearer. I've heard that it gives your heart the courage to make sacrifices and look at painful truths."

"Agnes will need to sacrifice pleasure to study, and courage to pass her college entrance exams," Mr. Pittman interjected.

Suddenly, Mr. Jackson leaned over and took my hand to get a better look at the ring. "Why it's a Persian seal ring," he exclaimed. "It's a Lamassu."

"A what?" I said.

"The carving on the bloodstone is a bull with wings and the face of a human. The Lamassu is the protective deity of Persepolis."

A long silence followed.

"She's baffled," Mrs. Jackson finally said. "And I don't blame her. We're all confused. You must excuse him; he is an eccentric professor of ancient Persia."

"Do you suppose that the ring will protect her after she is no longer in our custody?" Mr. Pittman asked.

"I should think so," Mr. Jackson said with a laugh. "I should think so."

"Well, Lucille, you see," Mr. Pittman continued. "We could have left her in the bath at Poti."

The Pittmans and Jacksons laughed heartily, but I didn't find the joke in it.

"This ring will be a little piece of Persia that I carry with me every day," I said. "I hope it protects me in America when I'm by myself, without Father."

Our last evening on board the S. S. Philadelphia there was a party in the second-class cabin. They had a piano, but no pianist.

"We could use some music," Mr. Jackson said. "Perhaps Dora and Lucille could sing."

"Agnes, I remember hearing you play 'Stabat Mater dolorosa,' the thirteenth-century Catholic hymn to Mary," Mrs. Pittman said. "Why don't you accompany me and Mrs. Jackson as we sing?"

"But it's the world's greatest Latin hymn," I replied. "I'm afraid I'd do a disservice by remembering it rather badly."

"Nonsense," Mrs. Jackson said. "You're wearing the martyr ring and should play nobly."

I reluctantly played as Mrs. Pittman sang soprano and Mrs. Jackson alto. When we finished, the guests applauded and thanked us for our impromptu performance.

"Quite a feat," Mr. Jackson said, "and completely unrehearsed."

As we left to go to our cabins, Mrs. Pittman put her arm around my shoulders. "We'll be in America tomorrow. Our journey together will be over, and we'll be going our separate ways. It's been such a pleasure to take you with us." She gave me a squeeze.

"Tomorrow is June twenty-sixth. It's hard to believe that after six weeks it will be my first day in America. I can hardly wait to get off this boat, but I have no idea what to expect."

"Who will you be staying with?"

"I'll be staying with Mother's relatives first. Her sister Sophea passed away and her brother Foster lives in Chicago, so Grandmother Rhea will meet me. Uncle Will is driving us to Englewood, New Jersey, where my Aunt Sophea's children live. After a month I will go to Pennsylvania and stay with Father's family. He has nine brothers and sisters, and there are thirty-two aunts', uncles' and cousins' names to remember."

"Yes, it would be easier starting with your mother's relatives."

I tossed and turned all night, and barely slept. *I can't remember what they look like. Will they recognize me? What if they forget to come?*

The next morning, we steamed into New York Harbor, saluting the Statue of Liberty.

"I feel quite patriotic," I said, "even though this isn't my country."

"My dear, you'll soon find out that you actually are an American," Mr. Pittman said.

All the passengers were out on the deck watching the twin Hudson Towers of New York City emerge through the haze. On the dock below, greeters awaited, and I could decipher two faces that seemed familiar. "Oh thanks to God," I exclaimed. "They're here."

I was so excited I could hardly wait to greet Grandmother Rhea and Uncle Will, and I pushed my way through the crowds till I was in Grandmother's arms. After hugs and kisses, Uncle Will led me to customs to tend to my trunk. The Pittmans, having gone ahead, waited for me outside of customs.

"It's time to say goodbye," Mrs. Pittman said.

"I promise I'll come to New York and see you off to Persia a year from now," I said.

"Good luck on your entrance exams," Mr. Pittman said. "I'm afraid we kept you from your studies."

"You'll do fine," Mrs. Pittman said. And they were gone.

Soon I was sitting in the back of Uncle Will's Model T, speeding at over forty miles an hour. I felt disoriented from lack of sleep. Everything looked so unfamiliar and so many questions raced through my mind.

What will we do all summer? Will I fit in?

A Lamassu, a human-headed eagle-winged bull, the protective deity of Persepolis.
(Historical image collection by Bildagentur-online / Alamy Stock Photo)

Chapter 6

SUMMER 1909 WITH
THE DULLESES AND THE WILSONS

WE DROVE THROUGH THE GATES AT 400 PALISADE
Avenue and up a long driveway to a large stone house. "Rosenvik," the
palatial Dulles estate, was tucked back in the woods, away from the
street. I was suddenly self-conscious of how shabby I looked in my
traveling clothes. Winifred and Beulah, the maid and cook, met us on
the front steps, and we were quickly joined by the Dulles children, who
lined up in a row by the door—Dorothy, Edith, Rhea, and Winslow.

"She's your cousin Agnes from Persia," Uncle Will said. "Her mother
is your Aunt Annie, Mother's sister."

"Rhea and Winslow were too young to remember you when you
were here five years ago," Grandmother said. "Edith and Dorothy, of
course, remember playing with you."

"I'm fifteen," Dorothy said. "I'll be applying for college next year,
probably Smith."

"Edith is twelve," Uncle Will said. "Rhea is nine and Winslow is our
rambunctious five-year-old."

"Can I go now?" asked Winslow.

"No," Uncle Will replied. "We'll sit on the porch and have cookies and lemonade with your cousin."

"Sit down everyone and enjoy a cookie," Grandmother said nervously.

Sitting across from Uncle Will, I noticed for the first time how handsome he was with his broad forehead, clear blue eyes and firm lips. He looked very smart dressed in the latest men's fashions. Mother was so enamored by him that she gave Rose the middle name Dulles. Uncle Will turned toward me and a startled look came over his face. *Had he read my mind?*

Dorothy and Edith sat down on either side of me. Edith suddenly gasped with laughter. "Your shoes are so old fashioned," she said.

"What?" I replied.

"Your shoes, they have round toes and the curved pillar-like heels we used to wear. No one wears shoes like that anymore."

"The shoes we wear now have pointed toes and lower heels so that it is easier to walk in them," Dorothy explained. "See the shoes I'm wearing? This is what girls wear now."

My cheeks burned, and my tongue went limp in my mouth.

"I think I'll show Agnes the flower garden," Grandmother interjected. "Come Agnes."

We strolled through the large flower garden in back on a criss-crossing network of brick paths. The garden was filled with brambles, daisies, sweet peas, and roses of different shades of pink, orange, yellow, and red.

"Let's pick some red brambles and sweet peas. We'll walk over to Brookside Cemetery and visit your Aunt Sophea's grave," Grandmother said.

As we walked to the cemetery, Grandmother talked of Sophea's death in 1907. "After battling typhoid fever for six weeks, she died of pneumonia. She was only thirty-nine years old and left baby Winslow and the children without a mother. Fortunately, I was here to care for them."

"I remember when Mother received the cablegram announcing her death," I said. "Two days earlier we had received the box of Christmas presents that she sent to Tabriz. When Mother mentions Aunt Sophea, she says, 'Like a flower of the field, the wind passed over it,' from Psalm 103:16-18. She was very beautiful, wasn't she?"

"Yes, she was, and I keep a beautiful bed of flowers on her grave in her memory."

The slab was inscribed: "Sophea Rhea, wife of William Dulles, 1866-1907, Till the day break and the shadows flee away."

"Song of Solomon 4:6," I said.

Grandmother smiled through her tears. "So dear that you know the scriptures."

In Tabriz by the graveside we always sang, so I started to hum "All Things Bright and Beautiful." Grandmother joined in, in her thundering hymnal voice. We sang together loud and strong until we reached the front door of Rosenvik: "Each little flower that opens, Each little bird that sings, He made their glowing colors, He made their tiny wings." Singing with Grandmother made me feel better.

Before we entered, Grandmother touched my hand and said, "It's good having you here. Promise me to tell your mother that you visited her sister's grave. It will warm her heart."

I found Winslow in the playroom and asked him to lend me his colored crayons to make Mother a picture of Aunt Sophea's grave.

"We don't have crayons in Persia," I told Winslow. "You are lucky to have such nice toys. I'll buy some for Bobby and Annie and send them to Tabriz for their Christmas present."

When I mentioned the crayons at dinner, Uncle Will immediately responded, "No, don't buy the Eagle Pencil brand that Winslow has; they only have twelve colors. Buy the Binney and Smith, the 'Crayola.' They have thirty different colors; the most of any brand."

"Will, you're a businessman and a senior executive of three companies," Grandmother exclaimed. "How did you become so interested in crayons?" All of us laughed.

It took four of us, Uncle Will, Winifred, Beulah, and myself, to get my trunk upstairs to my room. Grandmother watched and helped guide us up the stairs so we would not scuff the carved mahogany panels along the stairwell.

"Only unpack what you need for the next two weeks," Grandmother called up the stairs. "We're going to Long Island after then."

Beulah led me down the hall to a room and when she opened the door the sweet smell of the flowers wafted through the window.

"This room overlooks the flower garden," she said.

"The pink lilies on the wallpaper match the flowers on the bedspread and lampshade," I exclaimed. "Undoubtedly the attention to detail of my dear Aunt Sophea."

"If it suits you, this will be your room whenever you stay at Rosenvik."

"It suits me just fine," I answered. "Imagine, my very own room."

Grandmother came to the door. "Let's look through your trunk," she said. "You'll want to wear clothes like those the other girls your age wear."

One by one she took out my dresses, shirtwaists, and skirts. "The hems of the dresses have been adjusted several times I see, and the colors are faded," Grandmother said. She took a white dress and lifted it to her nose. "A bit yellowed, but the smell of the water it was washed in brings back such memories; a hint of sulfur in the waterway where no doubt Kizbus washed this." With a nostalgic smile on her lips, she closed her eyes for a moment and sighed. "Let's see what you have for the winter. Oh goodness, only a green wool skirt and a red sweater, and both looking well worn."

"Yes, I wore them every day the past four winters," I said.

"It looks as though you're better equipped in the lingerie department—five nightgowns, five pairs of drawers, two chemise slips. But no corsets or corset covers?" She turned and looked at me with her eyebrows raised.

"I'm wearing the only ones I have."

Grandmother Rhea shook her head. "The final verdict, my dear, is that we must go shopping. I can't possibly let you go to Vassar like this. I'm busy tomorrow, but I'll have Uncle Will take you to Macy's on his way to work. On Tuesday we can go together. I'm sure it will take a full two days to shop."

The next day when I came downstairs for breakfast Uncle Will looked up from his newspaper, flashing a quick smile. "Good Morning, Agnes. I hope you slept well." His eyes darted about, quickly surveying my clothes. "Don't you have a nicer dress to wear to the city?"

"No, I'm afraid I don't."

"Even if you did there's no time to change. Please sit down and eat your breakfast. We'll leave in twenty minutes."

"Are you sure this will do? I can ..."

"Yes, you're fine for now. The salesgirl at Macy's will dress you up in something pretty before I take you to lunch."

Uncle Will was waiting in his Model T as I grabbed my purse and kissed Grandmother goodbye. Then we sped off to New York City at over forty miles an hour.

"I called Macy's and explained that I have a meeting at nine o'clock and need to drop you off before the store opens," Uncle Will said. "A salesgirl will meet you at the door and let you in."

"I'll be alone in the department store? I won't know what to do."

"That's why I've enlisted a salesgirl to take care of you. Macy's is at Herald Square, Broadway and 34th, and my office is at 115 Broadway, over four miles away. I wouldn't be of much help to you in the women's department anyway."

Uncle Will suddenly pulled up to curb and the car lurched to a stop. "We're here."

"This is the department store?" I looked out at a stone building that covered a whole block. "It's ten stories high."

"Macy's is the largest department store in the world. I'm sure you'll find what you need here. The salesgirl is waiting there at the door for you. Go and meet her. I need to be on my way to the office."

I stepped out and looked desperately after Uncle Will's car as he sped off. *I'm here in New York City by myself?*

A young woman in a navy dress opened the door. "Come in, Miss Wilson," she said. "Welcome to Macy's. My name is Miss Fitzgerald and I'm here to help you shop for pretty new clothes. We'll take the elevator up to the Women's Department." Miss Fitzgerald led me to what looked like a closet.

Can't we take the stairs? What if the elevator slips off its cable and falls down the shaft?

A uniformed man sitting on a stool pulled the iron accordion cage door shut and shifted a metal rod from zero to five. The elevator shuddered and ascended as the man called out the floors. "Men's Department. Haberdashery. Children. Women's Department."

"Thank goodness we're finally at our floor," I murmured.

"I'll take you to the dress section," Miss Fitzgerald said. "What size do you wear?"

"I don't know. I've never bought clothes at a store."

"Yes, I can tell what you're wearing is handmade. Made by your mother?"

"Yes," I said, smiling proudly.

"Strange how so many women still do that when buying clothes in a store saves so much time," Miss Fitzgerald said in a condescending tone of voice.

"We don't have fancy department stores in Persia," I retorted, "only bazaars."

Miss Fitzgerald stopped and turned to me. "I had no idea you were from Persia. Well, you're in New York now, and I promised Mr. Dulles I would make you look presentable. Let's look at dresses."

There were rows and rows of dresses hanging on racks as far as I could see.

"You look bewildered," Miss Fitzgerald said.

"There are so many to choose from," I said. "Where will I start?"

"I'm here to help you. First, let's find a pretty dress that you can wear to lunch with Mr. Dulles. Here's a beautiful white chiffon dress with a charming lace bodice," Miss Fitzgerald said.

"Is it silk?"

"Chiffon. It's less expensive than silk." Miss Fitzgerald continued to take dresses off the rack.

"This pink one has a pearl brocade collar and organza netting tied with pink bows. What a charmer. Oh, and this turquoise one is one of my favorites, simple but elegant. While you're changing, I'll find shoes to match."

"I can't afford much with the little money I have."

"Mr. Dulles has instructed me to put everything on his account. You needn't worry."

My cheeks were burning. *Uncle is paying for my clothes?*

Miss Fitzgerald led me to a room with a hanging curtain and a standing mirror. I drew the curtain closed and stood in front of the mirror, looking at myself for a few minutes, feeling at a loss. I slowly took my frock off and slipped the white dress on over my corset. The chiffon fabric floated over my body and down to my ankles. I turned my back to the mirror and fastened the buttons, then I turned to face the mirror. "I look like a princess," I gasped. I turned from side to side to watch the dress flow back and forth, then walked slowly step by step as a princess might approach her throne.

"I guess I'll have to look for a tiara too," Miss Fitzgerald said, coming into the dressing room. "Here are matching shoes for the white dress in two sizes. Slip them on and let me know which one is the better fit."

I chose a pair and she was off again. "This is fun. I'll try on the others." The pink one made me look like the belle of the ball, and the blue one made me look older and sophisticated.

I was wearing the blue one when Miss Fitzgerald returned. "Oh my goodness, I thought I entered the wrong dressing room at first. The dress is so flattering on you. It makes your gray eyes appear blue. Here, let me put these matching ribbons in your hair and slip on the shoes."

I gazed at myself. *I'm stunned, but happy.* "I don't know which one to choose," I wailed.

"Don't be silly; you can take all three. They aren't expensive like silk dresses."

"Oh, I couldn't. It's too much of an extravagance. Mother and Father would object."

Miss Fitzgerald laughed. "Miss Wilson, you can't wear the same dress to each dance you attend."

"Each dance?" *I've never gone to one dance.*

"Yes, I'm sure Mr. Dulles will take you to dances with his daughters. Each of them has four new dresses for summer dances that I picked out for them."

"Four?" I sat down on the stool. *Dorothy and Edith have four fancy dresses for the summer?*

"You seem overwhelmed. Why don't you pick the one you want to wear to lunch with Mr. Dulles."

"The blue one," I said.

"I thought so." Miss Fitzgerald smiled. "Mr. Dulles also wants me to find some shirtwaists and skirts for school. Stay here until I return. There are other lady customers on the floor now and I can't have you coming out here in that old frock."

I can't be seen in the beautiful blue cotton dress that Mother made for me? There's nothing wrong with it. I don't look like a beggar for goodness sake.

Miss Fitzgerald returned with seven skirts of different colors and seven white tailored shirtwaists. "This year the skirts fall softly to your ankle without a lot of excess fabric. The high neck is still the fashion, but the shirtwaist bodice is now more tailored than last year. A practical addition is the sewn-in fabric belt. I also brought you a pair of leather school shoes and the short boots that are now the rave."

"Yes, these are what I need for school. Thank you."

"I must tend to other customers now. I'll stop in on you a little later to see if you need other choices."

Need other choices? There are already too many choices. Surely Uncle will be angry if I take them all. And I can feel Mother's disapproving glance. I'll take the blue dress and two shirtwaists.

Miss Fitzgerald returned after a half hour with two more shirtwaists. "How did they fit? Are you happy with my selection? Here are two more I'd like you to try on. I promised Mr. Dulles I'd have you ready by quarter to twelve."

"I'll take the blue dress and these two shirtwaists on the chair."

"Miss Wilson, you don't understand," Miss Fitzgerald said sternly. "Mr. Dulles will be quite angry with me if I've not provided you with an adequate wardrobe." We stood staring at each other for a couple of minutes, then she sighed. "I'll hold onto everything until you've discussed this with Mr. Dulles over lunch. Please at least try these last two shirtwaists to see if they appeal to you." She quickly left.

After I tried on the other two shirtwaists, I put on the blue dress and shoes. Miss Fitzgerald returned with bobby pins and a brush to fix my hair and secure the bows. "You are ready for luncheon with Mr. Dulles, as ready as you'll ever be."

Uncle Will was waiting in his model T by the curb in front of Macy's. He shook his head and laughed to himself as he opened the passenger door. "We'll be back after lunch to pick up Agnes's selections," he shouted to Miss Fitzgerald, who smiled and waved.

"The city streets are busy," I said.

"This mixture of cars and horse-drawn buggies makes it difficult to maneuver, but the worst problem is the broken-down automobiles. They plug up the road and you simply have no other choice than to find an alternate route."

"What's that?" I exclaimed when we approached a huge clock tower.

"The Metropolitan Life Tower. It the tallest building in the world, just completed this year."

"I thought the Eiffel tower was the tallest in the world."

"It's the tallest structure, not the tallest building, and I've heard that Paris will tear it down soon. It's a rather unsightly."

"The Pittmans and I felt the same way."

"Here we are, the U.S. Realty Building. I moved my office here in 1908 after it was completed. The building next to it is the Trinity Building. They call these two skyscrapers the 'Twin Towers.' They are indeed twin examples of Gothic splendor. Look for the gargoyles, both inside and out. The famous Trinity Church and cemetery are just down the street. I'll take you there after lunch."

"The lobby looks like the entrance to a European castle," I said, admiring the ribbed ceiling, stained-glass windows, and a coat of arms.

"It never fails to impress visitors who come to my office," Uncle Will said. "The location has done wonders for my businesses. We're going to the top floor for lunch at the Lawyer's Club."

Another elevator, but this one with bronze cage doors. Men with suits crowded in with us, and I was pushed to the back. I held onto Uncle Will's hand and closed my eyes.

Uncle Will laughed. "Don't hold your breath or you'll faint by the time we reach the tenth floor."

When the elevator stopped and the cage doors opened, Uncle Will let the other men leave before he led me out. "Elevators are a new and scary thing for you, aren't they?"

"Do they ever fall down the elevator shaft?"

"It's never been reported. Here's the next elevator to the twentieth floor."

"Another elevator?" *It's going up ten more stories.*

"The view of the financial district is spectacular. It's well worth it."

Again, I held Uncle Will's hand and closed my eyes as we ascended. When the elevator stopped and the cage doors opened, we emerged into a hallway with a huge bear rug with the head and teeth intact. The floor was one large room with tables interspersed between gold Gothic pillars with bronze accents. Windows covered most of the exterior walls, except for one side where a large stained-glass window commanded the wall.

A man in a smart black suit darted in front of us. "Mr. Dulles, let me show you and your guest to your table," he said.

Our table was near a window, and looking down made me dizzy, so I looked around the room instead. I noticed that the men in tailored suits at nearby tables had turned in their chairs and were staring at me.

"I'm one of the few girls here," I said.

"Yes, this is a men's club; women are only guests."

"They're all staring at me."

"Don't be intimidated. They're trying to figure out who you are as usually I'm seen here with Helen Rollins, who you'll soon meet. Besides, you look quite beautiful in your new dress. Miss Fitzgerald certainly does a superb job."

"It's the first time that I understand why the Muslim women in Persia are happy to cover up in chaddars."

Uncle Will laughed so convulsively that he almost spit out the gulp of water he had taken and continued to cough for several minutes afterward. "We'll start with fried oysters," he gasped at the waiter when he came by.

After the waiter left, Uncle Will leaned toward me and looked into my face intently. "Agnes, about Miss Fitzgerald. She called me this morning after you'd tried on some shirtwaists and said you only wanted two."

"Mother and Father would not want me to be greedy. Luke 12:15 says 'Be on your guard against all sorts of greed; for life does not consist of an abundance of possessions.'"

"You do want to fit in with the other girls, don't you?"

"Yes, I do want to be accepted by the American girls, but ..."

"Then you must dress appropriately. Although you may like your clothes from Persia, you can't wear them anymore or the girls will make fun of you. We will stop at Macy's on the way home and pick up the other clothes that Miss Fitzgerald had you try on."

"I'm afraid that Mother and Father will be angry."

"I'll write to them and tell them what I've done and that I insisted on it."

Tears came to my eyes and I wrung my hands. *I don't want to displease Uncle Will, but Mother and Father will be angry with me.*

I could feel Uncle Will's tension as he stopped his automobile at Macy's. "Stay in the car. I'll only be a few minutes." As I waited, I watched the women coming out of Macy's wearing smart suits, flowing dresses, and wide-brimmed hats. They were all so handsome.

Maybe Uncle Will is right. Having nice things to wear gives pleasure to other people's eyes. It is not such a bad thing, as long as you don't have too much. Uncle Will is so generous. What can I say to thank him?

The next day, Grandmother Rhea and I spent the whole day shopping. I got three wool skirts, a pair of tan shoes, a red kimono, a dear little gray-and-white liberty cape, and thick kid gloves. After shopping, Uncle Will met us at Keen's Steakhouse on West 36th Street for lunch.

"This used to be an all-gentlemen's house until Lillie Langtry, King Edward's 'other woman,' took them to court for not letting her in. She won the case in 1905," Uncle Will said. "How times have changed."

The 4th of July was on Sunday, so there were no celebrations until the following day. Monday morning Uncle Will's brother, Reverend Allen Dulles, and his wife Edith arrived with Allen and the other children. We spent a noisy afternoon together shooting off what seemed an inexhaustible supply of exploders, firecrackers, and torpedoes. Allen and I pretended that we were secret agents trying to blow each other up. Winslow watched from Grandmother's lap, jumping up and down excitedly. Afterward the air was smoky and bitter smelling, with the sulfur stinging our eyes and noses.

At sunset we drove down to the Hudson River to watch the fireworks display. I shivered in the evening breeze and Allen put his jacket over my shoulders. "Promise you'll write me from Vassar," he said.

"Of course, I'll write to you," I replied. "What's more, my Uncle Rob is a professor at Princeton, and when I visit him, I'll have you come to the house."

After Allen and his family left for Auburn, Winifred gave me three large envelopes from Tabriz. I squealed with excitement as I ran upstairs to my room and tore open an envelope. Mother wrote that the Russian army had set up barracks on the grounds of the Royal Prince's Palace in Tabriz and had raised the Russian flag above the Arg. Father had taken a postcard of the Arg and painted the Russian flag on it. I giggled. "Father is always making light of a bad situation. How I miss his gentle humor."

Our trunks were sent ahead to West Hampton Beach on Long Island. Uncle Will rented a five-bedroom vacation house with a long porch in the back facing the ocean. After supper we sat on the porch, gazed at the stars and sang songs with the waves and surf as our music.

In the morning Uncle Will set up umbrellas and chairs in the sand.

After an hour watching beachgoers, Dorothy stood up and said, "Let's go swimming."

"But I can't swim," I stammered. "I don't even have a bathing suit."

"You can't swim?" Edith exclaimed.

"You can borrow one of my bathing suits," Dorothy said.

"There is a rope tied to that buoy offshore that the older women, who never learned to swim, use for wading," Uncle Will added.

"Nowadays most girls learn to swim," Edith said. "You'll need to learn, or people will think you are old-fashioned."

"If you want to, you can wade out with Edith and me," Dorothy said. "We'll go out until the waves touch our chins and we can still touch the sand with our feet."

I donned a sleeveless puffy black top and a pair of black bloomers that Dorothy gave me. When I looked in the mirror, I giggled. "Mother would never let me go out in public in Persia like this. It doesn't seem right to be so immodestly dressed. I know, I can wear the big beach towel over my head like a chaddar and walk to the shoreline. Then right before I go into the water, I'll toss it on the sand."

After I dropped the towel, I ran into the water and shrieked, "The water is so cold."

"It's the ocean," Dorothy responded flatly. "Even in the summer it's cold. Take my hand."

We waded out together among the throngs of bathers and reached a point where the water was up to our shoulders. Suddenly a big wave came in and lifted me off my feet. I fell backwards, plunging into the water, and came up sputtering and spitting out sand and saltwater. My mouth was gritty, and my throat burned.

Dorothy and Edith were laughing. "It's funny seeing you go into the ocean for the first time," Edith said.

Dorothy offered me her arm. "Here, hold on and don't let go. Let yourself rise up with the waves as they come in. Your feet will only be off the bottom for an instant."

Although I tried to do just as she instructed me, I managed to get whole buckets of water down my throat and into my ears. I was relieved when Edith said, "I've had my fill of the waves and I'm cold. Let's go to shore."

When we reached our beach chairs, Uncle Will smiled and said, "Agnes, I rented you water wings for the rest of your stay here."

Since there was a dance at the West Hampton Country Club that evening, Uncle Will invited Helen Rollins, his lady friend, to come up for the night. "Let's bring Dorothy and Agnes with us," Miss Rollins suggested.

"What fun it will be," Dorothy exclaimed. "We don't know any boys here, but that doesn't matter. We'll just dance with whoever asks us."

At Uncle Will's suggestion, Miss Rollins helped me change into the lovely white dress he bought me in New York. "You look beautiful," Miss Rollins said. "I'm sure that you will turn the boys' heads."

"But I don't know how to dance," I said.

"Just watch at first."

When we entered the dance room, a band was performing lively music and couples danced a fast-paced walk in the form of a square. "It's called the One-step," Miss Rollins whispered in my ear. "Quite easy; anyone can do it."

Several boys asked me to dance, but I simply replied, without further explanation, "Thank you, but I can't dance." They looked surprised at my answer—one stood in front of me frozen for half a minute, not able to respond, and another looked down toward the bottom of my dress wondering if I was missing a leg or a foot, I suppose. A couple of boys were kind and asked if I'd prefer to sit out the dance and eat a piece of white Angel Cake instead. This meant talking and eating, and I was in my element.

"Why didn't you dance?" Dorothy asked the next day. "I told at least two boys to ask you."

"Since I am a missionary's daughter, I did not want to do anything that other people would find inappropriate," I replied.

"But no one else at the dance knew you were a missionary girl," Dorothy replied. "Besides, everyone dances."

Grandmother, overhearing our conversation interjected, "Agnes, it's not considered immodest to dance in America. If you'd feel better about it, write to your mother and father and ask for their permission, but I'm sure that they intend that you become fully Americanized. This is your home now."

This is your home now? Those words jarred me into silence. I sat on the porch and wrote to Mother and Father, asking them if I could learn to dance. Women never danced in public in Persia. What would they say? They had sent me to America because I disgraced them. Would they think I was being disrespectful?

In the afternoon, instead of going for a ride with the others I stayed at the house and sat with Grandmother on the porch. A rainstorm was threatening, and the bathers and screaming children had gone home. In their place sandpipers had taken over the shoreline and were frantically running out as the waves receded and running in when one approached.

"I've been meaning to find a time to talk to you," Grandmother said. "How are you settling in?"

"You and Uncle Will have been so kind and generous," I replied. "I just feel awkward sometimes. I feel foolish because I can't swim or dance."

"You'll learn to do those things; just give it time." Grandmother placed her hand gently on my knee. "As for dancing, you really must learn. Didn't you dance with your young man in Persia?"

I swallowed hard before replying, "Do you mean Howard?"

"Of course, Mr. Baskerville. Your mother told me all about him."

"We never danced together. He was only my geometry teacher."

"Your mother said he asked for your hand in marriage. Surely there was more to it than that."

"He kissed me on the cheek, and he misunderstood my feelings about it."

"Your mother wrote that his death was very traumatic for you."

"I was upset because they made arrangements for me to come to America with the Pittmans. There were only a few weeks to pack." My eyes welled up with tears.

"I'm upsetting you, dear. I'm sorry."

"It was my fault Howard joined the army." I sobbed as tears streamed down my face. "Father told him over and over it was a rash decision, but he wouldn't listen."

"Now, Agnes. Young men do sometimes make rash decisions. You shouldn't blame yourself."

"He didn't know how to lead soldiers to fight. He could only teach his army to march, and not very impressively at that."

"You're becoming agitated, I'm afraid. Let's talk about something else."

"But it was not in vain. The roads were opened. Food came to the starving people."

"No, it was not in vain."

The others returned from their auto ride, and we heard them coming in the front door.

"Why don't you go for a walk down by the beach," Grandmother said.

I took in a long breath and started down the wood plank walkway to the beach. I sat at the end and took off my shoes and stockings. The sand was cool as it slipped through my toes. The beach was empty, and each wave crashed onto the shore, then slowly receded, hissing, like breathing in and slowly letting your breath out. I let my breath follow the waves. Finally, I heaved a long sigh, and the tight knot in my throat relaxed.

To think that three weeks ago I was on the other side of the Atlantic and now I'm here in America. Almost more than any other day, I think of home and the dear beloved ones there.

Out in the bay I spotted a rowboat and realized that it was adrift without a rower. The waves tossed it back and forth as it emerged from the shelter of the bay into the rough waters of the open ocean. "No one to guide you home little boat. Like me, you are adrift at sea, not knowing your fate. Would you drift forever out at sea? Would you overturn? Would you slip softly onto a beach in some other land, or would you be shattered into a hundred pieces on jagged rocks?"

I gasped and cried out loud, "Oh, how I miss home." As tears poured down my cheeks, the storm suddenly broke and drenched me from head to foot.

On August 3rd Uncle Will put me on the train for Pennsylvania. The rest of the summer I would be staying with Father's family, the Wilsons. Grandmother Wilson, three of his five brothers, and two of his four sisters lived in Indiana, Pennsylvania, and Father's other two brothers were close by in Saltsburg. Fourteen of my Wilson cousins would be there, four of them about my age.

I'd never been on a train by myself, and I carefully read over and over the instructions that Aunt Jennie had sent me: "In Philadelphia transfer to the sleeper bound for Pittsburgh. Get off at the Blairsville Intersection. Margaret will meet you there and ride with you on the train to Indiana."

A newspaper was left in my cabin by a previous passenger, and I was about to throw it away when I spotted the headline: "Shah of Persia Deposed, Son to Rule under Regency." The cheerful letters from Tabriz mentioned nothing of these events in Tehran. *My family could be in peril and they may not tell me so as not to cause me worry. All I can do is hope and pray for the best for my family and the poor land, I love so much.*

I was so afraid I would not wake up in time for my station stop in Blairsville that I hardly slept. Cousin Margaret found me wandering the platform in Blairsville and escorted me to the train for Indiana. It was a small, slow, regional train and after a short conversation I fell asleep on her shoulder. When I woke up in Indiana, Uncle Harry was waiting for us with the rest of the family in his Model T.

Grandmother Wilsons's house was on the corner of Church and Vine Streets, across from the Presbyterian church. My grandfather, Andrew Wilkins Wilson, had been a successful merchant and owned a dry goods store on Philadelphia Street. He built the stately three-story, wood-clad house to raise their ten children. The house was freshly painted gray with white trim, and the windows on the first floor were decorated with china plates and lace curtains.

Grandmother Wilson was a petite, frail woman with a prominent nose and a constant smile. Although she still had a carriage and horses, the house had plumbing and electricity, which not all homes in rural towns had. Uncle Harry, a banker, had lost his wife to appendicitis in 1889 and moved back into Grandmother's house with his children, Margaret and Lad. Aunt Jennie was their stepmother. She left college to care for her niece and nephew after their mother died and refused to marry until the children did. She was the boss of the house.

"Agnes makes it six," Grandmother declared over dinner, "and you know I'm not happy unless there are six Wilsons at the table."

Margaret was three years older than me and found it her duty to keep me entertained. Each day, we played tennis, and one morning we were joined by a visitor from Minneapolis named Donald Moorhead.

"Do you know Joe Cochran?" I asked, assuming he'd shrug his shoulders.

I almost fell over when he replied, "By coincidence, Joe turns out to be in the same class as me in high school." That evening I excitedly wrote a letter to Joe telling him about meeting his classmate and hoping to see him soon. "It's a relief knowing that I have you, a friend from Persia, here in America."

On August 17th a Wilson family reunion was held at the Indiana Fairgrounds, a gathering of one hundred and eighty relatives. Uncle Rob gave a speech on the family history and said a prayer in honor of Grandfather, who died in 1897. Grandmother Wilson sobbed, and her daughters took turns offering her their handkerchiefs.

At the reunion picnic Margaret and I sat with my cousin Anna.

"Jack Daub, my boyfriend, is in Pittsburgh for the summer," Anna said. "He's a junior at Princeton this year."

"Did my letter about Howard reach you?" I asked.

"Yes," Anna replied, "but now that you're here, you don't have a boyfriend, do you?"

"We'll have time to talk about Howard in Saltsburg," I replied nervously. "I'll be staying with you for two weeks."

"But Agnes has a boyfriend named Joe in Minneapolis who knows the Moorheads," Margaret interjected.

"How on earth did you meet someone from Minneapolis?" Anna asked.

"Joe's a friend from Persia, who now lives in Minneapolis. After his parents died, he came to America. "

After the reunion, I took the train with Uncle Rob and Uncle Andy and their families to Saltsburg.

Uncle Andy and his wife Aunt Bessie lived in a big Tudor house on the campus of Kiskiminetas Springs School. "Kiski School" was a boys' preparatory school that Uncle Andy founded. They had four daughters—Sarah, who was two years older, Anna, who was my age, and Gladys and Edith, who were over five years younger than me.

Uncle Rob and his wife Ellen had a summer home on the edge of town but lived at Princeton University during the academic year. They had one son, Howard, who was nineteen, and five daughters—Eleanor, who was my age, and Sarah, Anne, Jane, and Julia, who were younger. Family outings and picnics in Saltsburg with my ten cousins were raucous, and there were constant games and other activities—hiking in the hills, swimming and boating in the Kiskiminetas River, tennis, and Clock Golf, a game where players stand around a circle and putt into a central hole.

One evening there was a surprise party for Aunt Bessie's and Uncle Andy's wedding anniversary. There was a band with violins and banjos, and everyone danced the Virginia Reel, except for me.

The week before, I had received a letter from Mother and Father saying that they left the decision up to me as to whether I wanted to learn to dance. It was a hard decision, and I had to think about it a long while. Grandmother Rhea encouraged me to learn, and my cousins thought it strange that I even hesitated to try. I wanted to please them, too, but I thought Mother and Father would be best pleased if I did not dance.

The next day, Anna asked, "Why didn't you dance like everyone else?"

"It's not something I feel comfortable doing," I answered.

"But if you don't dance with boys, you'll end up an old maid."

"I don't want to do anything that would not become a missionary's daughter," I replied. "I won't dance."

My birthday was September 10th and Grandmother Wilson had Aunt Agnes' family over for dinner. There was white cake with seventeen pink candles, and lots of lovely presents, including a little Persian mat in a letter from Rose and telegraphic greetings from Dorothy Dulles. When Grandmother Wilson lit the candles on the cake she said, "Make a wish."

"Can I make two wishes?" I replied.

"Very well."

"My first wish is that I pass the Vassar entrance examinations. And my second wish is … Oh, I forgot." Everyone looked at me surprised. I took a deep breath in and blew out the candles. I was about to say my second wish was to go home to Persia. How sad that would have made all my kind relatives who have tried to make me feel at home.

And finally the day came, September 13th. It was the day I would leave for Vassar. Father's family all came down to the train to see me off. It seemed hard to leave. In a short period of time they had come to be my second family, and I felt safe with them.

Vassar would be my first time without my family, and I was thankful that at least my cousin Anna would be with me.

I'm on my way to college, but first I need to pass the entrance examinations.

Grandmother and Grandfather Wilson's House, Indiana, Pennsylvania

Chapter 7

VASSAR, FALL SEMESTER, 1909

AUNT BESSIE AND UNCLE ANDY WERE WAITING FOR ME at the Blairsville Intersection with Anna. We were traveling together on the express sleeper train to Jersey City, New Jersey and then transferring to a train to New York. It was delightful sharing a cabin with Anna—so different from the lonely trip there, but I hardly slept, what with her tossing and turning on the upper bunk all night. Or was it the Vassar entrance exams that occupied my mind? There had been little time to study since coming to America, with my relatives engaging me in all their activities. *Why hadn't I found time to study?*

When we arrived at the Jersey City Station, I telephoned Uncle Will. "Englewood 297," I told the operator. I was relieved to hear Beulah's cheerful voice warble "Rosenvik."

"It's Agnes. I managed to use a telephone," I said, smiling with pride.

"Mr. Dulles and Mrs. Rhea are on their way to Grand Central Station, Miss Wilson. They'll meet you at the entrance."

As we hurried to the platform to take the train to New York, Anna muttered, "Why can't the train go directly from Pennsylvania to New York? It's so inconvenient to make a transfer."

"The Pennsylvania Railroad will connect in about a year," Uncle Andy said. "They are even building a new train station."

At Grand Central Station, Anna and her parents left me to take the train to Poughkeepsie, and I stood alone at the entrance of the station. The bustle and street noise made me uneasy and I was relieved when Uncle Will drove up with Grandmother in his model T. After lunch at Purcelle's opposite Lord & Taylor at 6th Avenue and 20th, Uncle Will drove Grandmother and me along the Hudson River to Poughkeepsie, home to Vassar College.

We arrived at the Idylle Inn and found Anna and her parents had already taken rooms. "You're sharing a room with Anna," Grandmother said. "Settle in and join us for dinner."

"Anna doesn't have to take entrance exams," I said. "Why do I have to?"

"Anna was graduated from Kiski School, whereas you were home-schooled in Tabriz. There is a difference."

"But what if I don't pass?"

"Then you'll go to high school in Englewood with Dorothy Dulles for a year and try again."

"But I don't want to go to high school. I want to go to Vassar with Anna."

"Then you'll have to pass the exams."

With entrance exams the very next day, I was so nervous that I could barely eat dinner. That night, after Anna was asleep, I quietly got out of bed and knelt to pray. "O Lord, please give me the wisdom to pass the examinations. 'I can do all this through him who gives me strength.' Philippians 4:13. Ad majorem Dei gloriam."

The entrance examinations lasted four days, and each day after finishing my head was spinning. The first day my hand shook as I tried to scribble answers to the questions, and I broke the pencil lead twice. The second day, when my head finally cleared of nervous confusion, I started to feel more confident in my answers and I wrote and wrote. By the third day my arm was so tired from writing that it was numb, and by the fourth day the pencil seemed to move of its own volition. *After all this I simply must pass these entrance examinations.*

For the next two days, I waited, engulfed in panic, to hear if I'd passed. Finally, on Monday afternoon, Grandmother and I walked to President Taylor's office to learn my test results. The minutes crept by as I waited for Dr. Taylor to call me. A door suddenly opened and a tall man with a stern face said, "Mary Agnes Wilson, come in, please." I trembled as I sat down on a wooden chair and a cold hollowness spread through my body.

"It's not every day we have a girl from Persia attempt to pass our entrance examinations," Dr. Taylor began. "And, of course, we can't admit everyone." Dr. Taylor looked down and flipped through some papers on his desk. "Did you find the exams difficult?"

"Difficult?" I stammered. "No, I mean ..."

President Taylor smiled. "I didn't think so. You passed all fourteen exams without condition."

"I passed?"

"Yes, you passed. Congratulations and welcome to Vassar."

I jumped out of my chair and shook Dr. Taylor's hand until he laughed and said, "And once again, welcome to Vassar."

"I must tell Grandmother," I said and ran into the waiting room. "I passed, I passed."

"I had no doubt that you would, dear," Grandmother said.

"I've honored Father, my family, the mission, and old Tabriz. I did not let them down."

Anna joined me for a walk up to Sunset Lake and through the glen. "Oh, the trees are so lovely," I cried, bursting with joy. "I've never seen anything so beautiful before."

"They're maple trees," Anna said. "This isn't the first time you've ever seen fall colors."

"The leaves are all the colors of the rainbow—yellow, orange, red, and purple."

I ran through the lawn kicking the large maple leaves into the air, and without hesitation Anna joined me in my maple-leaf dance.

That evening at the Idylle Inn, Uncle Andy told us about the Hudson-Fulton celebration that was taking place in New York City that weekend. "It's the 300th anniversary of Henry Hudson's discovery of the Hudson River and the 100th anniversary of Robert Fulton's paddle-boat. There will be a huge parade through the city and a display of war ships in New York Harbor, with fireworks at night. Wilbur Wright is to take his flying ship around the Statue of Liberty."

"I would certainly like to see that," said Aunt Bessie. "We should postpone our return to Saltsburg and book a room in New York."

"You won't be able to find a room, I'm afraid," Uncle Will said. "They've been booked solid for weeks. On the other hand, if you don't mind the train back and forth to the city, we have room at Rosenvik."

"Oh, we couldn't impose," Uncle Andy said.

Sitting next to Aunt Bessie, I could feel her kick her husband under the table.

I smiled as I thought of my Father's description of Aunt Bessie. "Never offer her something you don't want her to accept."

"A smaller celebration will be held the following week in Poughkeepsie," Uncle Will said with a wry smile. "That will of course mean staying here another week."

The next day, the dormitory "mother" of Lathrup Hall showed Anna and me to our room. We attended freshmen orientation with President Taylor and Secretary McCaleb, followed by an All Class meeting, and discussions with the athletics coaches and student association presidents. I spent hours pondering the freshmen course listings and finally registered for French, German, English, Latin, and Math for my first semester. A sense of pride welled up in my chest as I walked away from the registration desk. *To think of it, I'm actually going to college.*

As I unpacked my trunk and carefully hung up my clothes on one side of our shared closet, Anna remarked with surprise, "All your clothes are new."

"Yes," I said, "Uncle Will and Grandmother Rhea were very generous."

At the bottom of the empty trunk I found an envelope with Mother's writing. She had somehow secretly stowed it away before I left Persia. The letter said: "We'll miss you, but you are on your way to becoming an educated young lady. I know you are in good hands with Uncle Will and my mother. Don't forget to write to the Coans and Cochrans to tell them how to reach you. They live in a double-house at 1732 Clifton Place, Minneapolis, Minnesota."

I've already written Joe Cochran, but now I can write and officially tell the Coans and the Cochrans that I'm a freshman at Vassar. How wonderful it will be to see Frank and Elizabeth Coan, and of course my childhood friend, Joe.

Our first weekend in Poughkeepsie was the Hudson-Fulton festival. Replicas of Hudson's *Half Moon* and Fulton's *Clermont* were escorted by a fleet of government warships. As the vessels approached the landing, there was a twenty-one-gun salute followed by cannon blasts. In town the church bells rang, and whistles and sirens blew.

A chill ran through my spine as I remembered the cannon blasting away on top of the Arg in Tabriz, and the bullets that hit the side of the Vanneman's house at the mission and the back of the chair where I had been sitting. I closed my eyes. If I had not fallen to the floor, I would be dead now. Oh the terror of that moment and the war, all around us, inescapable. I shuddered and held tightly to Anna's hand.

"Are you alright?" she asked.

"I don't like the noise of the cannons and guns. It reminds me of the Persian Revolution."

After dinner we returned to the harbor for the evening festivities. Grandstands had been erected on either side of the Hudson River, and a section directly in front of the landing had been reserved for Vassar students. Each time another group of Vassar girls came up on the grandstand, it jiggled back and forth. At first we laughed at the jiggling. "I guess no one could come up by surprise," Anna said. Then a large group of seniors pushed their way to the top row and the swaying became more pronounced.

"This doesn't seem right," I said. "It's only our stand that's moving so much."

Suddenly the grandstand started shaking and wobbling. And then crash, the grandstand collapsed and fell into pieces, leaving a big mix up of people, seats, and boards. At first there were screams of panic, then moans and groans as we lay too stunned to move.

There was a girl screaming, "I think my arm's broken. The bottom half doesn't move."

"How do we get out of this mess?" Anna whimpered. "My knee hurts."

A policeman came running over and took charge of the scene. "Everyone, keep still," he said. "Help is on its way. If any of you move, you may make things worse."

"It seems like an eternity that we've been lying here," Anna complained.

"When I feel scared, I remember the scripture Psalms 46:1-3," I said. "God is our refuge and strength, a very present help in trouble. Therefore, we will not fear though the earth should change, though the mountains shake in the heart of the sea; though its waters roar and foam; though the mountains tremble with its tumult."

"How do you know how to recite stories from the Bible?" the girl with the broken arm asked.

"She's my cousin," Anna said. "Agnes, the missionary girl."

As the police picked us out from under things, I was amazed how calm and collected the girls were. Neither I nor Anna lost anything in the jam, and of our eight dormitory floormates, only three had slight injuries. Later we heard that of over a hundred Vassar girls, only the girl who broke her arm and ten others were in the infirmary with injuries. "We certainly have much to be thankful for," I said. "Except from now on I'll be known as 'Agnes, the missionary girl.' "

Later in October, a guest speaker from the Student Volunteer Movement, Dr. Zimmer, spoke about the appeal for Christian volunteers to serve as missionaries in less fortunate areas of the world. Afterward, in the Student Parlor, Dr. Zimmer spoke informally to the students and when I introduced myself, he said, "I tried to pick you out amongst the other students by your likeness to your father. He told me that you were here."

"You know Father?"

"Your father is well known in the missionary circles and I've known him for years. I'm looking forward to seeing him in three years on his furlough."

"How do you join the Student Volunteers?"

Dr. Zimmer took a card from his vest pocket. "It's easy. When you decide to join the Student Volunteers, sign this declaration card and submit it to our office. It states your intention to become a missionary and join our weekly meetings."

"It says 'The Evangelization of the World in this Generation.' "

"Yes, that is our motto. The Student Volunteers have recruited over four thousand college students for missionary service abroad since it started in 1886. I was one of the Mount Hermon 100, the first hundred to go. It was an experience of a lifetime."

A wave of exhilaration traveled through my body, and I was so excited I could barely see. "I could join the Student Volunteers and go back to Persia," I said.

That night I wrote a long letter to Father asking him about the Student Volunteers. "Do you think I should join?"

Father's reply came a month later: "The organization is well intentioned and has done well in drawing attention to the missionary need. However, they recruit students with an interest in missionary service, without evaluating whether these students have relevant skills to offer or the ability to learn the language of the country. It was through a Student Volunteer group at Princeton that Mr. Baskerville came upon his ideas of missionary service. The decision is up to you whether to join or not."

If Howard joined, then maybe I should not. He came to Persia not knowing Azeri and unprepared to be a teacher. I also need to become more educated before I return so I am equipped to be a good teacher for the Persian girls.

On a sunny Saturday, Anna and I took a long walk in the hills, starting out in the morning and bringing lunch along. On the way back, when running gaily down a hill, I slipped and twisted my ankle. After assisting me for some distance, Anna stopped a horse buggy that was passing by and arranged a ride back to Vassar. The infirmary gave me strict orders to stay in bed all day and by dinner I could walk with only a little stiffness.

"Jack asked me to a dance at Princeton during Thanksgiving break," Anna said. "I thought of inviting you to come with me, but with a sprained ankle you'd have another excuse not to dance."

"Yes, after my fall I doubt if I'll be in shape to dance any time soon."

"When will you see Joe?"

"He wrote last week asking me to meet him in Albany in June. He's going to his brother Harrison's graduation at Williams. I'll use the bed rest to my advantage to write him a long letter."

I hadn't answered Joe right away. For some reason I had trepidation. Although I looked forward to seeing Joe and found it convenient to call my childhood friend "my boyfriend," I had a fear that by meeting him I was making a commitment.

Thanksgiving break: I was excited as I boarded the train to Englewood. Uncle Will had invited his nephew Allen Dulles to come from Princeton and stay at Rosenvik. Wednesday evening before Thanksgiving, in the midst of a snow blizzard, I was surprised when Allen asked Uncle Will, "Could you take Agnes and me for a ride in your auto? A drive through the Palisades in the snowstorm would be an adventure."

At first it was very romantic riding next the Allen in the back seat while Uncle drove, but then a tire blew out. Allen and Uncle Will managed to fix it while I stood outside the car with little mounds of light fluffy snow accumulating on my hat and the shoulders of my coat. Before we got back in the car, Allen dusted the snow off me and kissed my cold nose. He was such a gallant young man, but I was sure I was not "special" to him.

After the Thanksgiving meal, Grandmother asked me to help her serve coffee and once we were alone she asked, "Agnes, what did your mother and father say about dancing?"

Not again. "They said that it was up to me to decide."

"Well, if they have no objection and you want to learn, then we need to give you a dancing lesson. I'll ask your Uncle Will."

I was excited when Uncle Will motioned for me to join him in the study. "I'll teach you the 'One Step.' Now face me and take my left hand with your right hand. And now put your left hand on my upper right arm. We will start slowly. Watch my feet at first."

We did not have music, but that was fine as it was hard enough concentrating on his feet. Holding my hand, Uncle Will stretched my right arm to the side. "You'll be stepping forward and I'll be stepping backward," he said.

We took four steps, a quarter turn, two steps to the side and a full turn. "Now I'll walk forward as you walk backwards." We took four steps, a quarter turn, two steps to the side and a full turn. "You see we are just making a little square. Now a little faster." I managed haltingly two more squares. "You're doing fine. Only stop scowling and smile."

"I'm concentrating so hard."

"We still need to speed it up a bit more to the usual pace." Moving more quickly, we made it through at least a dozen squares. After we finished Uncle Will swirled me around in circles and I felt like a fairy princess. "Now you're ready to dance with Allen," he said.

"No, please no, not yet. I need to practice."

"Then he'll have to wait until our New Year's dance. It's a tradition here at Rosenvik."

On Saturday, we went to New York in Uncle Will's car and had lunch at the Manhattan, afterward going to a play at the New Theatre at 62nd Street and Central Park West. The theater opened at the beginning of November, and Uncle Will rushed there to buy $2 tickets for all six of us, the best seats in the house. The theater was a work of art, with gilded and painted ceilings, crystal chandeliers, and a heavy crimson velvet curtain with gold tassels. The play was "Springtime," starring Mabel Taliaferro, a comedy that takes place in Louisiana in the early 1800s. A seventeen-year-old girl, promised to her Father's elderly cousin, instead falls in love with a handsome young man. It was delightfully full of Southern charm. A newspaper review called it "light as thistledown and lovely as youth itself," and it certainly was.

As soon as the play ended, we rushed to the train station, and I soon arrived back at Vassar. My floormates were not returning until the next day and the halls were eerie quiet. Safe and alone in my dormitory room, it was time to practice the One Step. I faced the standing mirror and tried to imagine Uncle Will there with me. I slowly made my way through a square, then another faster, then faster. After ten rounds I flopped on my bed and giggled. "I'll be the best dancer at Vassar. I'll meet a handsome young man, like the girl in the play, and I'll fall head-over-heels in love."

For the next month, I left dinner early every night to practice the One Step in my room alone before Anna returned.

The sidewalks were in icy and covered with new-fallen snow, and my feet were slipping as I trudged along to the post office in down-town Poughkeepsie. I carried the package of Christmas presents for my family —scarves and gloves for Mother and Rose, Crayola crayons and miniature Statues of Liberty for Annie and Bobby, and a cloth-bound journal for Father. "My first Christmas away from my family and house in Persia," I muttered. "It will be so strange celebrating Christmas with relatives instead."

My sister Rose will be with the family in Tabriz. How I wish I was more like her, so sweet and unselfish. I'm quite the opposite, always thinking of myself. I want to become a better person, but my motivation is only a form of selfish pride.

Tears welled in my eyes, and my eyelashes froze together in the cold wind. Then, turning a corner, I slid off the walk and into the street, falling on my side. A passing gentleman stopped and helped me up just in time before a carriage coming around the corner nearly ran me over.

Before Christmas, I took the train to visit Uncle Rob in Princeton. Cousin Howard walked with me from train station to their home at

93 Stockton Place, a stately brick house just across the street from the university. When Uncle Rob met us at the door, his smile was so like Father's that it brought tears to my eyes.

My younger cousins were busy in the parlor stringing popcorn garlands for the Christmas tree. Fortunately, Eleanor wanted to go for a walk. "Let me take you for a tour of Princeton campus," she said. "Christmas decorating bores me."

"Allen Dulles is a freshman here," I commented. "I'll be able to tell him I visited and found the fine Princeton buildings so very close together."

"How did you meet a young man already? You've only been in America a few months?"

"I met him in Paris. He's a relative of sorts. My cousins in Englewood are also his cousins. That is, his father is Uncle Will's brother."

"I see. Related, but not close enough to prohibit romance," Eleanor said and smiled slyly.

On Christmas Eve, I arrived at Rosenvik to find the Dulles family trimming a majestic Christmas tree in the Green Room. It was cold and windy, and snow falling without, but warm and cheery within. Christmas morning after breakfast we congregated to open presents around the tree.

"What piles of them there are," I exclaimed.

"It seems a hopeless job, I know," Grandmother said, "but if we work bravely, we might manage to open them all."

Grandmother gave me ice skates and a large box from Uncle Will contained another dress from Macy's and shoes to match.

"Your friend Miss Fitzgerald helped me," he said and winked.

"I'm quite overwhelmed with everybody's kindness and generosity," I said with tears in my eyes. "Christmas presents in Persia are always such simple, necessary things."

The next morning Uncle Will took us skating. "I've never skated before," I said.

"We've taken that into consideration," Uncle Will replied.

As I started cautiously out on the ice, Uncle Will said, "Don't feel defeated if you fall, only if you can't get up again."

Dorothy and Edith skated very well and went round and round the rink laughing with their friends, but I didn't care. I wanted to conquer this alone. I was walking along on the skate blades at first and made it a full circle around the rink. "I get on pretty well for my first time on the ice," I muttered, congratulating myself. Although I lost my balance and fell over several times, I was able to get up again.

After I had successfully made it around the rink three times, Uncle Will skated up behind me. "All-in-all you should consider this a great success," he said as he took my hand. "Don't worry. I'll skate slowly with you."

On the way home, I thought Dorothy and Edith would make fun of me, but instead Dorothy said, "You skated pretty well for the first time." And Edith smiled at me and nodded.

On December 27th, there was a big dance at the Armory. I went with the Dulleses, cold all over with fear and dread. I wore one of the dresses that Uncle Will bought for me at Macy's, a lovely, thin, white, flowing chiffon with an embroidered bodice. When I came down the stairs Grandmother said, "You look like an angel."

I stood with my cousins, Dorothy and Edith, on one side of the dance floor. As we were talking and aimlessly scanning the crowd, I saw a boy approaching us through the corner of my eye. He tapped me on the shoulder. "My name is Rowland Vermilye," he said. "May I have this dance?"

"Agnes Wilson. Yes, I'd be pleased to dance with you."

Dorothy and Edith were laughing as Rowland gently took my hand and led me to the dance floor. I never heard the music with my heart pounding hard against my chest and my head throbbing. I stepped on his foot once and was mortified, but he smiled sweetly and said, "You are not the first girl to do that; my feet must be too large." As I passed Uncle Will and Miss Rollins on the dance floor, we exchanged smiles.

That night after the dance Uncle Will asked, "How did you like dancing with Rowland Vermilye?"

"Rowland Vermilye? Goodness I forgot his name I was so nervous."

Uncle Will laughed. "If we run into him with his family at church, please remember to acknowledge him. They are good friends of the family. We will be going to another dance tomorrow."

"Another dance? So soon?" I was exhausted from nervous energy after this first dance.

The next night, I went again in fear and dread. As soon as the band started to play a boy asked me to dance. Then, for each dance after, a different boy tapped on my shoulder, introduced himself, and took me to the dance floor. Sadly, when it was over, I could not remember any of their names, but at least I was able to go with others, new and strange, and be a part of it. I had conquered a great fear and had accomplished a personal victory.

Preparations for the Dulles's annual New Year's dance at Rosenvik started a week in advance. Bakers brought sheets of cakes and pastries that filled the kitchen with tempting odors, and I joined my cousins in sampling when Grandmother and Winifred were not in sight. Furniture was removed from the entry hall, dining room, parlor, and sitting room to make a large open space, and oriental rugs were rolled up and removed to expose the wood floors. Elegant floral arrangements appeared on the mantels and on stone pillars on every corner. The house was a garden of flowers and ferns.

The night before the dance, the children's job was to "dance" oatmeal into the wood floors to make them slippery. After we'd completed our jobs, I joined Dorothy, Edith, and the younger children taking turns running and then sliding across the floor, making it a contest to see who could slide the farthest.

The night of the dance I dressed in my pink chiffon dress and wore pink ribbons and white carnations in my hair. As a special touch I slipped the bloodstone ring onto my ring finger to give me courage.

Standing in a row, the Dulles children and I met the guests as they entered. When Miss Rollins came, all of us gasped. She wore a shimmering pink silk dress with a bodice covered with pearls in a floral design, and her hair piled in ringlets on top of her head with pink and white rose buds. I felt a twinge of jealousy as Uncle Will took her hand and kissed her cheek. I wanted to look just like Miss Rollins someday.

Finally, the Dulleses from Auburn arrived, including Allen, who was on his way back to Princeton. I danced with Allen for eight dances and Uncle Will for two. It was a gay, bright, enchanting evening, a whirl of music and light. I was giddy with delight to be with Allen again and kept close by his side the rest of the evening. My head was spinning with excitement and my cheeks were hot and glowing all evening.

After the dance, I could barely sleep and decided to write in my journal and reflect on the past six months: "To think that I've been in America for six months, when it seems like years. My relatives have done so much to make me feel at home here. Grandmother Rhea and Uncle Will worry so much about my fitting in, buying me dresses and teaching me to dance. And yes, I can dance now and start to enjoy myself with others. But I still don't fit in with the other girls at Vassar. My cousin Anna is my only friend there and I must try to make friends with other girls. The highlight of 1910 will be seeing Joe Cochran in June after his brother's graduation from Williams. I can hardly wait."

A sudden gust of wind rattled the window and startled me. I slapped my journal closed. I felt strangely guilty with my family in Persia, while I was having such a full joyous life, eating cake and chocolates, dressing up, and going to dances. And poor Howard, how quickly I had forgotten him. But I hadn't forgotten. How could I? I was wearing the bloodstone ring and it reminded me of him.

The window rattled again, and a chill ran down my spine. *When another man touches or kisses me, there is always Howard's ghost present in the shadows. Was it my guilt for making him love me that haunts me? I remember so vividly standing around his coffin, silent and softened by grief, his face so calm and noble in death. I should try to rid him from my memory.*

Can I?

Chapter 8

SECOND SEMESTER AT VASSAR, 1910

ENTERING LATHRUP HALL AFTER CHRISTMAS BREAK, I was greeted by other girls, talking and laughing in the hallway. Anna was back from her vacation in Saltsburg and excited to see me.

"Jack came down from Pittsburgh after Christmas and stayed through New Year's Day," she said. "See what he gave me for Christmas." She extended her arm to show me a charm bracelet with three gold heart-shaped charms dangling from it. "He asked me to go to the Princeton Junior Prom in March." Anna was smiling broadly with a glow in her eyes.

"Did Aunt Bessie and Uncle Andy say you could go?"

"Mother thinks Jack is a good catch and urged me to go. Father, of course, insists on a chaperone."

"How will you arrange for a chaperone?"

"I've already written to Uncle Rob and Aunt Ellen to make arrangements," Anna replied, smiling sweetly and fixing her eyes on mine. "And I'd like to ask you a favor as well. Could you tell Miss Kilpatrick that Jack and I are engaged?"

"You think telling her that is necessary?"

"Otherwise she might not approve of my going."

My stomach felt as hard as a rock and my throat tightened. "But that would be lying."

"We are just about as good as engaged."

"But it's not true; you're not engaged yet. What if he changes his mind?"

"That won't happen."

"Mother and Father told me never to tell a lie—never. The Bible says, 'Lying lips are an abomination to the Lord.' Proverbs 12:22."

"Sometimes you have to lie so you don't hurt other's feelings," Anna replied. "Remember when I told you Jack said you were pretty? Well, I was lying. He never said that, but it made you feel good, didn't it?"

Anna's words stunned me like a slap in the face. "Frankly, I don't care what Jack thinks about me. I know I'm not pretty."

"Will you tell Miss Kilpatrick or not?"

"I don't want to and I won't. I'm afraid she will know it is a lie and won't ever trust me again."

"You are so unsophisticated. When your family was in America on furlough five years ago, my parents offered to have you and Rose stay with us and go to Kiski, but your father refused to let you. Mother and Father said that they were afraid you'd turn out like this."

"They did?"

"Yes. My parents said it was a mistake to take you back to Persia and that you'd never adjust to American life. They were right."

"It's true that I'm different from the other girls, but I'm learning how to talk to them and get along."

"They all think you are strange and don't want anything to do with you. They call you 'Agnes, the missionary girl.' "

"Yes, I know they do."

"Well, I'm your cousin and I'm also the only friend you have here. And as your only friend won't you do me this simple favor?"

"I can't lie. I'm a missionary's daughter."

"A missionary's daughter, who can't dance with boys because of fear of ruining her reputation," Anna sneered.

"Over Christmas vacation I went to three dances in Englewood and I danced with boys."

"Oh, so the missionary's daughter has already ruined her reputation. Then she can lie too."

"I won't do it, Anna. I simply can't."

"Well, if you don't tell Miss Kilpatrick I'll tell everyone about Howard Baskerville. How you wouldn't marry him, so he joined the Persian army and was killed. You feel guilty about it, don't you? That's why you want to hide it from the family. Well I'll make sure the truth comes out."

A wave of heaviness passed over me and the blood rose to my face. "Please don't tell anyone about Howard. Father didn't want anybody in the Wilson family to know. I only told you. It was to be our secret."

"Well you have a choice then, don't you? Talk to Miss Kilpatrick or I will tell everyone about Howard."

"I won't tell Miss Kilpatrick, and that's final." I turned away, no longer being able to look at Anna's angry eyes.

Anna stomped the heels of her shoes hard on the floor in succession. "Oh, you are impossible." She turned and abruptly left the room slamming the door behind her.

"Oh, Anna please don't tell the Wilson relatives about Howard. Father would never forgive me if Grandmother Wilson heard about it."

Sadly, Anna really was my only friend at Vassar and she was so different from me. All she thought about was marrying Jack. She had no ambitions of her own. Whereas I intended to have a career, not just marry and have babies.

That night I made a New Year's resolution to make at least three friends at Vassar. Before Christmas I had started to make friends with Mary Phillips, a freshman who I often sat with at Christian Association meetings. At the next meeting, I mustered the courage to approach her.

"Would you like to come with me for service on Sunday at the First Presbyterian Church in Poughkeepsie?"

She looked at me with surprise and then smiled, "Why, yes. I'd like to."

As we walked back from church, Mary said, "I come from Chicago and don't fit in very well with all these East Coast girls. They're all so sophisticated."

"And you think you have more in common with me?"

"Yes, you seem very honest and sincere, like Midwest folks. Besides, I think it is interesting that you are from Persia and I want to know all about it."

From that day forward Mary and I spent many evenings together talking about Persia. I even taught her some words in Azeri. Then one evening Mary announced, "I want to go to Persia with you some day." *Mary is a true friend who appreciates me and my differences.*

For a week before semester examinations I panicked and stayed up past midnight every night studying. As Anna and I were walking back to Lathrup after our mathematics examination, the sun's glare made it difficult for my tired eyes to focus. I squinted at something unusual in the sky. "It's a star with a tail," I exclaimed. "In the middle of the day?"

"Oh, I must have been so busy studying for exams that I forgot to look for the Daylight Comet," Anna replied. "Allen Platt, the science teacher at Kiski School, told me about it during Christmas break."

"What's a comet?"

"Mr. Platt said it's a large chunk of rock and ice that reflects sunlight. It's not on fire."

"Will it collide with the earth?"

"No. He said it is too far away."

The German exam was not at all easy and it took me the full two hours allotted. Afterward, I ran to the lecture hall to hear a talk by Booker T. Washington. The other students were already seated, and I finally found a seat where I could only get a good view of the back of his head. He spoke about the meaning of Success and Courage, and then spoke about helping others. "The highest test of civilization of any race is in its willingness to extend a helping hand to the less fortunate. It is not a sacrifice to give one's life in work for others; there is no greater joy. It is only by serving our fellow men that we can rise into the spirit of Christ."

I was so touched by his words that tears ran down my cheeks. To think that I almost missed his speech, something so much more relevant to what I wanted to do with my life than speaking German. It was that night that I decided that the most important thing that I could do for others would be to return to Persia as a missionary teacher and help educate Persian women so they could advance in their society. *This is what I want to do with all of my heart.*

For semester break Anna and I went to Princeton and stayed with Uncle Rob. Aunt Ellen invited Jack Daub and Allen Dulles over for tea. On the train back to Vassar, Anna spoke in a continuous stream about Jack, but suddenly stopped when she noticed I was no longer listening to her.

"You seem to like Allen Dulles a lot," she said.

"Yes, I do. He was at my uncle's New Year's dance and he was my main dancing partner."

"Don't you have a beau in Minneapolis?"

"Yes, Joe is my friend from Persia. We have known each other since we were children."

"He's not really a boyfriend then."

"Joe is my boyfriend. We were 'pledged' for marriage by our parents as children."

"That is just parents' talk. No matter what they say they can't make him propose to you."

"Marriage isn't something that crosses my mind anyways. I'm too young for that."

"You've never shown me a picture of Joe. Do you have one?"

"No, but I have a mental image of him. He's a tall, slender boy, with sandy hair, blue eyes, and freckles."

That evening I decided to write to Joe and ask him to send me his picture. If I had one to show the girls, I'd be able to say I had a boyfriend, like Anna. I felt a bit odd asking Joe for his picture but decided needing to recognize him when we met in Albany this summer was a sufficient excuse. I quickly put the letter in the mailbox before I changed my mind.

Joe would make a fine boyfriend, but would we ever get married? How foolish and dreamy I was, and yet I had faith in dreams. They certainly came true with Howard Baskerville, but in his case, I foolishly dreamed that I could turn his head and it ended in disaster. I did hope that it would not be one-sided the other way, with me dreaming of Joe and he not feeling a thing for me.

Anna came bursting into my room, her eyes wide with fear and her face white as a sheet. She held *The New York Times* in her hand. "You need to read this," she stammered. She pointed to an article on the second page. Just as I was about to take the paper, she pulled it out of my hands.

"No, I'll read it to you. 'Halley's Comet Tail Contains Poisonous Gas. Today Sir William Higgins of the Yerkes Observatory announced the discovery of cyanogen, a deadly poison, in the tail of Halley's comet. The techniques of spectroscopy, in which light is analyzed to determine the composition of celestial objects, identified the poisonous gas. On

May 19th, the earth will pass through the comet's 25 million-kilometer-long tail. The French astronomer, Camille Flammarion, believes that as we pass through the comet's tail the cyanogen would impregnate the atmosphere and possibly snuff out all life on the planet.' "

"What? Another comet? I thought comets were safe. Is this a hoax?"

"I'm afraid not. Scientists think this one is dangerous, and they are never wrong."

"What is this world coming to?" I exclaimed. "God sent the plagues and the flood to destroy the unrighteous people on earth. Did he send the comet?"

Halley's Comet appeared in the night sky on April 10th, and Anna, Mary, and I slipped outside the dormitory to see its long and glistening fat tail. "I don't think Halley will hurt us," I whispered. "Nothing that beautiful could."

The following weeks, Anna took the newspaper from the library every day and brought it to our room, discreetly folded under her coat. We lay on my bed together and read the articles about Halley's Comet. Advertisements began appearing in newspapers, on boards, on shop windows around town for anti-comet umbrellas. Hope's anti-comet pills were selling for twenty-five cents each and advertised as "an elixir for escaping the wrath of the heavens." Panicked buying of gas masks and anti-comet pills ensued.

One afternoon Anna came to the room with a box in her arms. "It's from Mother," she said. "I know it's not chocolates. She's so concerned about my figure." Anna was strangely silent after she opened the box.

"What is it?" I asked.

"It's a gas mask, an anti-comet umbrella, and anti-comet pills. I can give you some pills if you need them. There are two large bottles."

I wrote to Mother and Father, asking them about taking the anti-comet pills. Father wrote back quickly saying, "The pills are likely only sugar and corn starch."

"Americans wear nice clothes and drive automobiles, they have telephones and electricity, but they have superstitions like the poor illiterate Persian peasants," I said.

Each night for the next four weeks, we went out to visit Halley in silence and held hands. The newspapers continued to report strange incidents attributed to Halley. On April 22nd, Mark Twain died. He was born in 1835 when Halley's Comet last passed by Earth and had predicted his death by its next visit. Then, on May 6th, England's King Edward VII died, and people speculated that it was linked the comet. Later that week, a shepherd in Washington state went insane with worry about the comet. A California prospector nailed one hand and his feet to a cross and refused to be rescued.

With all the tension in the air, I realized that it was the anniversary of the Persia Revolution and Howard Baskerville's death. In reoccurring nightmares, the cannon on top of the Arg was firing, and I was in the Vanneman's house, with bullets flying through the windows. I desperately crawled on my belly to a door, but when I entered the room, Howard's blood-soaked body lay on a bed. I reached to touch his lifeless hand and woke up in a cold sweat.

I found the bloodstone ring that Howard gave me carefully tucked away in my silk jewelry box and slipped it onto my ring finger. "The ring has a protective deity engraved in bloodstone," I told Anna. "The man-bull with eagle wings, the Lamassu of Persepolis."

"And what can it do?" Anna asked.

"It can give me courage," I answered. "I guess I'm superstitious too."

On May 19th, the day the Earth would pass through Halley's tail, the churches were filled with crowds of people attending all-night vigils. Mary and I joined a crowd of students outside to watch Halley, like any other night, but Anna refused to go out and sat in her room with her gas mask, anti-comet pills, and umbrella.

"Let's all join hands," I said to the other students assembled, and we stood together, strong and brave.

Mary asked to sleep in bed with me until the night was over. "If God chose for us to die tonight as the tail of the comet passes over us, then it shall be," I said, "but I believe God still has plans for us." I put my arms around Mary and fell asleep, comforted by the warmth of her body against mine. She stayed warm all night, and no one died from the comet's tail.

After that night a strong bond developed between Mary and me, and we were together most of the time. On weekends in spring, she spent the night with me, and after a late breakfast we went for lovely long walks and gathered violets.

One afternoon, while returning to Lathrup from Latin class, I saw Anna beckoning me from the window. Instead of speaking she fluttered a scrap of paper down to my feet bearing the brief words "Frank Coan in Parlor." I almost fell over I was so overwhelmed with surprise and excitement. Rushing into the parlor to greet my childhood friend, I suddenly recoiled when I saw him. He was so much changed it startled me. Frank was tall and thin—painfully so—with the general appearance of not being very strong, but he was still recognizable with his fine dark eyes and sinister smile. Yes, this was Frank, my friend from the mission in Urmia.

"I'm here to welcome you to America and personally send you regards from the Coans and Cochrans," Frank said. "Our families have been living together in Minneapolis."

"Mother told me. All together in one big house, just like in Persia."

"I'm now at Williams, and my sister Elizabeth is at Wellesley. Coan-incidently, we are both graduating from college next year."

"Coan-incidently. Frank you are the same as always, you silly boy. What will you and Elizabeth do after you graduate?"

"We'll both go back to Minnesota for a few years. Elizabeth plans to go the teacher's college, and I plan to attend a theological seminary. Eventually Elizabeth plans to return to Persia, perhaps through the Student Volunteers. I'm leaning toward missionary work for the YMCA in India. What about you? Any plans?"

"Goodness, I barely made it through my first semester, but I do plan on returning to Persia after I graduate. Perhaps with the Student Volunteers like Elizabeth."

"Elizabeth will be glad to hear that. She's currently their president."

"Oh, I must talk to her about it."

"The Cochrans are also doing fine. Clement is in the grain business in Minneapolis and Harrison graduates from Williams this year. And, of course, you likely heard that Joe has been accepted at Williams as a freshman next year." Frank gave me a sidelong glance.

My cheeks were burning, and I was sure he read the surprise in my face. "No, I didn't hear that," I stammered. "I'll have to write Joe and congratulate him."

"He's excited that he'll be closer to you." Frank smiled slyly and winked at me. "I hear the two of you have been devoted pen pals all these years."

"Yes, and I'm happy we kept it up. I didn't feel so lonely coming to America knowing I had Joe here, and of course, you and Elizabeth."

That evening I stayed up till midnight writing a letter to Joe. I was happy to have Frank's visit as an excuse since he had not yet replied to my last letter. How strange it was. I just ached to see Joe again and wanted him to be my boyfriend, yet I hadn't seen him for three years.

Later in May, Uncle Will and Harriet Rollins were married at the Rollins' summer home in Mamaroneck, New York. The bridesmaids, Dorothy, Edith, and I, carried bouquets of sweet peas and wore white chiffon dresses covered with organza netting and tied with blue bows. Before we went down for the ceremony, Miss Rollins presented us with crescent pins with pearls and sapphires. Being such a happy affair, I didn't understand why Grandmother Rhea was crying.

Dorothy took me aside and said, "Grandmother will be all right. Miss Rollins will let her stay at Rosenvik after the wedding."

"What?" I said. "It had never occurred to me that Grandmother Rhea might not have a home when Uncle Will married again."

"She has nowhere else to go. Father and my new mother are generous people. Besides, Miss Rollins asked her to take care of Rhea and Winslow."

The second week of June, I took the night boat to Albany, the Peoples Line 6.30 729th. Sitting on the deck as the boat slipped through the waters of the Hudson River, the moonlight and cool breeze helped to relieve my nervous anxiety. I was stopping in Albany *en route* to the Silver Bay Conference to see Joe. He had never sent me his picture, saying he'd given all his senior pictures away. I hardly slept a wink worrying that I wouldn't recognize him.

In Albany I disembarked at five o'clock in the morning and walked to the Albany Union Train Station at the corner of Broadway and Steuben Streets. Settling onto a bench in the waiting area with a book, I found myself dosing off.

A tap on my shoulder startled me awake. I opened my eyes to see a young man looking down at me. "Agnes?" he said.

"Joe?"

He was laughing heartily as he helped me up and enveloped me with a hug. "I would recognize you anywhere, even sleeping on the bench in a waiting room."

We stood looking at each other, smiling. Joe was a tall lanky young man. He'd lost his freckles and looked so much like his father and namesake, with his long forehead and stern, intelligent face. His brilliant blue eyes sparkled through wire-rimmed glasses. A warmth of nostalgia radiated throughout my body.

Other people stood nearby, watching us, and Joe introduced them. "This is my brother Clement and his wife, Agnes, my brother Harrison, and my sister Lilli."

"We don't have much time," Clement said. "We'll be taking the train to Chicago at one o'clock. Let's go for a walk along the Hudson River and an early lunch at Keeler's."

"I'll be going to Williams next year, as you know," Joe said as we walked. "It's a pleasant campus surrounded by rolling hills, with mountains close by."

"Will you be able to visit me at Vassar?"

"Of course. Williamstown is not far from Albany, then I can take the train or boat to Poughkeepsie."

"He'll have his nose in his books a good amount of time if he expects to go the medical school," Clement interjected, "so don't expect to see too much of Joe."

"Clement is thirteen years older than me," Joe said. "But he thinks he's my father sometimes."

"Just looking out for your best interests, little brother," Clement added.

My time with Joe was over way too soon. It was very emotionally stirring for me to see him again, and I started crying as I watched the Cochran's train leave the station. Seeing Joe again moved me in a strange inexplicable way.

The rest of the Vassar delegation was already on the Lake George steamer when I arrived in Caldwell, and I barely made it on board before it took off for Silver Bay. In addition to Mary Phillips, two other freshmen, Helen "Buzz" Howson and Marcia Livermore, were part of the Vassar delegation, and we were assigned to the same room at the Silver Bay Hotel.

Young fellows with blue S.B.H. emblems on their white lapels took our suitcases, and we were hustled into a huge dining hall where dinner was immediately served. During the evening platform speech, our schedule for the next five days was announced: "Your morning will start each day promptly at seven-thirty with breakfast. Then you will start the morning session at nine with Bible and Mission classes, followed by a platform address, then lunch. The afternoon is free for recreation—swimming, boating, hiking, or studying your Bible lessons. It is your choice. At five-fifteen p.m. the meeting for Bible secretaries is held, followed by dinner at six. Evening church service is at seven-forty-five, followed by a brief reception. Everyone is then dismissed for the day and lights are out at ten, no exceptions."

The next day I arrived to find the conference room filling up and, seeing an open seat, maneuvered my way to the front. To my surprise the person sitting next to me was Elizabeth Coan, Frank's sister from the Urmia mission. We jumped up and down, hugging and squealing.

"I'll be leading the morning Student Volunteer's meetings," she said. "I'm sure you'll want to attend. Frank told me you plan to join and return to the mission."

"Yes, after I graduate from Vassar. Do you have any recommendations on things I should do here at the meeting?"

"I recommend that you sign up for an interview with Louise Holmquist, one of the conference leaders. She always has good insight."

Louise Holmquist smiled and took my hand as we sat down for my interview. "I pray for you, that you will be a blessing to college life.

Live so that when you are gone from college, the girls remember you as one who showed them the Lord in all you did."

She seemed to know what I lacked and needed, and yet did not know myself. *Louise Holmquist and Elizabeth Coan are the most influential women I've met in America. Someday I want to be an eloquent leader of the missionary cause just like them.*

In the beginning of the week, the girls at the conference seemed afraid to speak. There was uncomfortable silence, as though something was wrong. Then, on the last Friday, Miss Terrance Taft spoke on "Perfect Obedience to God's Will."

"It is necessary to find out what His will is for your life," she said, "before it's too late."

Her simple words woke up something deep inside me, a novel revelation. Questions raced through my mind. *Was there a life plan for me that He had already determined? Is my purpose to be a foreign missionary His will, or is it just my own will? How would I find out what His will is for me?*

At the next delegation meeting, many people spoke as though they were all similarly awoken. One girl told us that while playing with the sand at the shore, she dug little wells in the sand and noticed how the water of the lake immediately flowed in to fill them, and if she dug deeper more water replaced the sand. She realized that if she dug her own Self out of her life that God would be able to fill it.

How I wanted to add a word of the thoughts that filled my heart, one little word of how I felt I was beginning to know God more than ever before, but my tongue was paralyzed. I could not manage to speak. *Coward, coward. Why did I not speak then?*

Our final delegation meeting was led by my new idol, Louise Holmquist. She sat with a lamp behind her, which cast her long, distorted shadow on the stage. As she pointed to her shadow she said, "How could I get from my sight this Self of mine? Why only by turning from it to the Light. With my eyes fixed on the Light, I am troubled by my Self no longer. What's more, if we keep our eyes on Him, other people will not see us, but only God through us.

"People can either be like automobiles with the power in themselves, liable to give out at any time, or they can be like the trolley, useless in themselves, but full of energy and usefulness when the lever is moved to touch the wire. God, like the wire, is always there full of power, ready to give us energy to fulfill our dreams. We only need to reach out to Him to use it."

"She is so eloquent," I murmured.

The delegation erupted, people raised their hands, talking all at once. Louise Holmquist stood and raised her arms in the air to silence the chaos. She looked like an angel with her ruffled white blouse, arms spread wide. "One voice at a time. One voice at a time," she said. "I don't know you all by name. You there in the back." She proceeded around the room, and when she came to me, she called me by name, "Agnes, your turn."

My heart was pounding in my temples. I can't remember what I said, something about thinking of Him every time I take a trolley, but what was more important is that I spoke up in front of everybody; they listened and took me seriously. Someday I hoped to speak in front of others like Louise Holmquist.

It was our last night at Silver Bay and our hearts were very full. How could it be over? We had just begun. After lights out, Mary and I lay on her bed and talked of many things, all Silver Bay had meant to us, all we had learned, of hopes and fears, and resolution of our doubts about God.

Early the next morning we loaded onto the Lake George steamer and sailed down the lake. Wistfulness overcame me as Silver Bay disappeared amongst the wooded hills. "It is an experience I'll always remember," I said.

In addition to deepening my faith, I had become closer to Mary Philips, Buzz Howson and Marcia Livermore. I had lived up to my New

Year's resolution to make three new friends at Vassar this year. And, they would become life-long friends.

On the train to New York, I told Marcia how much my interview with Miss Holmquist meant to me. "She said marvelous things to me as well," Marcia said. "She told me to live so that when I leave college that all remember me as showing them the Lord's ways in all that I did. Isn't that sweet?"

I looked at Marcia with amazement. "She said the same to me," I said.

For several moments we looked at each in utter disbelief. "Did she pray that you would be a blessing to Vassar?" Marcia asked.

"Yes, she said that too."

"Miss Holmquist made me think that I was someone special," Marcia said, "but I'm just the same to her as all the other girls."

My heart, which had felt so full, felt as though it had been crushed between two stones.

When I reached New York, I hurried to meet the Pittmans, who were on their way back to Persia. Over lunch, we talked about our trip to America together, and I was surprised at how nostalgic I was.

"I remember taking our first bath in Poti," I said. "How we visited Michelangelo's "David" in Florence, and the Eiffel Tower that Mr. Pittman disliked so much."

"Sadly, our furlough is over," Mrs. Pittman said, "but fortunately it is relatively safe to return."

"The Shah's son is in power now," Mr. Pittman added, "or more precisely the Russians. They've put up barracks in what once were the beautiful gardens of the Crown Prince's palace in Tabriz. I don't look forward to seeing that, but we will be pleased to see your parents and the others at the mission."

"And I hear your sister Rose is on her way to America with the Vannemans," Mrs. Pittman said.

"Yes, they left June 17th and expect to arrive in America at the end of August. How strange it must seem with only the little ones at home. My heart is aching to see them all."

"Two more years until your parents' next furlough. Time will pass quickly, you'll see."

I gave them a long letter for Mother and Father to hand deliver, a small doll for Annie and little bag of marbles for Bobby. It was a tearful goodbye with kisses and long hugs. As I watched their steamer leave the dock and set out to sea, I gasped, "I wish I was going with them. When will I be able to go back home? When will I go back to Persia?"

Chapter 9

SOPHOMORE YEAR, VASSAR, 1910

FROM NEW YORK I TRAVELED TO INDIANA, Pennsylvania to spend the summer, staying with Aunt Agnes, Father's youngest sister and her family. Uncle Stacy, her husband, was the post-master, and their children, Stacy Jr. and Jane, were four and two. Aunt Agnes managed her children on traditional Wilson family love principles, being always gentle and patient. Stacy Jr., really a dear little fellow, was often rough and boyish. Whereas Jane was quite affectionate, and her sweet kisses filled my hungry heart's longing for my little brother and sister far away in Persia.

One afternoon as I sat sewing, Stacy Jr. tugged at my skirt. "Tell me a story," he said.

"I'd be happy to do that," I said and put down my sewing. "The story is called 'The Belling of the Cat.' " Stacy sat on the floor in front of me, with wide eyes. "The mice called a meeting to decide how they could save themselves from the house cat, who kept plucking them off one by one. All the mice had ideas, but none seemed good enough. Then a young mouse stood up and said, 'Let's hang a bell around the cat's neck to warn us when it's coming.' One mouse exclaimed, 'He's a genius.' And the others crowded around the young mouse and patted him on the back. After all the congratulations and rejoicing settled down, an old mouse slowly stood up and said, 'It is a fine idea, but who will bell the cat?' The moral is that it's one thing to propose an idea, and it's another to carry it to fruition."

"What does 'fruition' mean?" Stacy asked.

"To bring to completion," I answered.

"Oh. I don't think Mother would let the mice bell our cat Chester."

"Why is that?"

"Cats are meant to catch mice. You should know that."

"Would you like another story?"

"Not now." Stacy proceeded to play jacks with himself, tossing the ball and collecting metal jacks from the floor in his hand.

"In Persia they play jacks with sheep knuckles," I said.

Stacy continued to play with his jacks, ignoring me. "Can you imagine how hard it is to hold big sheep knuckles in your hand and catch the ball?" Stacy continued to ignore me. I could tell he was very fond of my stories, but then he wounded me so by becoming unresponsive. It was foolish, I suppose, that I should care, but I did care. My heart was just too proud to ever show it longed and hungered for love from those around me. We all need love, just as we need food. Dear Mother and Father and sweet Rose, their love I could always count on, but they were far away. How I missed them.

I sometimes wondered what the relatives thought of me. When I was around them it often seemed that I was merely playing a part in a play, not being my real self. It gave me a dreadful feeling of being unreal. *Oh, you poor little struggling Agnes. Whatever will become of you?*

Every day, Cousin Margaret found it her duty to take me along with her, and I enjoyed her company even though she was three years older than I. One day we were invited to a picnic at the country club with a group of girls from town. Margaret had us sit with her classmate Caroline and two girls my age, Isabelle and Elsie. We waded in the creek and sat on the bank and engaged in "girl talk."

"Elsie, you know people around town are talking about you and Frank," Isabelle said.

"Are they? What are they saying?" Elsie asked.

"Several people saw Frank coming out of the jewelry store last week," Caroline said.

Elsie smiled. "Well if he bought an engagement ring, he hasn't asked me yet."

"I have my eyes on Robert Sutton," Isabelle said.

"The Sutton family is well-to-do," Caroline said. "He'd be quite a catch."

"John Sutton, Robert's grandfather, was my grandfather's business partner," I interjected.

"Since you're Andrew Wilkins Wilson's granddaughter, you'd be the perfect match for Robert," Caroline responded.

"No you don't," said Isabelle.

"Don't worry," I said. "I'm going back to Vassar at the end of the summer, and I intend to graduate from college."

Margaret looked at me, appalled. She'd warned me not to brag about going to college as not all girls in town were "so privileged."

"Agnes isn't used to being around boys," Margaret said. "Vassar is an all-girls school."

"Like a nunnery," Caroline said.

"I fear that I act quite awkwardly around boys," I said. "I prefer talking to men."

"I also prefer older men," Caroline said. "I'm interested in Ernest Stewart. His wife died five years ago, and he hasn't remarried. I asked Father to introduce us."

"But he's fifteen years older than you," Margaret protested.

"Fifteen years older, yes, and a successful attorney. He's everything my parents would want in a son-in-law."

"I thought finding the right husband was about romance," I said.

The other girls laughed. "Romance has little to do with it," Caroline responded. "Someday you'll find out for yourself."

I was perplexed. "I want love to be nothing but romance, to fall head-over-heels in love."

All the girls laughed.

On August 20th, I received a telegram from Rose announcing her safe arrival in America: "Here I am and send much love, Rose." How the days did drag by waiting for her to arrive. Finally, on August 31st, Margaret and I got up at quarter past five and went to meet her at the Blairsville Intersection. It seemed an unearthly hour, and we were dazed to see other people up too. As fate would have it, the train was an hour late, and how the time did creep as we paced the platform or tried to become engrossed in life at the train station.

At last in rushed the great express, with its long line of cars and out from all that train stepped only one little girl. It was sweet little Rose with her pink cheeks glowing under the roses on her broad-brimmed hat. On the train to Indiana, we talked and talked of old times and friends and places and all that had come to us that year, a long talk that continued until an early hour the next morning.

The next day, Anna and her sisters and Uncle Rob's children came from Saltsburg, and the gang of Wilson cousins went to the Indiana County Fair. We tied each other together with rope for fear of losing the group and threaded our way through the huge crowds, often stopping to make a ring around some innocent couple to sing "Ring Around the Rosie."

My birthday was the last event of the summer, and Uncle Harry brought me a big bag of chocolate "kisses" from Pittsburgh. "These are the rage," he said, "but so hard to find in the small-town stores."

The "kisses" were wonderful. We pulled a little paper at the top and there was the little chocolate, ready to pop in our mouths, and no messy fingers.

"Why are they called 'kisses'?" I asked.

"They say it is because the machine that makes them sounds like it is smooching each time it drops one onto the conveyor belt," Uncle Harry explained. "I went to the factory in Hershey and heard it myself."

Lunch was barely over when Uncle Dick appeared in his car to take Rose and me for a long ride. When we returned, the backyard was crowded with dozens of Wilson relatives. Birthday dinner was followed by a cake with pink-and-white shiny frosting and eighteen pink candles. My presents were many, useful, and pretty, but the best present of all was having my sister Rose with me.

"Think of it," Rose said. "You're eighteen, a real adult."

"Not just a girl, but a woman," I replied proudly.

Among the Wilson relatives were Aunt Annie, Uncle Alfred, and their boys from Detroit. Rose would be returning with them to live in Detroit for a year and go to high school before coming to Vassar. After being away from Rose for more than a year, and having only two weeks together, it seemed like the cruelest punishment to take her away.

Back at Vassar, Anna and I again roomed together on the second floor of Lathrup Hall, and my friends Mary, Buzz, and Marcia were just down the hall. Aimie and Dorothy Vanneman, my friends from Tabriz, were freshmen, but instead of living in the dormitory, they lived in a house close to campus that their parents had rented. The Vanneman house provided a home away from home. With the Vanneman girls at Vassar, the other girls stopped calling me "Agnes, the missionary girl."

My sophomore classes were Physics, German, History, and English. I had the added responsibility of the Mission class, that I was asked to teach. With the support of my friends, Aimie and Dorothy Vanneman, the class became quite popular.

We enjoyed a warm fall with hayrides, and the sightings of two comets were visible in the sky, the blue Comet Brooks and festive yellow-orange Comet Beljawsky, like decorations in the Halloween sky. I was relieved that there were no apocalyptic predictions associated with these comets, as with Comet Halley.

A month after returning to Vassar, I was overcome with joy to find a package in my mailbox from Joe Cochran, a freshman at Williams. His letter read:

My Dearest Agnes,

I'm beginning to learn the Williams College lingo. The students are called 'Ephs,' pronounced with a long 'e' and our mascot is Ephelia, the Purple Cow. I picked up this card with a lovely likeness of her in the student bookshop. There is the poem by Gelett Burgess on the back, and yes, I can tell you this right now 'I'd rather see than be one.' I hope this inspires you, knowing your love of poetry.

On the long train ride from Minneapolis to Albany, I thought a lot of my father, Joseph Sr., who died of typhoid in Urmia five years ago. My goal is to follow in his footsteps, become a doctor, and return to Persia. Having spent my childhood there and knowing the language, it seems the natural thing for me to do.

I'd like so much to see you Agnes. I've checked on schedules and I could take a train from Pittsfield, twenty miles from here, or the boat from Albany. It is about eighty miles either way. My deepest regards, Joe.

I wrote back immediately, asking him to come for the Vassar Ice Carnival in February.

Since Anna was always bragging about Jack at our table, I told the other girls in Lathrup that Joe was my boyfriend. But it wasn't true; not in the same sense as Jack was to Anna.

In Miss Hill's Bible Class, we studied Matthew 18:19: "If two or three of you agree to ask, it will be done for them by my Father in heaven." Our group decided quickly to pray for greater spirituality. While waiting for the others to complete their discussion, I watched the snowflakes accumulate on the windowsill.

Miss Hill suddenly broke my train of thought. "Agnes, are you thinking about Joe?"

The other girls laughed.

My cheeks became hot. "Yes, I was thinking of Joe. My face must reflect what I'm thinking quite transparently."

On December 17th, Anna and I left to spend Christmas break in Pennsylvania. Instead of going to Jersey City as we had before, we took a train from the new Pennsylvania Station that had opened November 27th. It was a "palace," covering two city blocks, from 7th to 8th Avenues and West 31st to 33rd Streets. As I looked around, admiring the huge lobby, to my delight I spotted Aimie and Dorothy Vanneman with their mother. We sat together on the train all the way to Philadelphia. We talked in English, Azeri, French—whatever was most convenient. Our conversation lost Anna, but she was happily crocheting the entire time.

Rose arrived from Detroit, and we shared a room at Grandmother Wilson's house.

"What book are you reading?" Rose asked.

"It's 'The Rosary,' " I answered. "Most of what I tend to read, I fear, are frivolous romance novels."

"Why exactly do you like those books?"

"I don't know, but I quite enjoy the most romantic love scenes. It helps me to dream about handsome men."

One evening, one of Lad's friends, John Thompson, came to dinner and gave us a piano concert, playing anything right out of his head.

"John is a piano teacher and recitalist," Lad said. "Why don't you play something for him, Agnes? He can give you some pointers."

I was nervous as I sat down at the piano bench, with the relatives looking at me so attentively. "I'll play Anton Rubinstein's 'Kammenoi Ostroi,'" I said.

John Thompson raised his eyebrows. When I'd finished, everyone clapped, and John sat down next to me on the piano bench and said, "You need to work on feeling the music in your body so that it is not so mechanical. My best prescription for that is falling in love."

"One can only play 'Kammenoi Ostroi' when you're in love," Grandmother Wilson added. "You'll need to work on that, Agnes."

Everyone had a good laugh.

"I do want to fall in love," I said. "I want to fall head-over-heels in love."

On Christmas Eve, Rose and I "worked like Turks" getting Christmas presents ready; a chemise for Margaret, an elaborately embroidered towel for Aunt Agnes, and doll clothes for little Jane. We helped stuff the thirty-pound turkey and decorate Aunt Agnes's tree. That evening Rose and I sat with Aunt Jennie, Uncle Dick, and his new wife, Clara, in the parlor.

"What have you decided to do after Vassar, Agnes?" Uncle Dick asked.

Oh, that awful dreaded question—"What do you plan to do after graduation?"

"I'll be graduating in June 1913 and intend to return to Persia that summer with Mother and Father after their furlough. I want to become a missionary like them."

"That would be my plan too," said Rose, "only later."

"Good for you, girls. Your father would be proud to hear that. But what about marriage?" Aunt Jennie asked.

"That's also a big question," I answered.

"I think she'll marry Joe Cochran. He's a missionary doctor's son from Persia. They are good friends," Rose said.

"And you Rose?"

Rose blushed and looked at the floor.

"Rose is so pretty that she will be able to pick and choose," I said.

"So right you are," answered Uncle Dick. Seeing Rose's continued embarrassment, he quickly changed the subject to his recent visit to Gettysburg and gave us a most thrilling description the heroic battles on Cemetery Ridge during the Civil War, reading directly from a pamphlet he had obtained.

"We expect to live in California," Clara said after Uncle Dick finished his story. "My sister Irene lives in Santa Ana and has invited us to stay with her."

Grandmother Wilson, sitting in the next chair, scowled and said, "I don't think favorably about your moving to California. It is too far away and would be a great break in the Wilson family life. I must have at least six Wilsons at my table for dinner or I'll feel lonely."

The evening before leaving Indiana we attended a dance at the country club.

"You are only going as spectators since you don't know any boys in town," Aunt Jennie said. Rose and I looked at each other in surprise. "We're not going to dance?" Rose said.

Even though we did not get a chance to dance, we enjoyed the music and small-town antics. First, a crazy old man got out in the middle of the room and danced alone, keeping time to the music with tambourines. The girls I met at the country club that summer were there. Elsie was dancing with Frank, and Isabelle was with Robert Sutton. I smiled to myself, thinking about stealing Robert Sutton away. Then a wave of frantic chatter filled the room as Caroline came through the door on the arm of Ernest Stewart and took the dance floor.

"He's old enough to be her father," I heard someone whisper.

It hadn't taken those girls much time to get the men they intended on marrying, but I pitied them. None of those girls would ever go to college, and they had nothing to do but think about getting married.

Still, I hoped it would be that easy for me to fall in love when I met the right man.

Afterward in our room, while brushing my hair, I asked Rose, "Did you learn to dance in Detroit?"

"Oh, yes," Rose answered enthusiastically. "The Detroit University School holds dances and invites girls from the Detroit Day School. Aunt Annie takes me to dancing lessons."

"Did you ask Mother and Father for permission?"

"No, Mother and Father wrote Aunt Annie to do for me what she thought was best. Aunt Annie and Uncle Alfred are the kindest, most generous foster parents I could hope for."

"You're lucky to have a chance to go to high school before going to college. I wished I had." *Yes, the transition would have been easier, but I made it through the struggle.*

Rose and I took the train to Saltsburg and stayed with Uncle Andy and Aunt Bessie at Kiski. James, the Kiski football coach and Sarah's fiancée, came over for tea. Jack Daub, Anna's boyfriend, had just arrived and swaggered into the room wearing a tie scarf and a checkered vest. He pulled out a gold pocket watch and opened it, acting very Princeton-like.

"Mind if I smoke?" he said, extracting a cigarette from a shiny gold cigarette case he drew from his vest pocket. He lit a match before Anna could answer. "Jimmy, how did your football team do this year?"

"Kiski did better than expected; second in the league," James responded.

"James is the best football coach Kiski has ever had," Sarah said proudly.

"You do say," Jack said. "I should invite you to Princeton to see a real football game."

Sarah squirmed uneasily in her seat. "I'm going to be sick," she said and suddenly rose and hurried down the hall.

"Sarah is sensitive to smoke," James said flatly.

Jack rubbed the butt of his half-smoked cigarette in the ashtray aggressively, putting it out. I decided that I didn't want a boyfriend like Anna's, with his smoking and bullying.

The next evening, Aunt Bessie held a party at the house, and I wore my fluffy white net dress with blue ribbons from Aunt Helen's wedding. Before supper they hung up a sheet and all the girls stood behind it with only their shoes exposed. The boys had to choose a girl to sit next them by her shoes alone. Roy St. Clair, a junior at Washington Jefferson, chose my white shoes.

"Lucky you," murmured Aunt Bessie. "The St. Clair family is one of the most respected families in the county. His father, Frank St. Clair, is a co-founder of Kiski."

Lad chose Rose, and James chose Sarah, and they joined Roy and me at our table, a jolly, congenial set.

"I have some jokes for you," Roy said. "Why don't they charge fares to policemen on cable cars?"

"Don't they?" asked Lad.

"They don't because you can't get a nickel out of a copper," Roy answered. After the laughter subsided, he continued, "What is the most generous animal?"

"A cow," said Rose. "It gives its milk for free."

"No," said Roy. "A skunk, because it gives every passerby a scent. One more, here comes our food. What is the shape of a kiss?"

"Round," Sarah said.

"No, a lip tickle. Elliptical, get it?" Roy turned toward me and brushed his little finger around my lips.

"A lip tickle it is," I said.

The refreshments were rare—Aunt Bessie's wonderful fried oysters, sandwiches, salad, olives, pickles, cake, and ice cream with chocolate and whipped cream. Aunt Bessie said our table got the prize for eating, and we certainly did well. Roy St. Clair and I continued to tell jokes most of the evening and kept the others well jollified. *My but he is fun.*

The next morning, Roy took me sleighing. It was a glorious day and our only disappointment was that we had to be back at three for tea. Roy and I did not joke as much as the previous evening, but I enjoyed being alone with him. At tea, Roy and I sat together again, and I mentioned I loved to walk, so when he left he coupled his goodbye with, "Don't forget, I'm coming up here to walk with you next summer."

I hoped that Roy and I would spend time together next summer, as we seemed so perfectly matched in attitude, but I doubted if I would see him. It seemed that in America people moved around quickly and you might only have a fleeting chance to know someone. *Would meeting that special man only occur by chance?*

Chapter 10

SOPHOMORE YEAR, VASSAR, 1911

THE VASSAR ICE CARNIVAL WAS THE THIRD WEEK OF February. As I took the cable car to meet Joe at the train station, I had butterflies in my stomach. To my dismay, his train had already arrived, and I anxiously searched for Joe amongst the passengers. Suddenly I felt a sharp tap on my left shoulder and instinctively looked to my left, but no one was there. Turning around, I found Joe standing to my right, sporting a wide grin.

"The most beautiful girls are always at the train station," he said. My cheeks were so hot they stung in the cold air. He laughed and said, "What fun it to see you fall for the tap on the far shoulder trick. And I love to make you blush."

We left his bags at the Idylle Inn and gathered with the others at Vassar Lake. Three big bonfires were blazing on the shore, with Japanese lanterns strung between them. As we sipped hot chocolate, my Vassar friends strolled by to be introduced. Others engaged in conversations peered stealthily around their classmates' shoulders to take a look at Joe.

The band started playing, which was our cue to take our places on the ice for the procession. All of the Vassar girls were dressed in white and the ten best skaters led the march, wearing spangled silver scarves. Each class skated across the length of the lake in couples, I with Mary

Phillips. As the Class of 1913 skated down the lake, we sang our "Odd Class Marching Song": "Come and sing for eleven and thirteen too; Come and give a hearty cheer; Join our song as we gaily march along, with hearts that know no fear; Left and right beneath the green and white; Oh everybody shout and sing, for eleven and thirteen too."

Suddenly the tip of my left skate caught the ice and my knee buckled. As I was falling, Mary caught my arm and I regained my footing just in time.

After the procession I found Joe standing by a bonfire. He brought his arm vigorously around my shoulders, laughing. "Yes, you can skate, my dear Agnes, but not very well. I feel it my duty as a skater from Minnesota to give you a few lessons."

Joe stayed the next two days and we skated together each afternoon. I was happy and proud that Joe had come down from Williams, and I was able to introduce him to my friends. Yes, I could say that Joe was my boyfriend now.

"He's very intelligent looking," Anna commented. "It's a shame he's not going to Princeton. We could have visited our beaus together."

In March, I held my Mission Class on the celebration of Noruz, the Persian New Year. We celebrated on March 21st, the vernal equinox, as is customary, with a large box of Persian cookies and candies that Mother sent from Tabriz. It contained a delightful assortment of confections: Gaz, sumptuous pistachio nougat; Sohan, exotic saffron brittle with almonds and pistachios; Ghotab, almond- and walnut-filled crescent pastries; and Koloocheh, date- and walnut-filled cookies.

Aimie and Dorothy Vanneman helped me set up the Haftsin table in our sitting room. It consisted of seven items with the letter "S" for Sin in the Persian alphabet: Sabzeh, wheat sprouts, for "renewal"; Samanu, sweet pudding, representing "affluence"; Senjed, dried fruit, signifying "love"; Seer, garlic, for "health"; Seeb, apple, representing "beauty"; Somaq, red berries, for "the sunrise"; and Serkeh, vinegar, for "age." I also laid a Persian poetry book by Hafez on the table, and by tradition we opened it randomly to tell our fortune for the next year. Mine was: "Ever since happiness heard your name it has been running through the streets trying to find you."

"Are you happy?" Aimie asked.

"Yes, I am," I replied, "Who couldn't be, surrounded by such wonderful friends?"

All the girls on our floor participated and asked if we could celebrate Noruz next year. I was so proud of my success. I finally felt my classmates accepted the difference in my upbringing and found Persian traditions interesting. It was so different from the previous year, when I didn't have friends and my classmates only knew me as "Agnes, the missionary girl." Now Mary, Buzz, and Marcia were my close Vassar friends, and there were also my "mission sisters," Aimie and Dorothy.

On Sunday, March 27th, I left for Easter break and took the train to Princeton to visit Uncle Rob and Aunt Ellen for a few days before going to Englewood. On the train, I read a newspaper article about a terrible fire in a shirtwaist factory in Manhattan. The Triangle Shirtwaist Company, at Greene Street and Washington Place, had locked the exits and stairwells on the 8th, 9th, and 10th floors to prevent workers, primarily women immigrants, from stealing. When a fire broke out late in the afternoon, the owners escaped to the roof, leaving the workers trapped inside. Some women crowded onto an exterior fire escape and it collapsed, sending twenty victims hurtling down a hundred feet to the pavement below. Others jumped to their deaths out of windows, their hair and clothes on fire. One hundred and forty-six died.

I couldn't get the women who perished in the fire out of my mind the entire train ride to Princeton.

As I ate dinner with Uncle Rob, Aunt Ellen and my cousins, we talked about the Manhattan fire.

"I had no idea the working conditions were so bad in America," I said.

"Working conditions in the sweatshops are deplorable," Uncle Rob said. "There are no laws to protect the workers or the conditions in which they work."

"There was a memorial at the Metropolitan Opera House," Aunt Ellen said. "Rose Schneiderman, a union activist, gave a speech calling for unionization."

Uncle Robert hit his fist on the table, sending the water glasses and silverware on a little jump with an aftermath of clinging. "That will get us nowhere. We need our government to take action. Frances Perkins, the head of the Consumers League, is lobbying to pass legislation to end child labor and require better working conditions. She witnessed the fire and saw women jumping to their deaths. She won't let this continue."

"Why, Rob, I've never heard you talk with such admiration about another woman," Aunt Ellen said, "but, you need to settle down. Enough about sweatshops."

"Yes, you're right." Uncle Rob heaved a deep breath.

"Agnes, pardon your uncle," Aunt Ellen said. "He gets very aroused by social injustice."

"He's just like Father," I said. "If it would help the cause, I can ask the girls in my Mission Class to write letters of petition to President Taft."

"Oh, don't bother with Taft," Uncle Rob said. "He won't do anything. Write to your New York senator. Root is his name, I believe."

As I rode the train to Englewood, to spend Easter with the Dulles family, I drafted a letter of petition that I would copy and have my classmates send to Senator Root in Washington. My first call to social action made me feel empowered.

After the Easter service at the Englewood Presbyterian Church, Uncle Will grabbed my arm. "Dr. Speer is over there. He told me he wanted to speak to you."

We rushed after a tall man in a black suit. I'd heard Father speak of Dr. Speer, the head of the Board of Foreign Missions, but this was so unexpected, I didn't know what to say.

"Agnes, do you remember me?" Dr. Speer asked. "I visited your family at the mission in Tabriz when you were a child."

I looked at the man's face, with its expansive forehead and compassionate eyes. "Yes, you do look familiar," I responded.

"We live on Missionary Ridge, not far from here. Perhaps you could join us for tea tomorrow afternoon?"

"Yes, I'd love to come for tea."

The Speers house was cavernous, with decorations and rugs from all over the world. They served tea on the back porch, facing an immaculate garden. Dr. Speer sat quietly, studying me for several minutes. There was something very spiritual about him, and his silent and calm demeanor seemed so natural that it did not make me uneasy.

"You look like your father," he finally said. "I hope you also have his strength and courage."

"I hope to," I responded, "but he is the strongest and most courageous man I know."

"Do you think you will become a missionary like your parents?"

"I hope that is God's will for me."

"God's will and man's discovery of that will are two different things. One may not be willing to discover God's will, or one may pursue a course that is not God's will."

"My question is, how will I learn what His will is for me?"

"God works along channels of personal desire and inclination to help you discover His will, not by coercive acts."

"I believe His will is for me to return to Persia as a missionary."

"Many ministers tell me that the great mistake of their lives was not answering God's call to missionary service. Don't let it be too late if this is what you want to pursue."

"I'm considering joining the Student Volunteers."

"I tell the Student Volunteers that realization of a missionary call requires the consideration of three elements: the needs of the world, the personal qualifications for missionary service, and the absence of insuperable obstacles. If the need is great and difficulties do not hinder you, and, most importantly, if you are qualified, then you ought to go to the missionary field. But if you are not qualified, you should not go. Good intentions aren't sufficient."

"How do I become qualified?"

"You already know Persia and the language, but you should learn to be a nurse, a doctor, or a teacher to be able to address their needs."

"I'll become a teacher," I said firmly.

Dr. Speer laughed and looked at Mrs. Speer. "Just like that, she's discovered God's will."

"Don't pay any attention to him," Mrs. Speer said. "You need to make sure this is what you want to do."

"This is what I want to do with my life," I responded. "I'll learn to become a teacher, a good one, and return to Persia as a missionary."

"My recommendation for you is to apply to Teachers' College at Columbia University. I work in the Presbyterian Building in New York, on the corner of Fifth Avenue and 20th Street. You can visit me there any time to seek my advice."

"It sounds as though you've planned out the life of our future missionary," Mrs. Speer said. "Is it settled then?"

"It's settled," I responded.

On the train back to Vassar, I thought over everything that Dr. Speer had said. It would be hard spending two more years in America before returning to Persia, but it was important that I train to be a good teacher so I could educate the Persian women.

Good intentions are not enough. Howard Baskerville proved that to me.

Back at Vassar, violets and daisies were blooming, and robins covered the lawns. Preparations were in full swing for the May Pole exercises and Daisy Chain parade. The Sophomores picked thousands of daisies in the fields around Vassar to make the daisy chain. It would be carried on Class Day by twenty-four Juniors, representing the most attractive girls in their class. As I picked flowers with Mary and Anna, I said, "Who from our class do you think will be chosen next year to carry the Daisy Chain? Do you think I will?"

Anna laughed. "A girl with a 'Wilson chin' would never be picked. Perhaps I will be selected since I look like my mother and escaped the dreaded chin."

"The girls who are chosen for the Daisy Chain parade are pretty on the outside," Mary said, "but none of them match Agnes's internal beauty."

As my sophomore year ended, I reflected on the progress I'd made; I was fitting in with the other girls, I had friends, and I could call Joe my boyfriend. It was a happy year. As I started to pack, I opened my silk jewelry box.

"The bloodstone ring that Howard gave me," I whispered. "April 20th came and went, and I didn't remember the anniversary of Howard's death."

I slipped the ring on my finger. *I haven't forgotten. How could I?*

Instead of going to the Silver Bay Conference that summer, I chose to attend Rose's high school graduation in Detroit. Uncle Alfred met me at the train station and drove me to their home, a large red brick house a few blocks away from the Jefferson Avenue Presbyterian Church where he was a pastor. Aunt Annie, Rose, and my young cousins, Alfred Jr. and Andrew, were waiting for me on a large porch off the side of the house.

"Aunt Annie and Uncle Alfred have been like parents to me," Rose said.

"The boys love her like a sister," Aunt Annie added. "They'll miss her when she leaves."

"We will be leaving Detroit too," Uncle Alfred interjected. "We're moving to Baltimore this fall where I've taken a position as pastor in another church."

"It will be easy for me to come and see you there when I'm at Vassar," Rose said. "I'll visit you every Easter."

"That will please us all," Aunt Annie said and squeezed Rose's hand.

They appeared so close, like a family, and I felt like a stranger. I was jealous of Rose.

The graduation ceremony at Detroit Home and Day School was attended by a number of wealthy families of Detroit. The parking lot was filled with Model Ts, not just black ones but some with gold plating.

"Tin-Lizzies as far as the eye can see," Uncle Alfred commented, "and gold-Lizzies too."

"The Ford's likely own one of them," Aunt Annie added. "I hoped Rose might get the attention of that Ford boy, Edsel, but she told me she was more interested in going to college."

At the graduation picnic on Bell Isle, we sat on blankets near the Detroit River, basked in the sun, and watched Andrew and Alfred Jr. run around in the field.

"It was good to get a feeling how you spent your first year in America," I said to Rose. "If only I'd had a chance to be 'Americanized' before I went to college, my adjustment would have gone more smoothly."

From Detroit, Rose and I took the train to Chicago. "Will you remember what Uncle Foster looks like?" Rose asked.

"Of course, he has Mother's gentle face and smile," I replied.

"Do you know why he never married?"

"Grandmother will tell you he's married to painting," I replied. "Mother said it's because after she and Aunt Sophea left Lake Forest, he felt he should move back home so Grandmother didn't live alone. He worked in Chicago and commuted from there."

Uncle Foster met us on the train platform. His sandy hair was speckled gray, but he was otherwise unchanged from seven years earlier; a short soft-spoken man, who smiled like a cherub and was irresistible when it came to hugging. Being with him, you immediately felt the comfort of family.

"I've been longing for a chance to see you since you arrived from Persia," he said. "After lunch, we'll take the train together to Forest Lake. We're staying with the Wheelers."

"Is that where you are living?" Rose asked.

"I spend my summers there," Uncle Foster replied. "I've been staying at the Union Club in Chicago most of the year, which is close to my business, the Holland Radiator Company. This fall I'll move to Englewood and take a position at Will Dulles's firm. I'll be living at Rosenvik with my mother."

"Then we'll see you for Thanksgiving and other holidays," I exclaimed.

"Yes, I'm looking forward to being with you," Uncle Foster said. "An additional bonus is the painting studio that Will is allowing me to have in the servants' quarters, even though he thinks I'd be a much more successful businessman if not for my painting."

"Who are the Wheelers?" Rose asked.

"Anna Holt Wheeler is your mother's best friend," Uncle Foster said. "She has been a main contributor to the Tabriz mission and entertains missionaries on furlough. We grew up across the street from the Holt mansion. Her husband, Arthur Wheeler, was a classmate at Lake Forest University. Their estate is called 'Thalfried,' German for 'peaceful valley.' "

"Is their house on a lake?" I asked.

Uncle Foster replied. "It's situated across from a ravine, half a mile from Lake Michigan and a quarter mile from town. I'll take you for picnics on Lake Michigan every weekend."

Anna and Arthur Wheeler met us at the door of their large, English Tudor house with open arms. "Our young missionary girls have arrived," Mrs. Wheeler exclaimed. "You must call us Aunt Anna and Uncle Arthur. You have your own bedrooms on the third floor."

At the end of July, Rose and I anxiously awaited the arrival of two additional guests at the Wheeler estate, Joe and Andrew Cochran. As we stood on the platform of the Lake Forest station, the train from Minneapolis roared in and the two lanky Cochran boys stepped off.

At dinner Mrs. Wheeler announced, "Next week we're taking a trip into the deep woods of northern Wisconsin. My father was Devillo Holt, a founder of the Holt & Balcom logging company. We'll be staying at the logging camp near Archibald Lake."

The logging company had preserved an old section of trees called "Cathedral Pines," a grove of towering two- to three-hundred-year-old trees. Joe and I walked through the grove and marveled at the flocks of blue herons that made the tall trees their rookery. The squawking of baby herons made us laugh.

"What a hideous noise in 'the Cathedral.' Like babies crying during church service," Joe said.

"Some of these trees were here before this country was even founded," I said.

"Yes, and let's hope that the logging company leaves these noble trees to be enjoyed by our children and grandchildren."

In the evening, with the sunset burning in the water, we sang songs out in the boat and listened to our voices echo off the shore. It was magical and romantic being with Joe.

After we returned to Lake Forest, the entire Coan family came to Thalfried for a weekend reunion—Rev. Frederick Coan, his wife, Ida, and their children, Elizabeth, Frank, Howard, and Katharine. I was eager to have a chance to talk to Elizabeth about teachers' college.

"After graduating, I didn't feel prepared as a missionary teacher," Elizabeth said. "I'm going to Teachers' School in Winona before I return to Persia."

"Dr. Speer advised me to apply to Columbia Teachers' College," I said.

"In 1914, I'll sail for Persia and look forward to you joining me a few years later," Elizabeth said. "We'll be a powerful twosome."

On Sunday, after the service at the First Presbyterian Church, Joe and I took a walk down Deerpath Road to Forest Park. As we walked along the paths, I said, "It's funny, but I suddenly remembered Mother's story of how Father proposed to her right here."

"Right here?" Joe exclaimed.

"Yes. Father was on furlough from the mission where he'd gone alone. He came to visit Grandmother Rhea, who all the missionaries told him about. Mother and Father took a walk to the lake, and out of the blue Father knelt on one knee and proposed. She had only known him for three days."

"She said 'yes' on the spot?"

"No, she told him she barely knew him, but consented to letting him write to her. Father courted her for four months, and then she gave him the answer he wanted."

"What if I were to propose to you right here and now?"

"Joe, don't tease me," I gasped.

"How do you know I'm teasing?"

"Because neither one of us is ready for marriage."

"Fair enough. But tell me one thing. Would I have to propose to you here like your father?"

"No, I think not. Goodness knows when we'll be back here again." I smiled at Joe coyly.

"Right, we won't be able to wait that long." Joe reached for my hand and squeezed it.

When we returned to Thalfried, Mrs. Wheeler met us at the door. She took one look at me and said, "What have you two been up to? The strangest things happen along walks to the park here. I won't write your Mother quite yet, but you can always have the ceremony here at Thalfried."

"I'm so transparent," I whispered apologetically to Joe, whose neck was red above his upturned collar. Fortunately, the others were gathering for Sunday dinner and did not seem to notice.

We had a dinner of roast chicken with gravy, potatoes, and beans on the porch in the back on a long picnic bench. Joe sat across from me and our eyes met often.

Oh, those brilliant blue eyes. I do wish you ask me to marry you someday.

Then, as quickly as the Cochrans and Coans had descended upon us, they were gone, and it was just Uncle Foster, Rose and I with the Wheelers. That night as we prepared for bed, Rose asked me to brush her hair. She sat in front of me, facing the vanity mirror, and I could see her face, which suddenly lit up with a smile. "I hope you and Joe get married someday," she said. "The way he looks at you, you know he's in love. You'd make the perfect missionary couple."

I smiled back at Rose. "Maybe Joe and I will return to Persia together someday. But first I need to make sure I have adequate training to do missionary work."

Chapter 11

JUNIOR YEAR, VASSAR, 1911

"I'M NERVOUS ABOUT STARTING MY FRESHMAN YEAR AT Vassar," Rose confided as our train left the station in Indiana, Pennsylvania for New York.

"Don't worry, I'll teach you the ropes," I replied. I instructed her on the logistics of the Blairsville Intersection, getting around the New York train stations, and taking cable cars. "You'll need to learn how to get to Indiana and to Englewood from Vassar on your own," I told her. "I won't always be with you."

In New York, Grandmother Rhea and Uncle Will met us at the elevated cable-car station at 125th Street and Broadway. We sped off in Uncle Will's car to Englewood, Rose and I sitting in the back seat.

"Did you girls see the headline in the newspaper today?" Uncle Will asked.

"Why no," I replied.

"The Mona Lisa was stolen from the Louvre."

"How would anyone be able to sell it or keep it a secret in their home?" Rose said.

"I can't imagine the Louvre without the Mona Lisa," I bemoaned. "It must be found."

"The French will blame the Germans, and the Germans will say the French did it as a distraction from international issues," Uncle Will said. "If it's just a hoax, the Mona Lisa will reappear as mysteriously as it disappeared." But the Mona Lisa did not reappear.

In mid-September we drove to Poughkeepsie. When we registered at Vassar, I asked Miss Kilpatrick, "Could Rose room with me? I could make sure she adjusts to college life."

"Rose will have to live off campus until the second semester," Miss Kilpatrick replied with a sympathetic smile. "I have a sister too and know what it means, but this is the way it must be." And with that, our cherished plan of rooming together fell through. Instead, I roomed with Anna in 410 Lathrup Hall, with my friends Marcia, Buzz, and Mary down the hall.

Lessons kept me busy—Junior English, Economics, Philosophy, Biology, French 17th Century Literature, Baby Psychology, History of Comparative Religions. I tutored French and proudly sent my first ten dollars to Tabriz for the Boys' School Christmas entertainment.

Despite the time my lessons occupied, I anxiously focused my thoughts on my future. Elizabeth Coan urged me to join the Student Volunteers, and I finally decided to become a member. With great resolve, and not much trouble, I found the card that Dr. Zimmer had given me freshman year, signed it, and sent it to the Student Volunteer Office at 50 East 70th Street in New York City. I also followed Dr. Speer's advice and applied to Columbia University Teachers' College.

"There, I've done it," I said, throwing my hands over my head in victory. "I'm on my way to becoming a missionary. I've paved the path for my future, and nothing can get in my way now."

Rose had a rather hard first semester at Vassar, finding it difficult to adjust to both college life and her course load. Living off campus first semester, she also found it difficult to make friends.

"What's wrong, Rose?" I asked. "Don't you like Vassar?"

"Lessons are interesting, and my teachers couldn't be better, but I have a hard time fitting in with the other girls."

"But Rose, Aunt Annie did a fine job of making sure you were adjusted to life in America. You can dance and ice skate, things I couldn't do when I came here."

"The other girls talk about their boyfriends all the time, and I don't have one, so I feel left out."

"Make one up."

"How can you make up a boyfriend? Eventually the girls will find out. Besides, I wouldn't feel comfortable lying."

"I know. What about Andrew Cochran? He's at Williams with Joe."

"I like Andrew, but we were never close friends."

"Here's what I'll do," I continued. "I'll write a letter to Joe tonight and invite him to the Vassar Ice Carnival in February. I'll tell him that you asked me to invite Andrew too." I felt clever having come up with such a good plan.

The day before the Ice Carnival, Joe and Andrew arrived at Lathrop. I smiled at the sight of the two handsome Cochran brothers sitting in the parlor. They almost looked like twins; tall, lanky young men with erect posture, sandy hair, long foreheads, and brilliant blue eyes. Joe gave me a firm hug, and I looked past him to watch Rose extend her right arm to Andrew. She seemed to lose her balance when instead of shaking hands he hugged her. Rose's cheeks turned scarlet. As we sat and talked, I noticed the other girls peeked stealthily into the parlor as they passed the door. I smiled. *All is going as planned.*

The Ice Carnival proceeded as usual, with the class processions across the ice at Vassar Lake followed by a big banquet. The next day was open skating and the lake was crowded with couples. Rose and Andrew looked happy as they skated together, and when they stopped on the shore to warm up at a bonfire, Rose's classmates surrounded them.

After Joe and Andrew left by cable car for the train back to Williams, I breathed a sigh of relief. I had set the stage for Rose's acceptance by her classmates. Would she ever tell them Andrew was her boyfriend? Probably not. Rose was too saintly honest.

Since deciding to actively pursue a career in missionary work, I wanted to inspire other students to do the same through my Mission Class. With such a large class this year, I enlisted Aimie and Dorothy Vanneman, along with Rose, to assist me. We knew we had succeeded in inspiring the students when they volunteered to make pillowcases for the hospital in Tabriz.

Several of my Mission Classes were about the religions of Persia.

"In the 7th century, Shiite Islam came to Persia as a result of the Muslim conquest," I told them. "With over three hundred mosques, it is the most predominant religion of Tabriz. The main Christian group is the Armenian Gregorian church. Zoroastrianism, the native pagan religion of Persia, is practiced by the 'fire worshippers.' It's named after Zoroaster, an ancient Persian prophet, who wrote the Avesta, the ancient Zoroastrians scriptures."

"Why are they called 'fire worshippers'?" Mary asked.

"Zoroastrians worship fire, the god Atar, and water, the goddess, Apas. Fire brought them warmth in the bitter winters, and water made life possible for the ancient people on the barren plains of Persia. They sacrifice animals to Atar and believe their souls merge with the god 'Soul of the Bull.' That's why they are called 'fire worshippers.' "

"Do they believe people have souls?" Anna asked.

"Yes. They believe that after death human souls linger on Earth for three days before crossing over the perilous bridge to the underworld, where they face the possibility of resurrection. When a person dies,

Zoroastrians believe that demons rush into their body, so the corpse is immediately disposed of in the Tower of Silence."

"What is the Tower of Silence?" Buzz asked.

"It's an open-roofed, circular tower, thirty feet tall and fifty feet in diameter. The bodies are carried up a ladder, thrown down the tower onto a grate, and left for the birds to eat."

The girls gasped.

"We climbed up to a Tower of Silence outside of Tehran and looked into it, but it was empty," Rose added. "I told Father that I was glad the Tower of Silence was empty, and he said he was glad too."

"I find it strange that people would leave a body of a loved one to be ripped apart by birds," Anna said.

"We all have strange ways of dealing with the dead," Rose added. "For thousands and thousands of years people have died. People simply don't know how to cope with it."

"Rose, what you said is very simple," Aimie said, "but somehow it strikes me as profound."

The next Mission Class was on Mohammedanism and society in Persia.

"The difference between Jesus and Mohammed is some Christians believe Jesus is the son of God, whereas Muslims believe Mohammed was a prophet who communicated with God," I said. "Both faiths believed in one God. The Christian scripture, the Bible, is not followed as literally as the Qur'an."

"In Persia, few people can read," Rose added. "Father spreads the Christian word by giving sermons at the mission church and talking to villagers in the countryside. Similarly, the one hundred and fourteen suras of the Qur'an are taught verbally by priests in the mosques."

"Some of the suras specify the work and customs appropriate to women and relationships to men," I continued. "Culturally, women do not have a high place in Persian society. Women are separated from men in mosques and have separate entrances into their homes, even different living quarters in wealthy households."

"In the streets, women are covered from head to foot with blue, black, or striped clothing," Aimie said. "They wear a shalwar, baggy trousers narrowing at the ankles, with stockings attached, and a chaddar, a large piece of cloth worn over the head, surrounding the upper body like a shawl. A veil is worn that entirely covers the face, with latticework allowing the eyes to see where one is going."

"They are beautiful women," I added, "but none expose their beauty in public."

"How different it must be," said Mary. "Yet, I'd love the chance to go there and meet the Persian women."

Rose insisted that we spend Easter vacation with Aunt Annie and Uncle Alfred in Baltimore, where they had recently moved from Detroit. Uncle Alfred was a pastor of the First Presbyterian Church in Baltimore, and he gave a beautiful Easter Service. We spent the rest of the week shopping, and I had a sewing girl make a white satin dress for me. I tried it on and draped a green silk scarf over the shoulders that Dorothy Dulles had given me for Christmas.

"It's perfect," Rose exclaimed.

"The Dulleses are holding a dance at the Blankenhorn Hall in Englewood next week," I said. "If I go two days early *en route* to Vassar, I could show off my new dress."

On Friday, April 12th, the day before the dance, I arrived at Rosenvik. I was surprised to find Uncle in his study, talking on the telephone and everyone else waiting tensely in the parlor. They smiled cordially, and Aunt Helen motioned for me to sit. We waited silently for Uncle to finish his phone call.

Uncle Will entered solemnly, saying, "My cousin William is not on the *Carpathia*."

"Oh, Will," said Aunt Helen and immediately stood up and put her arms around him. Uncle Will began to shed tears and his chest heaved.

"He was only thirty-nine. The dog perished too. It was too enticing for him, the chance to sail first-class on the Titanic." Uncle Dulles hid his eyes in his hands.

Aunt Helen turned her head to us and said, "Children, please go upstairs. We'd like to be alone."

"Who died?" I asked Dorothy.

"William Crothers Dulles, Father's cousin."

"What is the Titanic?"

"The largest luxury ship to sail the globe. Unfortunately, the captain didn't know how to navigate around an iceberg. Thousands are dead. Don't you read the newspaper?"

"Where did he sail from?"

"Southampton."

"That's where my family will sail from three months from now."

I couldn't sleep all night, worrying about my family coming in August for furlough. Their ship might hit an iceberg too, and they'd be lost to the sea.

The next morning at breakfast, Uncle Will said, "I've cancelled the dance. It wouldn't be fitting given the tragic events of the week and a death in the family."

I had hoped to show off my new dress, but I was deeply saddened by the loss of Uncle Will's cousin and all the other passengers on the Titanic.

On June 19th, with the school year over, Rose and I left for Saltsburg for cousin Sarah's wedding. The ceremony was performed by Uncle

Rob at high noon on a hill on the Kiski School campus, a beautiful summer day with an immense crowd of relatives and friends gathered. Sarah wore a white crepe gown and carried a bouquet of Talisman roses, creamy yellow buds with pink edges.

"The wreath of orange roses over her veil is a Wilson family tradition," Anna told me.

After refreshments, there were speeches and well wishes to the newlyweds. Toward the end, Uncle Andy stood up and said, "It's been a joyous occasion and we thank you all for celebrating with us. Since the whole family is here, I'd like to make another happy announcement. Our daughter Anna is engaged to Jack Daub."

The crowd broke into applause, and Anna and Jack stood up to receive their congratulations. I had known it for about a year, and even though I was lukewarm to Jack, I felt strangely jealous of the applause and attention Anna was receiving. Her glance caught my eye and she gave me a smug smile. I wanted to tell her that I wasn't jealous and that I'd never marry anyone like Jack, but I did not.

Right after the wedding, Rose and I headed to northern Pennsylvania for the Y.W.C.A. Eagles Mere Conference. With all my cherished memories of Silver Bay, and having never heard of Eagles Mere, I was reluctant to go, but I was in charge of the Vassar delegation, so I needed to attend. It was a long trip to Williamsport, changing trains in Harrisburg, and I was happy that Rose was with me for companionship. Just after six in the evening, we arrived amidst the Blue Ridge Mountains.

"With views like this, it was worth the long trip," Rose exclaimed.

"We're not there yet," I said. "We still have to take a train up the mountain to Sonestown. They said it takes an hour. We're staying at the Forest Inn with over four hundred other attendees."

"I'm hungry. I hope we don't miss dinner."

"Where's the train station?" I asked a man on the dock. "We're going to Eagles Mere."

"The last train left at six," the man replied. "They discontinued the later trains last year."

"Whatever shall we do?" Rose cried.

"You can stand by the road over there and see if someone going up the mountain will give you a lift," the man said.

"Can we walk?" Rose asked.

"Dear, no," the man replied. "It's thirty miles uphill, and it will be dark by the time you're halfway there. Bears will eat you."

"Bears?" Rose exclaimed.

"Yes, the bears come out at night."

"Let's go stand by the road," I said to Rose. "I'm not scared of bears, but we can't walk thirty miles up the mountain."

With a thunderstorm approaching, we walked about two miles up the road, both of us glum and silent. Then a man with a horse drawn wagon came up behind us, and Rose turned and started waving franticly at him. "Sir, can you help us get to Eagles Mere."

"Sir?" he replied, laughing. "I'm just a farm hand. Eagles Mere is a four-hour ride up the mountain."

"Oh, please, sir," Rose replied.

"Shucks, how can I refuse a pretty girl like you? I sure can't leave you here. Get in the back. We're all going to get drenched with that thunder shower coming in."

Rose and I huddled together, lying in the back of the wagon. An hour later, the storm opened up.

"There's an oiled tarp under the seat. Cover yourselves," the man shouted back.

Rose and I covered ourselves with the musty-smelling tarp, but our clothes and hair were soaked with rain already. After the storm passed, Rose lay back with her knees bent, forming two peaks in the tarp. "Mount Ararat," she said. Rose had always done this in Persia as a small child and I laughed until my sides ached.

"This wagon reminds me of the first few days of my trip to America, sitting in the back of a wagon and the troika. It was so difficult to sit back there alone day after day."

Rose looked at me with surprise. "I was in back with Aimie and Dorothy. We told stories and played cards every day. I'm so sorry you went the year before."

"So am I. If only I hadn't made Father so angry, I would have been able to go with you. But I'm happy we're together now."

When we arrived at the Forest Inn, it was eleven at night. Louise Holmquist was waiting on the steps to meet us and help us to our room. "We didn't have supper, but we arrived safely," I said.

"All is well," Rose added. "At least we didn't get eaten by bears."

I could hear Rose tossing and turning in her bed, so I knew sleep was not coming to her either.

"Rose?"

"What is it?"

"Did people talk about me at the mission after I left?"

"Yes, of course they did. They asked if I'd heard from you and how your trip was going, if you made it safely to America."

"No, I meant about me and Howard."

Rose was silent for some time, then she rolled on her side to face me. "Mother wrote a long letter to Reverend and Mrs. Baskerville, telling them everything about Howard's death and the funeral. I was in the parlor with Annie and Bobby when she sealed the envelope. Then she looked up and said, 'Children, Howard Baskerville is no longer alive. Father asks that we never speak of him again in this house.' Her voice was so stern that Annie put her hand on Mother's Bible lying on the table and said, 'I promise to never talk about Howard again,' and Bobby did the same."

"What about you?"

"Well, I just spoke about Howard, so you should know I didn't put my hand on her Bible. If you are asking if I would talk about him here, in America, the answer is no. I feel that his death was a curse on you and the family that is best forgotten."

The next morning, I attended a course on the Chinese Revolution taught by Dwight Edwards, a young man who helped found the first Y.M.C.A. in Peking.

"In 1911, the six-year-old emperor Puyi was overthrown during the Xinhai Revolution. It ended two thousand years of the Qing dynasty," he said. "I was there to witness it happen."

"And do they have a parliament and a constitution?" I asked.

"Both. The flag is the banner of 'Five Races Under One Union'— red for Han, yellow for Manchus, blue for Mongols, white for Muslims and black for Tibetans. They advocate racial integration and tolerance."

"They fought for democracy and won. If only Persia had such leaders," I said.

Rose chose to attend a talk by Reverend James Ramsay Swain on "The Decisive Hour of Christian Missions." When I met her for lunch, she came to the table arm-in-arm with Louise Holmquist. My stomach sank. *She's latched onto Rose.*

"Miss Holmquist wants me to become an apostle, like Paul, to my classmates at Vassar," Rose said. "When I leave, they will remember me as one who showed them Christ in everything I did."

I heard that before. Poor naïve Rose. Yet I was once young and impressionable too.

That afternoon, as Rose and I walked around the Eagles Mere Lake through a field of giant boulders, I said, "I wish I had the strength to move one of these. Then I would know I have the strength to succeed."

"I plan to succeed by sticking to my dreams," Rose said.

"And what are your dreams?"

"To go to a foreign land and be a missionary."

"Back to Tabriz?"

"I'd like to live somewhere I haven't lived before, learn new things about people. But I will go where the true need is."

Rose's dreams were different from mine, and admittedly more admirable.

After the Eagles Mere conference, we took the narrow-gauge train down the mountain and were soon on the Pennsylvania Railroad back to Indiana. It was a long trip nonetheless and I was restless. Father, Mother and the children were boarding their steamer in Southampton on July 17th and I was scared for their safety after the Titanic sunk.

"Please let them cross the ocean without hitting an iceberg," I prayed.

Rose and I spent two weeks in Indiana, staying with Aunt Agnes and Uncle Stacy and their children. Aunt Jennie and cousin Margaret saw to it that we were entertained with picnics, tennis, and swimming, but I counted the days until July 24th when the family's boat would arrive in New York.

It was sad to see Grandmother Wilson so frail and failing. "She often stays in bed most of the day now," Aunt Jennie said. "I prepare her meals and help her sit up and eat. I'm afraid she grows weaker every day. I hope Sam gets here in time to see her alive."

"Poor Grandmother," Rose said. "We'll visit her every day and remind her that Father is coming to America to see her."

Two days before the boat was to arrive, Rose and I traveled to New York and stayed at Rosenvik while we waited. Early in the morning Uncle Will drove us to New York to meet the family at the wharf. "When will the boat from Southampton arrive?" I asked a porter.

"They arrive when it suits them," the man replied. "It will be the 'Olympic' and she'll dock over there."

Rose and I paced and paced the dock, back and forth, until Uncle Will squinted toward the rising sun and said, "I believe that speck there on the horizon is their steamer."

Rose and I held each other's arms and started jumping up and down. "They made it; they made it," we cried.

Uncle Will laughed. "You ladies are acting like little children. I may go wait in the auto so no one thinks we are related." But he didn't leave us.

Finally, as the sun rose, the speck became a steamer with four stacks and two masts.

"Goodness, the steamer I took, the Philadelphia, had only two stacks," I said.

"Yes, this one will carry almost three thousand passengers, yours was about half that," Uncle Will explained. "But it also means that it will take a long time for the passengers to come down the plank. Best be patient."

As Olympic docked, we searched the faces on the deck.

"There," Rose said, pointing at a young girl with thick blond curls, waving. "It's Annie."

"Annie?" I gasped. "Goodness she was only eight when I left. She's no longer a child."

Finally, we saw the family start down the plank together. Rose and I started screaming and waving. "I can barely wait," I said. *Oh, Father. How I hope that you have forgiven me. I've tried so hard to be good, even if I did learn to dance.*

As the family emerged from the crowd, Rose and I ran to greet them. Rose was in Father's arms first, and Mother gave me a long hug. As I tried to hug Father, Bobby and Annie surrounded me. He could only lean in to give me a light kiss on the cheek before they were led off by the customs agents to claim their trunks.

As I watched the family complete customs inspections, I marveled that Mother and Father had barely changed, but I hardly recognized the children. Annie was quaintly pretty, with thick curls, and dear little Bobby, an adorable eight-year-old with his blond hair and big blue eyes. Once they were through customs, we sped off, packed together in Uncle Will's Model T, to spend six lovely weeks at Rosenvik, one big family.

I walked softly down the third-floor hallway and peeked into the large guestroom where Mother was humming while she unpacked her trunk. "Mother?"

"Come in, dear. You startled me at first. I'm not used to hearing your voice."

"Where's Father?"

"Out on the veranda with Uncle Will. You'll have a chance to talk to him later."

"I wanted to ask you about Father. Is he still angry with me?"

Mother turned and brushed back the hair on the top of my head, looking softly into my eyes.

"Your father is wise and he is no longer angry with you. 'Fools give full vent to their rage, but the wise bring calm in the end.' "

"Proverbs 29:11."

"Undoubtedly the Lord has forgiven you too."

After staying at Rosenvik for six weeks, Rose and I left with the family for Indiana, Pennsylvania, to help them settle into the house they rented for the year's furlough. As soon as we arrived, we rushed over to see Grandmother Wilson. She lay in bed with her eyes closed, her breath shallow.

"Mother, I'm here," Father said and took her hand gently in his. Her eyes slowly opened and sparkled with a glow of joy as a weak smile spread across her face. After an hour, Bobby started to squirm, and Father bade us to leave him alone. He spent many hours alone with Grandmother Wilson over the next weeks.

Uncle Harry had arranged for a five-bedroom house at 36 South 6th Street for our family. Bobby and Annie were ecstatic about their new home, and Mother was cheerful as usual, but Father wore a cloak of sadness after seeing Grandmother Wilson. He found it impossible to engage in his usual gentle humoring at dinner each day after staying by her bedside.

"I hate seeing Father so sad," I told Mother.

"It's best we all start the grieving process," she replied. "Your Grandmother has only days left on this earth."

Grandmother Wilson died October 12th, only a few weeks after Rose and I returned to Vassar. The next day was Sunday, and we went to the Presbyterian Church in Poughkeepsie with Anna to say prayers for our Grandmother Wilson.

"I'm so happy she was able to see Father again," Rose said.

"Grandmother was bed-ridden all summer," Anna said. "It was sad waiting for the end."

"She waited for Father to return," I said.

"What happens when people die?" Rose asked, tears streaming down her cheeks.

I took a Bible from the pew and opened it. "In Revelations 7:15-17 it says, 'They are before the throne of God and serve him day and night in his temple; and he who sits on the throne will shelter them with his presence. Never again will they hunger; never again will they thirst. The sun will not beat down on them, nor any scorching heat. For the Lamb at the center of the throne will be their shepherd; he will lead them to springs of living water. And God will wipe away every tear from their eyes.' "

Rose squeezed my hand. "Grandmother is happily with her Master."

Chapter 12

SENIOR YEAR, VASSAR, 1912

AS SOON AS WE ARRIVED AT VASSAR OUR SENIOR YEAR, Anna and I ran up the stairs to the top floor of Lathrup Hall. We were sharing six bedrooms, three on each side, a sitting room, and a kitchenette with Marcia, Buzz, Mary, and our new friend Kitten.

"Our double alley is wondrous," I exclaimed.

"We'll have parties until the wee hours," Buzz said.

"And elaborate breakfasts every weekend," Mary added.

My senior classes included Social Psychology, Physiology, Ethics, and Shakespeare. Despite my full schedule, I planned to go to Joe's Phi Gamma Delta fraternity party in October. Marcia offered to help me decide which dress to wear.

"I want to look beautiful," I told her. "Well, as beautiful as I can muster."

She chose a coral dress with an embroidered bodice. "It gives a soft pink glow to your cheeks," she said.

Joe met me in Albany and arranged for a car to take us to Williams together. Williamstown was a quaint sleepy town nestled in the bosom of the Green Mountains. In the dim afternoon sun, the rolling hills were cast in a purple hue and covered with trees bearing leaves in crimson, yellow, and orange.

At the Williamstown Inn, I dressed for the evening Glee Club Concert and dance. As I admired myself in the mirror, I said, "I want to be the most beautiful girl on the dance floor, at least in Joe's eyes." The finishing touch was the bloodstone ring, the one Howard had given me. As I slipped it onto my finger, shivers ran up my spine. I only wore it for special occasions, and putting it on made me gasp with excitement, as though something magical could happen that night.

Joe looked smart in a black suit, a white shirt with an upturned collar, and a blue bow tie. He brought me a corsage of a white rose trimmed with baby's breath and ferns, and he fumbled as he pinned it to my chest. I held my breath and let it out suddenly, which made us laugh. Standing close to me, he smelled of sandalwood soap.

"What do you think of Williamstown?" I asked over dinner.

"I thought I'd be bored at first, but I am so busy studying that I quite like the quiet and peaceful surroundings. The fraternity gives me all the social life I need; that is, except for visits with you."

"And lessons?"

"Biology, Chemistry, and Math to prepare for medical school, of course. With two more years at Williams, four years in medical school, and a few years of clinical practice, it will be at least eight years before I would be ready to return to Persia."

"I know you're so determined to follow in your father's and grandfather's footsteps and be the third-generation Cochran missionary, but 1920 seems a long time away."

"If you wait for me to finish medical training, we can go back to Persia together. I'd like that." Joe reached across the table and took my hand; he gently squeezed it. "What an interesting ring you're wearing, is it Persian?"

"Yes, a professor of Persian antiquity said it is a man's signet ring engraved with a Lamassu, the deity of Persepolis," I replied.

"How envious I am. I wish I had something precious from my homeland."

As we ate, I thought of the summer of 1901, when Grandmother Rhea and my family visited the Coan-Cochran house in Urmia.

"I'm hoping for a third-generation of Cochran missionaries," Joseph Cochran, Sr., said.

"Well Joe and Agnes seem well suited," Grandmother Rhea said.

"Joe has my blessing," Father added.

"It's settled, then," Dr. Cochran responded, and all the adults laughed.

At the time, the adults seemed quite serious about it, but then we were only eight years old and did not understand the adults were humoring us.

Joe opened his pocket watch and broke my reverie. "Oh, we must be off. We don't have much time before the Glee Club concert."

The Glee Club performed in Chapin Hall, and Joe's fraternity brothers saved us seats in the balcony. The concert program contained the name and lyrics of the songs: "The Purple Hills," "The Royal Purple" and the alma mater, "The Mountains." Afterward, Joe and I followed the crowd to the dance, everyone singing and our breath forming a big cloud of fog in the cold mountain air: "The Mountains, The Mountains. We greet them with a song ..." Musicians from the Glee Club approached from behind and joined in with guitars and banjos.

As we entered the dance hall, the music began, and Joe took my hand and led me onto the floor. I swallowed hard. Fear seized me as though it was my first dance. *Why am I afraid now? Please don't let me stumble.*

Joe confidently and smoothly guided me across the floor. "You're doing fine," he said. "Just relax and let me lead."

"You can lead me anywhere," I whispered, but I don't think Joe heard me over the music.

When the band took a break, we got in line for punch.

"You look very lovely tonight," Joe said. "Your cheeks are so rosy."

"I'm warm from dancing," I said. "How did you learn to dance so well?"

"All Grandmother Hale's doing. Mother loved to dance, and Grandmother saw to it that I took dancing lessons. At the time, I was afraid to tell my friends, but now when I see how awkward my fraternity brothers are, I thank my dear Granny."

After the dance, Joe held my hand as we walked to the inn. "Tomorrow is meant to be an all-day and all-night affair, so value your sleep tonight." I hesitated before going in, and he smiled and kissed me on the cheek. Sweet Joe had taken the bait.

I sighed as I closed the door behind me. It was so romantic dancing with Joe, I wanted to dance forever. I held my arms out as though holding him again and danced to music in my head. My heart was stirred by Joe in a way it never had before.

The next day was the Williams-Wesleyan football game. "You'll have the opportunity to sing 'The Royal Purple' again," Joe said as the band started up.

Joe and I joined in with the crowd, "Some vaunt the crimson, some the blue, And some their honest green; We're to the regal color true, Of Berkshire's Purple Queen ..."

Although I couldn't follow the football game, the frequent bursts of song kept me in my element.

After the game, Joe said, "We're going to a play. The Cap and Bells is the student theater group. By necessity, boys take the women's roles, and they are sometimes very funny."

The play was a humorous sketch with a six-foot male heroine in a blue satin dress, high-heel shoes, and a wig of long blond hair. There were mild love scenes with several male courters.

On the way back to the fraternity house Joe said, "Not too risqué for you, Agnes, I hope."

"I had to close my eyes for most of it, I'm afraid," I responded.

Joe chuckled. "You watched all of it, missionary girl. I saw you."

The banquet at the fraternity house started at eleven at night and lasted until three in the morning. There was a large sliced ham, roasted chicken, potatoes, carrots, salad, cake, and ice cream with chocolate sauce. Everyone ate like savages, talked boisterously, and laughed merrily. Then there were more songs.

"These are traditional Williams songs, but the Glee Club does not perform them in public," Joe explained.

The first was a wine drinking song: "Come, fill your glass up, To Williams, to Williams, to Williams." The second song was about sometimes sleeping in silk pajamas, and sometimes not.

As they were singing, I noticed a purple throw on a couch and stealthily ventured over to claim it. As the fraternity boys finished their last refrain, I stepped boldly in front of them and flung the purple throw over my shoulder and let it flow down my back to the floor. "I'm the Berkshire's Purple Queen," I announced to the awe-struck crowd. As I made my way around the room, addressing all the members of my court, they burst into a rousing chorus of "The Royal Purple."

Joe laughed hysterically. "Oh, Agnes, I truly did not know that you had that in you."

The next day I woke to gentle knocking. "A Mr. Cochran in the lobby," the innkeeper said through the door.

"Tell him I'll be there in a few minutes." *Oh my goodness, I overslept.* I dashed water on my face from the washbasin, brushed my hair, and hurried to dress. I smoothed the wrinkles from my skirt as I sallied down the hall to the lobby.

"Church service is at ten o'clock," Joe announced. "I know you'd never miss Sunday service." I noticed a smirk on his lips.

As we walked briskly, Joe put his arm over my shoulder and said, "Did the Berkshire's Purple Queen get her beauty rest?"

"Not quite enough," I responded.

"The innkeeper told me that you'd skipped breakfast, but don't worry. There's a big lunch planned after church."

Other members of the fraternity party made room for us in their pew, but Joe and I needed to sit so close together that our legs touched.

The feeling of his leg against mine was so distracting that I barely listened to the sermon.

In the afternoon, Joe and I took a horse-and-buggy ride in the countryside and ended up at a sweet little chapel. The door was open, but no one was within. Our footsteps echoed as we walked to the altar, and we dared not speak above a whisper. "I'd like to get married in a quaint little church like this one," Joe said.

"Or in the mission church in Tabriz," I added.

That evening, the fraternity held a long hayride in the countryside under the stars. Joe sat close to me to keep me warm. At eleven o'clock we returned to the fraternity house.

"Are you tired?" Joe asked.

"Surprisingly not," I answered.

"Then let's sit somewhere quiet and talk for a while."

We started reminiscing about childhood in Persia and before we knew it dawn was upon us. Joe was about to take me to the inn when we heard a loud commotion in the social room. We found that everyone was up dancing, so Joe and I joined in and after an hour we sat down to a big pancake breakfast. Shortly afterward, it was time for Joe and me to leave for Albany.

On board the train back to Poughkeepsie, I played with the bloodstone ring on my finger.

I've never had so much fun. I knew something magical would happen when I wore this ring.

Joe followed up with a lovely letter, telling me all sorts of trash about being the belle of the party, for purely being crazy and taking the part of Berkshire's Purple Queen. I held Joe's letter to my heart and murmured, "Oh, how the days will creep by until we're together again. There is something special between us."

To accommodate the forty-seven girls enrolled in my Mission Class, it had to be held in Freshmen Parlor. Without the help from Aimie and Dorothy Vanneman and Rose, I wouldn't have been able to manage a class that large. I wanted to interest the girls in missionary work, to stimulate them to help women in poorer countries around the world through education. "There is such desperate need for girls to be educated so they can improve their lives," I told them.

I was surprised when Elizabeth Coan appointed me Vice President of the New York Student Volunteers. At first, I was proud and grateful for the honor, but I later learned that it meant time-consuming correspondence. My first project was to request permission for girls from my Mission Class to go to the Student Volunteer Conference at Cornell in December. It was my wildest dream to get as many as fifteen interested in attending. In the end twenty-seven wanted to go, and I had to select the attendees. How rewarding it felt to know that my class had stimulated so much interest.

In mid-November, Dr. Speer invited Father to speak on the Persia Revolution at the Presbyterian Board of Foreign Missions in New York. "I'll come to see you and Rose at Vassar afterward," he wrote. Rose and I were excused from classes for the day and toured Father around campus.

"The Presbyterian Board certainly packed my schedule full during my one-year furlough," Father said, "but I'm glad I could make time to see you. I still find it hard to believe that Agnes is graduating from Vassar already. Mother and I, of course, plan to come to your graduation ceremony in June."

I smiled, knowing that soon I would have a chance to make Father proud of me.

"I'm hoping to hear if I've been accepted at Columbia Teachers' College any day," I said. "I toss and turn every night, thinking about it."

Father smiled slyly. "Robert Speer is rather certain you will be going to Columbia next year."

"If I don't, I want to return with the family to Tabriz in August."

"You will get a letter from Columbia in a month or two."

"I'm so distraught not knowing what I will do after graduation, what my future will be."

"One should learn patience in your youth, as it is harder when you get older. 'It is good that a man should both hope and quietly wait for the salvation of the Lord.'"

"Lamentations 3:26."

Father smiled and kissed me on top of my head.

Mrs. Vanneman had a dinner in Father's honor at her house in Poughkeepsie. We found ourselves drifting in and out of conversations in Azeri and English, centered around the mission in Tabriz. When I mentioned I'd received an invitation to go with a Student Volunteer group to Northfield for Thanksgiving, Father urged me to go. "It's important for you to make contacts with influential people. Mr. Fitt is the managing editor of *Record of Christian Work* and his wife, Emma, is the daughter of Dwight L. Moody, the famous evangelist who founded Mount Hermon School. I've known them for many years. We'll miss you, of course, at Thanksgiving, but I will only return home on Thanksgiving morning and leave the next day for another conference."

After Father's brief visit, he left for Philadelphia to give a lecture.

"Father is in such high demand," Rose said. "It's like being the daughter of a celebrity."

"Everyone in the religious community seems to be requesting that Father visit them while he's in America on furlough," I said. "I've missed him so much, and now I feel that they are depriving me of him."

"It makes me proud to be his daughter," Rose added.

I nodded, as my chest swelled with pride.

Arthur and Emma Fitt invited Elizabeth Coan, me, and other leaders of the Student Volunteers for Thanksgiving at their home in Northfield, Massachusetts. The next day was a house party and hayride for thirty college seniors. Mary Phillips came from Poughkeepsie, and Joe joined us from Williams.

In the morning, I went with Mrs. Fitt to help her pick up food for the house party and when we returned, a crowd of students had gathered in the yard for the hayride. Mary stood at the front door and motioned frantically for us to come into the house. It was only when the door shut behind us that I saw Mary was white with fear. "Vassar called while you were out. They said that you received a telegram from your Uncle Rob that read: "Train accident. Your father not as bad as paper said.""

"Paper?" I exclaimed.

"There's one in Arthur's study," Mrs. Fitt said. "Wait here."

"What's happened to Father? Please let him be all right."

Mrs. Fitt quickly returned with a newspaper. "The article on the train wreck is on the front page."

My throat was so tight I could barely breathe.

"What does it say?" Mary asked.

"Train Derails in Glen Loch, Pennsylvania—four dead, fifty injured."

"And your father?"

"There are only names of the dead. Father is not one of them."

"That should be a relief."

"Mrs. Fitt, could I use your telephone to call my mother?" I asked.

"Yes, of course," Mrs. Fitt replied. "I'll stay with you while the others go on to the hayride."

"I'll stay too," Mary said.

Mother picked up the phone on the second ring. Her voice was shrill. "Wilson residence."

"Mother, it's Agnes. How is Father?"

"I didn't know how to reach you. Father is in the hospital in West Chester, Pennsylvania. He injured his spine, but is able to move his hands and feet, so the doctors have ruled out paralysis."

"Did you talk to him?"

"No, he can't come to the phone. They thought it might be a week or two before he could go home. Your father had the nurse tell me not to come to West Chester."

"Does that mean he will be home for Christmas?"

"I think so." She sighed. "I'll write when I have more news."

After hanging up the phone, Mrs. Fitt said, "Why don't you and Mary join the others on the hayride? We'll drive and catch up with them."

Joe was happy to see me. He was pale with sympathy when I told him what had happened to Father and stayed close by my side, as did Elizabeth Coan and Mary Phillips. My whole body was numb and my senses were dampened. "Oh, I hope he's not in pain," I said, close to tears.

"Your father's so strong," Joe said. "I'm sure he'll recover."

"Relax your shoulders and breathe," Elizabeth suggested.

I was holding my shoulders with my arms crossed and when I let go, I heaved a deep sigh. "Yes, it will be okay," I managed to say.

"Feeling better?" Joe asked. I nodded, and he slipped his arm around my shoulders.

"I'll see Father in three weeks when I go home for Christmas. It would not be worth going home now while he is still be in the hospital."

The train ride back to Vassar was unnerving. Each time we passed over a trestle, I closed my eyes and held my breath. Mary chattered away about her plans for Christmas at home in Highland Park, Illinois, and how she planned to go back and teach there after graduation. At some point she apparently realized I wasn't listening and stopped talking.

When I saw Rose back at Vassar on Sunday, she did not have much additional news.

"Father was on a speaking tour in Philadelphia and coming back to have Thanksgiving dinner with us at Aunt Agnes's house. When we got to the train station to meet him, we were told there had been an accident at Chester, just out of Philadelphia. A bridge collapsed. The train derailed and fell down a steep embankment. All day we waited for news of Father. Finally, at eleven o'clock at night, Uncle Dick came over with a telegram saying Father was among the injured and had been taken to the hospital. He let the rest of the family know."

Mother wrote to us three weeks later. "Father came home today in the care of an orderly. Uncle Dick and Uncle Harry carried him upstairs to bed. His condition is worse than he let me know. The X-ray showed two vertebrae between his shoulders are broken and the ligaments torn. He's wearing a brace from his armpits to his waist. Recovery is expected to take many months."

"We will see how bad it is when we go home from Christmas," Rose said. "Maybe this will mean that their furlough in America will be extended."

A week later, the Student Volunteer Conference was held at Cornell University in Ithaca, New York. It had meant months of planning and correspondence to arrange for a delegation of Vassar students from my Mission Class to go, and then a snow blizzard hit New York. All the trains were delayed or cancelled. Our trip seemed doomed, but I was determined to get my delegation on a train to Ithaca. Somehow all of us made it there.

After we arrived and sat in front of the fireplace at the lodge with hot chocolate and cookies, one of the girls said, "I feel better that we braved the storm." And the others nodded in agreement.

The next morning, I was eating breakfast with our Vassar delegation when I felt a gentle tap on my shoulder. "Mrs. Labaree?" I cried and jumped up into her outstretched arms. "What are you doing here?"

"Robert and I are in America on furlough. Elizabeth Coan asked me to be one of the speakers at the conference."

I introduced her to the girls in our Vassar delegation. "Mrs. Labaree is from the mission in Urmia and writes poetry about Persia."

"I'm a Vassar girl too," she said. "The class of 1902."

Seeing Mary Labaree was the highlight of the meeting. I was so proud to introduce a real missionary woman to the students of my Mission Class.

"Robert and I had a chance to see your father and hear him speak in Philadelphia at the Presbyterian Conference before the fateful train home," Mrs. Labaree said. "How is he doing?"

"Mother tells me he is still recovering in bed."

"Goodness, that would drive your father crazy. He is the most active and industrious man I have ever known."

"I've never seen Father sick, except for an appendicitis ten years ago."

"I brought some of my poems about Tabriz. I'll write them down for you to give your father as a Christmas present. I'm sure anything Persian will be a great comfort to him."

After years of going to relatives for the holidays, I actually had the sensation of leaving for home when I boarded the train for Pennsylvania. Even with Father's injury, Rose and I were excited about having a Christmas with the whole family.

When we arrived in Indiana, Uncle Dick picked us up from the station. He had come over to the house earlier to help Father downstairs and sit him up in a chair in the parlor. "He wanted to be up and out of bed when you entered," Uncle Dick said.

Rose and I ran toward Father with our arms wide open, ready to hug him, but he recoiled and stretched his arms out to prevent our onslaught.

"Girls, no hugging quite yet," he said. "I have pain, but they say it should subside in a few months. Then it will be all about gaining my strength back." We resorted to kissing his cheeks and forehead.

Father was sitting up a bit, but he looked so tired and weak, so alarming for a man of such strong physique. It made me shudder to see him wince in pain when he moved. Without Father's vigor, my holiday spirits were dampened.

"It's hard to see Father that way," I told Mother as I helped her in the kitchen.

"Yes, dear," Mother replied. "Your Father is not the best patient either. He's convinced he is still rugged and strong, indestructible, of herculean mind and body. He insists that he doesn't need a wheel-chair, but that will need to change. I don't have the strength to help him walk about."

"Will he eventually be able to walk again?"

"Only God knows. There is so much uncertainty about the extent of healing one can expect and how long it will take. We pray for his recovery, but we must accept and be happy with whatever progress he makes."

"We'll all pray for Father," Rose said.

" 'He gives power to the weak and strength to the powerless,' " I said. "Isaiah 40:29."

Grandmother Rhea and Uncle Foster had moved to Indiana and were staying with Uncle Harry and Aunt Jennie in the old Wilson house. They helped us celebrate Christmas, bringing added cheer to the household.

"Grandmother and Uncle Foster are going to stay with us until we leave for Persia," Mother told us.

Father enjoyed sharing jokes with Uncle Foster around the dinner table, as long as Uncle Foster didn't make him laugh too hard. "Oh, my ribs are breaking," he moaned when he started to belly laugh.

On Christmas Day, there were the usual mounds of presents. To my surprise, amongst the gifts from relatives and family, there was a package from Joe. He gave me a picture of himself hiking the Appalachian Trail and a beautiful purple cashmere scarf. The card read, "Merry Christmas, Berkshire Queen."

"Glad to see you and Joe Cochran are still keeping in touch," Grandmother Rhea said. "We planned this ten years ago." Then she chuckled to herself.

While Rose and I were helping Mother clean up in the kitchen after the Christmas dinner, Mother said, "I have some news about the Dulleses to tell you. After Grandmother and Uncle Foster moved to Indiana to be with us during our furlough, Uncle Will broke the news to them that he and Helen decided to sell Rosenvik and move to New York City. They now live at the Hotel Gotham at 5th Avenue and 55th Street."

"It is hard to imagine Uncle Will selling Rosenvik and living in an apartment," I said.

"Sometimes a new wife wants her own home, without the memories of the first wife. Aunt Helen also wanted to live in New York City and be close to Symphony Hall and the theaters, rather than live in Englewood. It's a rather large, elegant apartment I've been told."

"I'll miss going to Rosenvik. I spent my first holidays in America there."

"Grandmother will miss it too. She lived at Rosenvik for twelve years and raised her grandchildren there. The problem is that when Father and I go back to Tabriz, there will be no place for Grandmother to live."

"What about Uncle Foster?" Rose asked.

Mother shook her head. "The misfortunes on this family multiply," she said. "Uncle Foster has been diagnosed with tuberculosis. The doctor recommends that he go to a sanitarium in California."

"Oh, my goodness," exclaimed Rose. "How did he become ill?"

"You girls are old enough to understand," Mother said. "It is likely that he was infected by a sick lady he frequented in New York on Soubrette Row."

"Is he contagious?" I asked.

"Yes, but he controls his coughing around others," Mother replied. "It's all he can do. He deserves our love and affection despite his illness. Don't forget that."

Father was calling for Mother from the other room. As Mother untied her apron, she said, "Remember girls, be careful not to talk about Rosenvik around Grandmother. It upsets her."

Later in our room I said to Rose, "It makes me sad. I spent so much time at Rosenvik over the past four years."

"Grandmother will be eighty soon," Rose said. "I worry she won't have a place to live or anyone to care for her. Maybe if you go to Teachers' College Grandmother could live with you in New York."

"I couldn't imagine," I said, startled by her suggestion. "How would I have a social life if Grandmother is living with me?"

Chapter 13

SENIOR YEAR, VASSAR, 1913

UNTIL FEBRUARY IT HAD BEEN A WARM WINTER, AND the artificial lake Vassar constructed for ice skating had not frozen over. Then, the first week of February, a snowstorm dropped a foot of new snow and everyone was out sledding. Five Vassar girls took a toboggan down Sunset Hill and lost control. The toboggan veered, skidded over the lake, and fell through the thin ice. A freshman on the toboggan managed to get to shore and help two other girls out. She then held a third girl's head above the icy water until help came. One girl got stuck under the ice and drowned. Even though the lake was only nine feet deep, it took an hour for them to find her body. She was from Poughkeepsie and thousands turned out for her funeral.

"How could this happen?" I asked. "Once it was a joy to walk around the lake, and now we're all afraid to go near it."

"I can imagine the girl's panic, being trapped under the ice, trying to come up for air and not being able to," Anna said.

"Gulping water, her lungs filling, her body so cold," I said. After her funeral, the girl under the ice also appeared in my nightmares of Howard Baskerville. He lay in his coffin, wearing a black suit with a white carnation in his lapel. The girl lay next to him.

We thought the Ice Carnival would be cancelled, but the Vice President of Standard Oil had funded the pond's construction and demanded that it take place. Everyone was scared to skate on the lake, but fortunately the temperature was below freezing for the next ten days and on February 18th celebrations went on as planned.

Joe came down again from Williams, and there were the usual bonfires and Japanese lanterns. We skated across the lake in Egyptian costumes, wearing different colored scarfs for each class. As I skated off the ice, Joe gave me a big hug and held me close. "Your last Vassar Ice Carnival, Egyptian Princess."

I smiled weakly.

"You're more quiet than usual," Joe said. "Is something wrong?"

"I'm so preoccupied with Father's health and the future of our family," I replied. "They're not going back to Persia at the end of summer."

"You'll have more time with your family before they return. That should make you happy. Is there anything else troubling you?"

"I'm anxious about my application to graduate school. What if I'm not accepted to Columbia?"

Joe patted me on the back. "Wait and see what they say."

In April, I finally received a letter from Columbia Teachers' College and was scared to open it. Alone in my room, I sat on the edge of my bed and gingerly pulled the single-page letter out. Taking a breath in, I unfolded it and read the first line: "Dear Mary Agnes Wilson. After careful consideration of your credentials, we are pleased to inform you ..." I jumped up and started screaming, "I've been accepted. I've been accepted."

That evening in Lathrop dining hall, I had to bite my lip to hide my grin. After everyone was seated, I took my knife and softly tapped my glass of water to get everyone's attention.

"I have an announcement to make," I said. "I've been accepted to the master's degree program at Columbia Teachers' College." Everyone applauded and congratulated me. It was one of the happiest moments of my life.

I wrote a letter to Joe, and another to Mother and Father, telling them. "I hope this makes Father happy," I said to Rose. "I hope he's finally proud of his wayward daughter."

I was pleased to also hear that Marcia was accepted at Columbia University for graduate school, and Buzz planned to work at Howson & Howson, her father's patent law firm in New York. Sadly, other friends were going home and farther away. Mary was going home to Highland Park, Illinois, to teach elementary school; Kitten was returning to Vermont to marry her fiancé, Sinclair; and, of course, Anna would marry Jack in Saltsburg that summer. As Commencement week approached, we took pictures of each other every few minutes and promised to have a reunion of our Vassar double alley someday.

At the Senior Award ceremony, it was announced that I had been chosen to graduate with honors and awarded Phi Beta Kappa. I was also selected to be one of the six commencement speakers. What overwhelmed me the most was that my classmates selected me for the Borden Travel Scholarship. "I went through grueling interviews with three professors," I told Rose. "The Borden Award means I can travel to study in a different country. I'll be able to go to the Sorbonne, just like Margaret Dulles." I was overwhelmed with all of the recognition.

The night before Commencement Day, I was nervous about giving my speech and excited about graduation. I barely slept, but at sunrise the air was filled with the smell of freshly cut grass and blossoms on the yellow-wood tree. At eleven o'clock, the Seniors lined up on the lawn in twosomes, all wearing white dresses. Anna and I walked together, carrying shower bouquets of pink roses and lavender sweet peas.

"I was surprised to see your father here," Anna said.

"Six months ago, I didn't think it would be possible for him to come to my graduation," I replied, "but he's here. I want to make him proud of me, more than anything."

Being the first of the six commencement speakers, I felt the audience's eyes on me as I took the podium. On the last step, I stubbed my toe and almost tripped, but a teacher standing nearby grabbed my arm just in time to prevent my falling. "I'm sure everyone in the audience saw it," I muttered and took a deep breath to recompose.

The title of my speech was "The Streets of a Persian Town," and I had written it especially for Father: "Persia used to exist for most of us as a picturesque compound of Lalla Rookh and Rubaiyat, a luxurious profusion of roses and nightingales, with graceful domes and minarets for a background. But the events of the last few years have made us feel the inadequacy of such conception ..." At the end of my speech, the crowd applauded, and Mother helped Father stand in ovation. He was smiling and wiping his eyes at the same time.

Sitting down next to Anna, I gasped a sigh of relief and a wave of exhilaration bathed my whole body. "I have fought the good fight. I have finished the course," I whispered. "2 Timothy 4:7."

The Trustees' Alumnae banquet followed the graduation ceremony, and Anna and I were greeted by Mother, Father, Uncle Andy, Aunt Bessie, and Anna's fiancé, Jack Daub.

"I was very moved by your interpretation of Persian affairs," Father said.

"It warmed my heart that you still care about Persia," Mother added, "even though you might never go back."

"But I will go back," I responded. "I intend to go back once I complete my master's degree in teaching." As I spoke, I felt a gentle tap on my shoulder.

"You didn't think I'd miss your commencement," Joe said. "I would not have missed it for the world. You all look stunning, and your commencement speech was wonderful."

"Mother, Father, do you remember Joe Cochran?"

Mother laughed. "I'd recognize a Cochran a hundred feet away. My, haven't you grown up to be a handsome young man. Oh, Sam, doesn't he look just like his father."

"Bessie and Andy, Joe's father was Joseph Plumb Cochran, Sr., a famous doctor in Persia," Father said. "He built a hospital in Urmia, the first respectable medical hospital in all of Persia." Then, turning to Joe, Father continued, "I hear that you plan to follow in your father's footsteps."

"I certainly intend to do so," Joe said, smiling radiantly. "And, I've invited Agnes to come with me back to Persia."

"Take her then and make a good missionary woman out of her," Father said with his typical gentle humor. I was mortified, but I could see from Anna's facial response that she thought it a pleasant revelation.

After Class Supper, Father took me aside. "A few last words of wisdom," he said. "As you excel in everything—in faith, in speech, in knowledge, and in all eagerness and in the love we have kindled in you, see that you excel also in the gracious act of giving kindness."

"2 Corinthians 8:7," I said and kissed Father goodbye.

"It was such a miracle that he was able to come," I whispered to Rose. "God gave him the strength."

My graduation present was a short vacation at Rye Beach with Mary and Marcia in a little bungalow, with Mother and Marcia's mother as our chaperones. We spent a week bathing, boating, and playing tennis. In the evenings, we had quiet hours reading on our homey, shackled veranda overlooking the water. Marcia's graduation present was a new Model T that her Father, a director of Mount Morris Bank, drove up to our bungalow the second day.

"You won't need an automobile living in New York," Mother quickly said when she saw Marcia's machine. "The cable car can take you any-where you need to go."

Mother never talked about money, but I knew my parents couldn't afford to give me an automobile on a missionary stipend. And with

Father an invalid, would he eventually resign from missionary service and be without a source of income? What would happen to my family then?

We were only at home in Indiana, Pennsylvania, for a week when we had to pack again for a two-month stay in Chautauqua, New York. Mother came upstairs to check on us. "I'm pleased to see that you are almost finished packing."

"Why are we going to Chautauqua?" Rose asked.

"The Chautauqua Institute requested that Father be the Presbyterian minister at their denomination house this summer. We accepted the assignment last fall."

"But Father can barely stand or walk," Rose said.

"Father committed to this before we came to America. It means a lot to him, and I want you girls to support him. You see, we are not guests at Presbyterian House; we are there to help as well."

"What do you mean?" I asked.

"I will help in the kitchen and serve meals. And you girls will help with the house laundry."

"What?" I exclaimed.

"You are doing a service. It will not be hard work."

Mother left the room and walked quietly down the hall, then down the stairs. She had delivered the unpleasant message and could go back to her work. Rose and I were silent, slowly folding clothes and putting them into our trunks, thinking about what this meant.

"I can't believe I'll be spending my summer after graduation doing laundry," I said. "I should be able to relax and celebrate."

Rose did not look up from her folding, only solemnly nodded.

"Our first summer in America with our missionary parents," I muttered. "It's going to be a nightmare."

The streets of Chautauqua were lined with quaint two- or three-story gingerbread houses, painted in an array of colors with contrasting colored trims and shutters—pinks, yellows, blues, greens, and purples. At every street corner was an inviting glimpse of the shimmering water of Chautauqua Lake.

"I'm in love with Chautauqua already," Mother said wistfully.

The car stopped in front of a three-story, red-brick building at 9 Palestine Street with the sign Presbyterian House over the door. On the first and second floor porches, people were swaying in white rocking chairs, keenly watching us as we unloaded. "Reverend Wilson," a man shouted.

Squinting in the bright sunlight, I made out a familiar face. It was Dr. Zimmer, who had visited Vassar my freshman year and gave me the card to join the Student Volunteers. He was soon down the steps, greeting Father and the rest of the family, and helped us take our trunks into the house.

Our rooms were on the first floor so that Father would not have to climb stairs. Rose and I shared a small sparse room facing the back lawn. "Look," Rose said. "I found a map of the building layout on our door. There are only thirty rooms. And look, it says, 'Sheets are changed on Mondays except by special request.' Laundry won't be that bad after all." Rose looked up, smiling, and started to laugh. "Agnes, you should look in the mirror and see your scowl. You're determined to hate it here, aren't you?" Rose was always so positive and sweet, and her face always reflected her inner peace, whereas my face always reflected my inner turmoil.

"I'll feel better once we have a chance to sail on the lake," I mumbled.

The common dining room at Presbyterian House was crowded with a dozen or so round tables with blue-and-white checkered tablecloths.

While Mother was busy serving, Father sat at the table nearest the door and welcomed the guests as they entered.

"This is going to be fun here," Annie said.

"Were you thinking it would be otherwise?" Father asked.

"Agnes has been complaining so ..."

Father immediately turned to me, changing his tone of voice. "Agnes, I've warned you about the influence your negative attitude has on others. We will need to talk about this, but on another occasion."

That evening, Father gave his first church service in the Presbyterian House chapel, a room off the dining room with small pews in symmetrical rows. The Institute had a special lectern made for Father so he could sit while giving his sermons. He sat in a big chair that looked like a throne with its burgundy cushions and a high back. Father cleared his throat and the room went silent. He spoke haltingly at first. "Welcome, I ..."

As he looked around the audience, his glance caught sight of Mother, with her loving face and encouraging eyes. His lips quivered under his thick mustache, then his voice began to boom as it always had before.

"I haven't heard Father preach since I left Persia four years ago," I whispered to Rose as tears welled in my eyes.

The subject of Father's sermon was "Friendship and Community, the Spirit of our Summer Together."

"In Colossians 3:12-15 it says, 'As God's chosen ones, put on compassion, kindness, lowliness, meekness, and patience. And above all these, put on love, which binds everything together in perfect harmony.'"

Father grew invigorated, his eyes glowing, as he reached the climax of his sermon. He rose from his chair, supporting himself with one arm on the lectern and stretching the other into the air. "In 1 Peter 4:9-10 it reads, 'Practice hospitality ungrudgingly to one another. As each has received a gift, employ it for one another, as good stewards of God.'

And let this house be blessed with that kindred spirit. Let God be in our hearts everyday of our sojourn."

The congregation surprised me by standing and applauding afterward. Father laughed, saying, "Well, it wasn't Hamlet."

"Father, I am so proud of you," I whispered.

The next morning at breakfast the guests at Presbyterian House stopped at the table to tell Father how much they enjoyed his sermon. "I'm sure now that you've shown that you are up to it. You'll get other requests as well," Dr. Zimmer said. And he was right. In addition to his regular daily services at Presbyterian House, Father gave three Sunday sermons in the large outdoor amphitheater to over four hundred people.

One morning, Father took me aside and asked me to sit with him in the small outdoor chapel. "I did not know what to think of your begrudging attitude about helping with laundry," Father said. "The other guests pay substantially for their stay here, and we stay for our service only. In 2 Corinthians 9:7 the Apostle Paul says, 'Each one must do as he has made up his mind, not reluctantly or under compulsion, for God loves a cheerful giver.' Now remember these words as you help with the laundry."

I sat and reflected on how Father and Mother had sacrificed so much for the people of Persia with their continuous unselfish service. I was spoiled with the maids at Vassar doing my laundry, being a guest of the Dulleses and Father's relatives in Indiana. I never had to do any housework.

When I came back to our room, Rose was reading.

"I've been thinking," I said. "We should help Mother with the housework when we are visiting in Indiana. She does so much."

"Why, I already help Mother with housekeeping," Rose responded. "She used to always insist on doing everything herself, but ever since Father's accident she lets me help her."

"I should have known you would do that," I replied. "You're always so sweet and unselfish, my dear sister. Why can't I be more like you?"

One afternoon Rose went with the children to swim in the lake, and I chose to sit on the porch with Mother, Father, and Grandmother.

"Father," I started hesitantly, "I have been thinking hard about God's will for me."

"Yes, and what did you determine that is?" Father asked, looking at me with anticipation.

"I feel my heart's calling is to pursue missionary work. It would be so natural for me to return to Persia, where I know the country and the language. But I don't know if this is God's will for me."

"You'll feel in your heart if you are on His path," Father responded. "You'll feel His inspiration as you proceed in your endeavor."

"And how will I know the right man to marry?"

Mother and Grandmother looked up from their books, and Father turned to Mother with his eyebrows raised.

"The decision that comes from your heart will be the right one," Mother replied.

"Put your own goals first, above all," Father added. "Never allow a man to convince you to do otherwise."

"Be careful in your decision who to marry," Mother continued. "There are women who live their whole lives regretting their choice of a husband. I am happy I am not one of them." Mother caressed the top of Father's hand.

"I would be proud if you followed in your Mother's footsteps and became a missionary," Grandmother interjected. "And there is always Joe Cochran. He'd make a good husband and you know I wouldn't like anything better."

"Grandmother," Mother retorted. "We agreed to let Agnes decide for herself."

I grew frustrated. "I feel uncertain how to learn what God's will is for me. I feel that I must make my mind up without His help."

Father scowled. "Agnes, that is not what I've taught you. Look into your heart. Don't expect a telegram from God telling you what to do with your life."

"But that's what I need," I replied. "I need it spelled out, explicitly."

Anna's and Jack's wedding was August 22nd, a *déjà vu* of Sarah's wedding the year before. Anna wore Sarah's wedding dress and veil, and the traditional wreath of orange roses. I was the maid of honor, and Anna's younger sisters, Gladys and Ella, were the bridesmaids. We wore light-blue crepe dresses and carried bouquets of pink carnations. Buzz and Marcia, our Vassar classmates, were ribbon bearers and wore pink satin dresses and white lilies in their hair.

On the same hill at Kiski School where Sarah and James were married, Father performed the ceremony, assisted by Uncle Rob. It was fascinating watching them together, so similar in appearance and gestures. "The two inseparable preacher brothers," Uncle Harry said.

Father's spinal injury still made it difficult for him to walk, but he could sit up and write for several hours each day. Dr. Speer, the head of the Presbyterian Mission Board, extended his furlough unconditionally saying, "We consider your books on Muslims and Bahaism to be very worthy and productive efforts. You are free to stay in America with our support until an improvement in your health warrants your return to the mission field."

Mother and Father talked often about the family's options for the future. Father's doctor remained uncertain about the potential for his recovery and gave him no affirmative prognosis.

"I should be fit to return to mission work next summer," Father declared.

Mother smiled sweetly and replied, "Yes, Samuel, we'll see how far you can walk in the spring."

The decision about the future of the family weighed heavily on Father. Being a person who never made decisions quickly and always considered all sides, he became quite restless with uncertainty by the end of the summer.

September 10th was my twenty-first birthday. "I'm officially an adult today," I announced at breakfast. Mother held a birthday party in the backyard after dinner, and I wore my fluffy white chiffon dress, with pink ribbons in my hair. Aunt Jennie brought a white cake with pink and white icing and twenty-one pink candles. "You match the cake perfectly," she said.

There were small gifts from the relatives—a silver pen from Aunt Bessie and Uncle Andy, a small black purse from Aunt Jennie, an embroidered chemise from Aunt Agnes, auto scarves from Anna and Sarah, and a five-dollar bill from Uncle Harry. Father slowly stood up from his chair and handed me a small wooden box with a gold stamp on top. He stood by my side, grinning as I opened it. It was a lovely round gold locket on a gold chain. I ran my finger over the etching on the cover. "It's beautiful, so intricate."

"Open it," Father said. Inside the locket were tiny photographs of Mother on one side and Father on the other, under thin sheets of glass. "Now you can always have me and Mother close to your heart."

I hugged and kissed Father, then Mother, and Aunt Jennie lit the candles on the cake.

"Close your eyes and make a wish, then blow out the candles," she said.

I closed my eyes and said, "I wish to return to Tabriz with Mother and Father." I blew, but only ten of the candles went out.

When I looked up, I saw Father sitting nearby with a crestfallen expression on his face. He turned to the others and cleared his voice. "Everyone, I have an announcement to make."

The boisterous crowd of relatives suddenly stopped their conversations and turned toward Father in anticipation.

"Annie and I have come to a decision about our future. Given my poor physical state, I have decided to resign my post at the mission in Tabriz. We will be staying here in Indiana, and I will continue to write and give lectures."

Father's brothers and sisters were ecstatic and enthusiastically congratulated him. I turned away, overcome with shock and anger. After some time, Father slowly made his way over to me. "Agnes, I know this came as a surprise."

Anger welled up inside me and I blurted out, "Now I'll have to stay in this country. I told everyone I was going back to Tabriz with you to teach at the mission. Now what am I to do?" I looked away from him and started to walk away.

"Agnes, look at me. I can barely walk. It has been a year since the accident, and I don't know if I will improve. I owe my resignation to the Presbyterian Board."

Tears welled into my eyes, and I ran into the house and up to my room. I lay face down on the bed and sobbed. "Now we're trapped in this country. I must find another way, some other way to return to Persia."

Chapter 14

TEACHERS' COLLEGE, COLUMBIA UNIVERSITY, FALL 1913

AFTER OUR TRAIN ARRIVED IN NEW YORK, ROSE AMBLED off toward the platform to Poughkeepsie and a sudden rush of uncertainty swept over me. There I was in the big city, quite unsettled in my own mind, and with only the vaguest notion as to which way to turn. Then I heard a familiar voice. "Agnes." I turned and there was Buzz Howson walking swiftly toward me. "Tell the porter to take your trunk curbside. Father is waiting in the auto."

The Howsons had plenty of room for me in their large, three-story, brick-and-brownstone home at 489 West End Street. They treated me like another daughter, including me when they went out as a family for entertainment.

My first step was to visit Dr. Speer at the Board of Presbyterian Missions and seek his advice on course work. He helped me select classes for my first year at Columbia Teachers' College, including three courses in Bible study at Union Theological Seminary, situated across the street. "This should give you sufficient foundation for missionary work," he said.

The Teachers' College courses flooded me with a light of great purpose. Dr. John Dewey's education classes introduced me to the concept of the school as a social institution through which social reform could be possible. "Education is not preparation for life," he said. "It is life itself."

Despite being rather slow, Dewey's lectures were stimulating as were his books, *The Pedagogic Creed*, *The School and Society*, and *The Child and the Curriculum*. "I strongly believe that students need to take part in their own education," he wrote, "that curriculum should be experiential and interactive."

Another instructor, Mrs. Romiett Stevens, took a personal interest in me and kindly arranged for me to visit a New York High School. "It was particularly interesting to me since I never attended high school," I told her. "Now I have a better understanding of what education is like in America."

Mrs. Stevens tried to impress me with the gravity of the state of education in America. "Seven percent of the people in America are unable to read and write," she said. "Even here in New York, a center of the highest development of education, only sixty percent of the children complete eighth grade."

"Less than five percent of the children in Persia are able to attend school," I responded, "and they are almost all boys. I plan to use my training to teach girls in Persia."

"You have quite a task when you return to Persia, don't you?" she exclaimed. "Your teaching will be a noble pursuit."

"Yes," I replied. "Paul said in Romans 12:7, that Teaching is one of God's Seven Graces."

After being at an all-girls college for four years, it was both exciting and distracting to have men in my classes. At Teachers' College the number of men and women were about equal in my classes, but at Union Theological Seminary the students were primarily men studying to be pastors. Many of the reverends-to-be were at least five years older than I and took great interest in the girls who attended their classes. It became my habit to enter the classroom early so as not to parade in front of my male classmates and feel their eyes on me.

My favorite Bible course was Apostles by Mr. Ross. Ready to grasp anything that served as a clue to navigating the labyrinth of my religious understanding, I found his lessons eye-opening. At one moment I thought I understood a concept, then an uncertainty seemed to present itself at every turn. I was waking up from my childhood conception of God, and the idea that being good and praying would bring me what I needed to be happy. I suddenly realized that there was a long journey to finding happiness. It meant inner reflection, self-analysis, studying the depths of my soul. It meant something I'd never done before.

Of all the Apostles, Paul's teachings helped me the most. I remembered a passage Father loved to read from Romans 12:2: "Do not be conformed to this world, but be transformed by the renewal of your mind, that you may prove what is the will of God, what is good and acceptable and perfect."

In October, I went again to Joe's fraternity house party at Williams. Joe was head of the Phi Gamma Delta fraternity house, and I was amazed at his transformation. He took command of situations with such dignity and managed the fraternity boys with authority and tact. The freckled boy who was my childhood friend had transformed into a mature young man and a natural leader.

Since I was the only girl back from the previous year, the fraternity brothers jumped to conclusions. "Do I hear wedding bells?" asked one. "When are you tying the knot?" asked another. Even more embarrassing, the fraternity boys demanded my repeat performance of the "Purple Berkshire Queen."

The program of events was much the same as before—concert, play, dance, football game, banquet, Sunday hayride. This time I really was not fit for the early Monday morning dancing, and Joe and I spent the time in his sitting room instead, having a tête é tête.

"Tell me about your studies at Columbia," Joe said.

"I'm taking primary and secondary education with John Dewey, who's lectures are slow and monotonously delivered, but brilliant all the same."

"Brilliant, how so?"

"The way he puts things. For instance, on the topic of 'Self' he says, 'The self is not something ready-made, but something in continuous formation through choice of action.' "

"Choice of action. Yes, I must admit that when I'm memorizing chemical reactions and biological terms, I remind myself that I do this by choice, to become a doctor and follow in my father's footsteps."

"Dr. Speer helped me choose courses that would properly train me as a missionary teacher. My favorite class is Apostles."

"The education courses I understand, but why the religious studies?"

"Religion does have a role in missionary work, after all," I responded. "I remember now how our fathers argued about what best served the Persians, religion or medicine. I'm afraid that we will argue about this too."

"Yes, we may. I look at things with my father's same scientific and rational eyes, while you see things spiritually and emotionally like your father."

"Yes, religion is more important to me."

"I must admit I'm not as devout as you are. I even study on Sundays."

"You're a heathen," I said and smirked at him.

Joe took the opportunity to take a sip of tea and change the subject. "I know that these types of questions annoy you, but what are your plans after Teachers' College?"

"I'm planning on taking a heavy fall semester next year and graduating in February, then I hope to spend winter in Paris. I've applied to the Sorbonne."

"What on earth will you study at the Sorbonne that you can't study at Columbia?"

"I won the Borden Travel Scholarship to spend time studying in a foreign country. I must take advantage of the opportunity."

Joe seemed quite perplexed. "But I applied to Columbia Medical School because I wanted to be near you. What will you do after Paris?"

"I plan to apply to the Presbyterian Board of Foreign Missions for a teacher position with hopes of going to Persia."

Joe looked silently down at the floor for a few minutes, then looked up earnestly. "I hope it can be more than friendship with you someday. I sincerely care about you."

"In Proverbs 17:17 it says 'A friend loves at all times,' " I replied, "and I do." Joe smiled and touched my hand. "But you must understand. I want to be respected as a missionary in my own right, not just the wife of a missionary doctor."

One day after Apostles class at Union, a young man stood waiting at the door. As I walked by, I was startled when he grabbed my arm.

"How do you do?" he said in a thick, Irish brawl. "My name's Frank Fitt. What's yours?" He had a prominent nose, closely set blue eyes, and prominent ears, the tops which bent over slightly. "Mr. Elephant Ears," I immediately nicknamed him to myself.

"Agnes. Agnes Wilson," I managed to say, almost laughing.

"Aye, an Irish girl. I knew by your looks. Would you care to join me for tea?"

"Tea? I …"

"Just tea." Frank laughed, likely at my lack of social spontaneity.

"Why yes, I would like to go for tea," I mustered.

"Well, let's go then." Frank politely took my arm and led me to a café a half block away.

"I'm from Limerick. Where are you from?"

"Tabriz."

"Tabriz, Persia?"

"Missionary parents."

"I see. Well, you look like a nice girl, and I could tell by your wide-eyed bewilderment that you are new here."

"My uncle from New Jersey brought me to the city several times, but I don't know my way around."

"Perfect. I will be your tour guide."

"How long have you lived in New York?"

"Since 1911. After I was graduated from Williams, I moved here to go to Union Seminary."

"Did you know Frank Coan? He would have been in your class."

"Aye, Frank Coan, tall skinny fellow, very kind."

Somehow, I was relieved that he knew Frank Coan. "If you want to show me the city, I'd like to see the skyscrapers."

"The Woolworth Building is the tallest, with sixty stories. It opened in April. Before then the Metropolitan Life Tower was tallest, with fifty stories, and its massive clock still makes it quite special. Then there's the Singer Building with forty-seven stories. Of course, coming in on the steamer you must have seen the twin Hudson Towers, twenty-two stories each. I'll take you to see the big ones after tea, if it would please you to do so."

"That would be a pleasure." I had a rush of anxiety about going out with a man I did not know well, but I convinced myself that it should be fine to go out with a fellow student.

Our first encounter was followed by walks through Central and Riverside Parks. Frank taught me the cable cars, the tunnels, the parks, and the museums. On rainy fall days Frank took me to the castle-like Natural History Museum on 77th Street or the Metropolitan Museum of Art at 5th Avenue and 81st Street. As I became more comfortable with Frank, I accepted invitations to evening shows on the "The Great White Way," as Broadway was called.

For my Bible classes, Frank was invaluable as part of my "thinking apparatus" and helped me clearly write my interpretive essays on the Apostles. He reminded me of Father; he had an amazing grasp of the scriptures and their underlying meaning. I was sure that someday Frank would be an incredible pastor.

The problem was that I was spending so much time with Frank that I reached my "high water mark." Although I enjoyed having a fellow student as a companion, it became clear that Frank wanted more in our relationship. While attending a tea at Union with Frank, Madeline, a classmate, took me aside and said, "Be careful with Frank. He latches on to girls and is very persistent."

Just before Christmas, Rose came from Vassar and stayed with me at the Howsons before going home with me. As coincidence would have it, Roy St. Clair from Pennsylvania was also in town and came up to call. We were both pleased to have him visit, since his jokes were so entertaining.

"Did you see the headlines of *The New York Times* today?" Roy asked.

"Why no," I answered.

"They found the *Mona Lisa*. The robber was arrested in Florence."

"Oh what joyous news," I said. "I had lost all hope. It's been missing for two years."

"Why didn't Father say anything to us?" Buzz exclaimed. "I'll get the newspaper from his study." She quickly returned with the paper. "The robber's name was Vincenzo Peruggia. Since he had worked at the Louvre, his presence did not alert the guards and he hid the painting under his smock. 'I only intended to restore *La Gioconda* to Italy, a painting that was stolen by Napoleon,' he said. After displaying it in Italy, the *Mona Lisa* will be returned to France on December 30th."

Mrs. Howson came into the parlor just then. "Agnes, a Mr. Fitt has come to see you."

Frank looked surprised when he saw I had company. "I came to see if you were interested in entertainment," he said.

"Frank, this is Roy St. Clair, a friend from Pennsylvania. He's attending medical school at Williams and Jefferson. This is my sister Rose. Frank is a classmate from Union Theological Seminary."

"Do join us for tea, Frank," Buzz said pleasantly.

Frank sat down and helped himself to a cup of Ceylon and a lady-finger. He eyed Roy suspiciously. "I had thought of taking you to see 'Grumpy' at the Wallack Theatre."

"Father and I went to see it last weekend," Buzz said. "It's quite entertaining."

"Where's the Wallack?" Roy asked.

"At Broadway and 30th. A cable-car ride down Park Avenue to 28th Street, then a brief walk."

"Frank knows New York like the lines on his palm," I said.

"Shall we go then?" Roy asked.

"Yes, let's go," I said. "Frank can escort Rose and we can go together."

I could tell that Frank was annoyed by this arrangement but was decent enough to show Rose a good time. "Grumpy" was a funny mystery play involving an old criminal lawyer, a lost diamond, and a mix up of camellias that implicated the thief. Roy came out laughing and talking loudly about the scenes and dialogue that he enjoyed. I was pleased that Roy had been there when Frank arrived. I wanted Frank to realize that there were other men in my life.

A few days later, Rose and I took the sleeper from New York to Pennsylvania to spend Christmas with the family. Father was able to sit without trouble and was writing a book on Muslims. I interrupted him once when he seemed in good humor. "Father, what are your plans when your health improves?"

"I may seek employment here in America," he answered, then looked wistfully out the window. "The doctors are encouraged by my progress, but they think further recovery is needed before I consider that."

It troubled me that Father was not enthusiastic about the future. *What would happen to Father? What would happen to my family?*

Chapter 15

TEACHERS' COLLEGE, COLUMBIA UNIVERSITY, SPRING 1914

THE MOMENT I MET STANLEY HUNTER WAS LIKE BEING struck by a lightning bolt. Frank was holding a tea in Union parlor for his mother, who was visiting from Limerick. I had made the mistake of mentioning the grand parade we had for St. Patrick's Day in New York, which set her off condemning America's frivolous treatment of a religious holiday. I was relieved when a man sauntered up beside us and asked to be introduced.

"Mother, this is Stanley Hunter," Frank said. "He's a classmate and a dear friend."

As I turned to also acknowledge Stanley, my mouth fell open. He was a tall young man with piercing blue eyes and a finely sculptured face, a broad forehead, a perfectly shaped nose, and an aristocratic chin.

A face like Michelangelo's David. He's the handsomest man I've ever seen.

Stanley caught my gaze and laughed. "Do I know you?" he asked.

"You haven't met Agnes?" Frank said. "She's a student in our Apostles class."

"It's hard to believe that I didn't notice you in class the first semester," he said and smiled.

His smile made me feel like I was melting inside.

Immediately I broke my resolution to spend my time studying rather than attend Union social gatherings. It was convenient being escorted by Frank as I could count on Stanley coming by to talk with his friend. Eventually, they politely brought me into the conversation, but Stanley never seemed heedful to what I had to say.

Strangely, it was a paper I wrote for Apostles class that first won me Stanley's attention. Dr. Ross made a fuss over my essay on Paul and read excerpts to the students in class.

After that, when Stanley was talking to someone at Union and I was within earshot, he teased me by saying, "And of course you've heard of Agnes's famous paper on Paul."

It always made me blush. Then Stanley would turn to me and say, "It's such fun teasing you. How pleasantly pink your cheeks become."

I responded by smiling and looking directly into his eyes. There was something exhilarating about flirting with a handsome man. I hadn't been flirtatious since Howard Baskerville, and it made me quite giddy, like a teenage girl.

Both Frank and Stanley were attentive to me at Union social gatherings and often sat on either side of me. On one occasion we were sitting together at a Union tea when I saw Dr. Ross pass by the doorway, and I left for several minutes, needing a chance to talk to him.

On returning to the tea parlor, my classmate Madeline whispered, "The 'rivals' held your chair for you," nodding toward Frank and Stanley. "Everyone finds their attentions to you quite amusing."

When I returned to the table, Frank announced, "We're going to toss a coin to see who gets the privilege of walking with you to Columbia Station."

"To the luck of the toss then," replied Stanley, mimicking Frank's Irish brogue and smiling at me. *Oh, that smile makes me weak in the knees. Please let it be Stanley.*

Frank fumbled in his pocket and produced a shiny nickel and cupped it in his right hand. "What will it be?"

"Tails," replied Stanley.

Oh, pray to heaven, let it be tails. I closed my eyes as Frank tossed the coin in the air and let it fall on the carpet.

"Open your eyes, Agnes. What is it?" Frank said.

I opened my eyes and looked at the floor. "Heads," I said trying to hide my disappointment.

Frank took my arm and slapped Stanley on the back with his other hand. "Better luck next time, old chap."

What fun it was to have two men "fighting" for my attention, but from what Madeleine said, I suspected that the joke was really on me.

The last Union social event of the year I attended with "the rivals" was a mixer with the more senior and newer students. Madeleine, the organizer, pinned a paper on each attendee's back; it had the name of their home state or country. The purpose was to give the newer students an opportunity to start conversations by asking questions about the place the older students were from. Frank, Stanley, and I were engaged in conversation when a group of new students joined us for introductions and questions.

"How long did you live in Persia?" one student asked me.

"I lived in Tabriz for sixteen years," I answered.

"And you?" another student asked Stanley.

"I've never been there," he answered. The students turned to each other, looking bewildered. Just then someone tapped Frank's shoulder, and when he turned around, we saw that the paper on his back said "Persia."

Stanley started laughing. "Madeline must have pinned 'Persia' onto Frank's back as a joke."

My face was burning.

"Wait. What does it say on my back?" Stanley asked, turning his back to me.

"It says 'Persia' too," I answered in astonishment. "No wonder the new students were confused."

"It's not funny," Stanley said, glaring at me. "Did you instigate this?"

"Of course not," I replied. "I'm as embarrassed as anyone."

"I think it's time for me to leave," Stanley said. He tore the paper from his back and abruptly left the room.

I was mortified and stalked over to Madeleine. "How could you do that?" I sputtered. "Now Stanley's angry with me because he thinks I had something to do with it."

"It was only meant to be a joke," Madeleine replied. "Somehow it did not work out that way."

"You have a curious sense of humor," I retorted.

Although Stanley continued to engage me in cordial conversation, the "rivalry" between him and Frank was over.

For the rest of the spring, Frank continued to be my chief Union companion and escort me to social events. I enjoyed his companionship, and his wonderful Limerick accent, but I decided firmly that he would only be a friend and a companion, nothing more. Stanley was whom I wanted. He made my heart throb and the blood surge in my veins.

'Scarcely had I passed them when I found the one my heart loves.' Song of Solomon 3:4.

One morning I found a note from Dr. Speer in my mailbox: "Please stop by my office this morning. R.S." I couldn't stand the suspense, so I headed straight away to his office at 5th Ave. and 20th Street. He looked up over his reading glasses from a book, his hand arrested in the midst of turning a page. "Oh, Agnes, so good of you to come so quickly. I wanted to talk to you about the Mott campaign."

"Yes?"

"John Mott is the leader of the Student Volunteer Movement, as well as the Student Christian Federation and the Y.M.C.A. The first week of March, he's coming to New York to give a full week of talks and Columbia is hosting the event."

"Yes, I plan to attend."

"There's an enormous amount of work to be done, and I think it would do you good to learn what it takes to organize these types of events. I'll have you meet with Guy Converse later today. He'll assign you a committee to lead."

Guy Converse was a short fellow with light-brown, wispy-thin, baby-like hair that fell on his boyish face each time he turned his head. As a result, he was constantly flicking it aside with one hand. Despite this distraction, he spoke assertively with a clear, pleasant voice and had a charming smile that he would flash whenever he paused.

The Mott Campaign took every minute of my time for almost six weeks; presiding at luncheons and subcommittee meetings, organizing sessions, and weighing in with noted religious leaders. There were one hundred and fifty members on the committee assigned to me. Our job was to reach all the students of each college personally by telephone, stimulate their interest in attending the meetings, and send them registration materials. We cut out all social affairs and "lived our religion" as the girls on my committee described it.

One Tuesday, March 3rd, the first talk by John Mott was held in Carnegie Hall and attended by three thousand students. Former President Taft presided over the meeting and introduced Mr. Mott, saying, "I came here tonight to recognize and pay tribute to another world power, working on behalf and representing America, John R. Mott. He is here to help along the college Christian movement."

Mr. Mott spoke on the danger of religious indifference. He declared, "Students of this day and age need to develop their ethical and religious nature. The injurious result of non-exercise of the moral muscles is a state of atrophy. If the moral faculties are not developed and used, they may be lost entirely. Use or lose." It was such a practical explanation and understandable to the students.

At Saturday's banquet with four hundred people, Guy suddenly ushered me to the head of the table to sit next to Mr. Mott. "At the last minute, Robert Speer called to say he couldn't come," Guy whispered in my ear.

Mr. Mott had a square face, intense eyes, bushy eyebrows and a frightfully stern mouth. He told a story of a trip he took to England for a missionary conference. "A colleague and I were approached by an official from the White Star Line. He had a copy of my book, *Evangelization of the World in a Generation* and asked me to sign it, which I gladly did. To our surprise he then offered to give us free passage to New York on his new ship, the Titanic. Not having packed appropriate clothes to be seated in the first-class dining room with millionaires, we declined and instead took the Red Line's SS Lapland, which had more humble accommodations. When we arrived in New York and learned the fate of the Titanic, we looked at each other in amazement. I said to my aghast colleague, 'The good Lord must have work for us to do.'"

"How miraculous," I exclaimed. With all his serious proselytizing I hadn't imagined that Mr. Mott had a sense of humor.

Guy Converse claimed the right of fueling our incipient acquaintance from the Mott Campaign with frequent offerings of flowers and theater invitations. In fact, that spring, I don't know how many things we did together—concerts, theater, receptions, premiers, walks, teas, tennis. After bringing me home, he started staying an hour or so and seemed to have no sense of time.

Buzz teased me. "I'm always pretty sure that he'll come out with a wedding proposal any day now." As it turned out, he was always without a sense of time for practical purposes—he had forgotten his watch at home.

Joe came to New York after Easter vacation on his way back to Williams, and Mrs. Howson kindly had him to dinner. After Joe left, Mrs. Howson said, "Mr. Cochran is my favorite among the young men that have been here, so confident and mature."

"Joe and I have known each other for years," I explained. "He's almost like a brother."

"Our maid was puzzled over the different gentlemen she has seen with you and asked me in the kitchen if this one was 'Miss Wilson's real fellow,' and I told her that I thought he was."

I blushed. How I hated it when people made assumptions. I recalled how the Phi Gamma Delta fraternity boys also made assumptions about Joe and me.

Maybe I shouldn't go to Williams for Joe's graduation in June. Joe's brothers, Clement and Harrison, will be there, and so will the Coans. They might make embarrassing assumptions too.

Joe was understandably disappointed when I told him I had decided not to come to his graduation, and it was impossible to reconcile him as I really had no legitimate excuse.

"Why are you afraid of people talking about us?" he asked. "My family and the Coans think of you as part of our extended family."

Why was I afraid of people talking about me? Was it because they talked about me and Howard Baskerville at the mission? Was I still ashamed?

I had let my closest friend down, and I regretted not going to Joe's graduation for the rest of my life.

Instead of going to Williams, I spent a week with my Vassar friend Marcia in New Rochelle. We went swimming at Hudson Park and played tennis. On warm afternoons, we sat together on the porch swing and talked for hours.

"Graduate school is so different from Vassar," Marcia said. "It's so distracting going to classes with boys."

"When I was younger, I never liked having boys around," I said. "Now it seems I can't get away from them."

"With Joe at Williams, who are you going out with?"

"Frank and Guy, companions from Union."

"Won't it be a bit complicated when Joe comes to Columbia for medical school next fall?"

"I expect to still go out with them as Joe will be very busy with his medical studies."

Mrs. Livermore opened the screen door and stepped out onto the porch. "Agnes, a Mr. Fitt has come to call on you. I'll show him back here."

Marcia looked alarmed. "Did you know he was coming?"

"No, I would have told you if I knew. I only gave him your address so that he could write to me."

Just then Frank and Mrs. Livermore appeared. Frank surveyed me, then Marcia, then the porch, looking uneasy, and finally sat down in a white wicker chair with pink flowered cushions. "I wanted to see you again before you leave for Pennsylvania," he said.

"We can always write," I replied flatly.

"I was studying at the Union library, the only one there. I could hear the bookcases creak, like the room was inhabited with ghosts."

"I wish I'd checked out some books to take home."

"Just write me and let me know what you'd like to read, and I'll send you a box. I could also make the trip to Pennsylvania and spend time with you."

"That won't be necessary."

"I'd like to meet your family while they are here in America."

I was slow to respond. "I'd prefer to be alone with my family. Father is not well, and I don't have much time with Mother and the children except in the summer."

"It's time that I meet your family and have a chance to talk to your father."

Marcia excused herself. "I'll return in a few minutes."

I looked at her desperately. She caught my glance and smiled sadly, as one might when seeing a butterfly caught in a spider's web.

"We've been seeing each other for nine months and your father should meet me. He should want to know if I am the right man for you."

"What?"

"Relationships move quickly these days, and your father and mother may return to Persia before I have another chance."

"A chance for what?"

"A chance for your parents to meet me."

"Not this summer."

Just then Marcia fortuitously returned to the parlor with a tray of tea and dainty cakes.

"Oh, Marcia, those cakes are so cunning," I exclaimed.

"Mary Phillips just arrived. She'll be down shortly after she freshens up after her long trip from Chicago." Marcia gave Frank a long look as he stood up. "You're not staying for tea?"

"No, I'll go now," Frank said and abruptly left.

"He makes me uncomfortable," Marcia said. "He's so tense."

"He's frustrated because he wants to say something but can't find the words. When he's like that he sometimes says things that he shouldn't."

Before I left for summer vacation, Guy came to say goodbye and gave me a big box of candy, which I took back with me on the train. I had gained some pounds over the year with all of the Mott campaign luncheons and Guy's frequent gifts of chocolates, so I resisted the temptation of eating any of the tasty morsels. "This will be a present for Annie and Bobby," I promised myself.

When I handed Bobby the unopened box of chocolates, he asked. "What guy did you get this from?"

"How did you know his name?" I answered.

Mother and Rose laughed as I'd written to them about Guy. "Just look at the confused look on Bobby's sweet little face," Rose said.

"The guy's name is Guy Converse," I added. "A nice friend, but not a beau."

"This is a big box of chocolates. I think he wants to be your beau," Annie said.

"Very astute, Annie," Grandmother interjected. "Never trust men with gifts of flowers or chocolates. And, I see you've gained, Agnes. Too many chocolates, no doubt."

"Agnes looks healthy and cheerful now that she's filled in some," Mother said in my defense. "Besides, being a little plump tends to be the desired look for young girls these days."

As I undressed in front of the mirror, I remembered putting on a corset for the first time in Europe with Mrs. Pittman's help. Even after wearing one for five years, I still found it unpleasant, but the corset hid the increasing size of my waistline. I made a resolution to work hard the rest of the summer to lose weight so I would look my best when Stanley saw me in the fall.

One evening after dinner, Mother and Father asked to talk to me.

"Agnes, we are worried that you are spending too much time going out with men instead of concentrating on your studies," Father said.

"These men you are seeing appear to have a romantic interest," Mother continued. "You'll get a bad reputation if you are just leading them on."

"They are devoted friends. That is all," I responded.

"It doesn't look that way to us," Mother said,

"Things are different than when you were a girl," I replied.

"Not that much different. When men give you flowers and chocolates, they are courting you."

"What's wrong with that?"

"What will happen when Joe comes to New York to medical school this fall?"

"I'll see him too."

"If I were Joe," said Father, "I would find a more devoted girl."

I thought about the men I met my first year at graduate school. How I wanted true romance, the type of romance that you read about in romance novels, where a dashing, handsome man suddenly embraces you, and you fall madly in love. Frank was too persistent and impatient, and Guy was too boyish. Neither was suitable for romance. Then there was Joe, so serious and staid, a loyal friend and as comfortable to be with as a brother. Joe was handsome in his own way, but we were on too familiar terms to have a romance.

Stanley Hunter was quite different from all of them. His very presence took my breath away. I tried to imagine his handsome face and feel his hand in mine as I took my morning walks. At night before I fell asleep, I tried to imagine what it would be like to have Stanley embrace me. I never dreamed that way about Guy or Frank, or even Joe. Thinking of Stanley stirred something deep inside of me that I'd never felt before. *'O that his left hand were under my head, and his right hand embraced me.' Song of Solomon 2:6.*

By mid-July, I decided to write to Stanley in hopes of a reply. I conjured up a theological question about a passage on Paul and added some light chatter about my summer activities. I sealed the envelope with a kiss and took it to the post office. My heart raced as I pranced home.

Stanley wrote me back about three weeks later, answering my question about Paul at some length, but nothing else. I held his letter in both hands for several minutes and carried it with me all day as I sung my little Persian love song that I wrote in Azeri to Anton Rubinstein's *Kammenoi Ostroi*. "My heart speaks the language of love. I love you. Yes, I love you."

The year before, Stanley had only asked me once to go with him to tea. This coming year I vowed to win his attention and become "his girl." *How do I let him know that I want him? My flirtations certainly worked for me before with Howard Baskerville. Surely I can win Stanley's heart in the same way.*

On June 28th, the Archduke Franz Ferdinand, the heir to the throne of Austria-Hungary, was assassinated by a Serbian, Gavrilo Princip, in Sarajevo. By the middle of summer, the European nations were embroiled in conflict. War was imminent.

"Can you believe such horror is possible in this day and age?" Grandmother muttered.

"Not having paid attention to world politics, I'm confused as to how the war even started," I said.

"It's the result of previously formed European alliances," Father explained. "There's an alliance between Germany, Austria-Hungary, and Italy and a separate one between Russia, France, Ireland, and Great Britain."

"What about Serbia?" I asked.

"After the assassination, Austria-Hungary declared war against Serbia. Germany's Kaiser Wilhelm the Second supported the invasion of Serbia for retribution. When the Kaiser's cousin, Tsar Nicolas II of Russia, mobilized its armies to support Serbia the real conflict began."

"Two cousins on opposite sides? Are they fighting against each other?"

"Yes. The Kaiser asked the Tsar to withdraw his armies, and he refused. As a result, Germany declared war on Russia."

"Why did France start fighting?"

"Germany asked France to stay neutral, but Russia promised France Alsace-Lorraine if they joined the war on their side."

"Why is Great Britain fighting?"

"Great Britain honored their alliance with France and declared war on Germany."

"I thought you said Italy was also in alliance with Germany and Austria-Hungary."

"Yes, that's very interesting. Italy decided not to join in with them, despite the Triple Alliance."

"What you are saying sounds like a simple explanation, but I don't think I understand why they are fighting this war."

"Not much to be gained on any side. Hopefully the dreadful skirmish will be resolved without a significant loss of life. Unfortunately, it's not a time to be traveling abroad."

The reality of the situation suddenly hit me like a tsunami. "Does this mean I won't be able to study in Paris this winter?"

"I'm afraid that it is very unlikely that the war will be resolved in six months' time."

"But my Borden Scholarship is for studying in a foreign country. I'd planned on studying at the Sorbonne second semester. Teachers' College expects me to leave in February."

"My recommendation is to write to Teachers' College and ask if you could stay on the second semester."

Despite having to give up my plans to study in Paris, I looked forward to another full year at Columbia. Instead of using my Borden Scholarship to study at the Sorbonne, I planned to study the human heart and lure in Stanley Hunter. As a young girl, when I won Howard Baskerville's heart, I was convinced that I could win any man. I was determined to find a way to win over Stanley Hunter.

The nights were sweltering hot in August, and it was hard to sleep.

"Are you coming to bed?" Rose asked one evening.

"No," I replied. "I think I'll stay up awhile and read the Bible."

Song of Solomon 5:2-4. "I slept, but my heart was awake. Hark! My beloved is knocking. Open to me, my sister, my love, my dove, my perfect; for my head is wet with dew, my locks with the drops of the night. I had put off my garment, how could I put it on? I had bathed my feet, how could I soil them? My beloved put his hand to the latch, and my heart thrilled within me."

I lay in bed trying to imagine Stanley's face, his hands touching me, his soft lips on mine.

Chapter 16

Teachers' College, Fall 1914

THE FIRST TIME I OPENED THE DOOR TO MY DORMITORY room on the 8th floor of Whittier Hall, I gasped. From my window an expansive view of New York City was spread before me. The room cost three hundred dollars for the academic year, including table board and plain laundry, but I decided that it was worth the expense to be close to work.

My first day, even before I settled in, Guy met me in the parlor with a bouquet of chrysanthemums and a box of chocolates. "Seminary classes haven't started, and I'm available to take you to entertainment the entire week," he said.

"I could use some cheerfulness with my plans for a semester in Paris crushed," I responded with a pout.

The rest of the week Guy and I went to several shows, "Miss Daisy" at the new Shubert Theatre, "Cordelia Blossom" at the Gaiety Theatre, "Twin Beds" at the Fulton Theatre and "The Third Party" at the 39th Street Theatre. Each time Guy came for me, he brought another bouquet of flowers and another box of chocolates. My dormitory room was fragrant with flowers everywhere; in vases, water glasses, and even the bathroom sink. I put a stack of boxes of luscious chocolate fudge and caramel candies in the parlor to share with the other girls, but after diligently abstaining all summer, I couldn't resist keeping a box for myself. It was a relief when Union Seminary started classes. Guy was a nice fellow and I enjoyed going to shows with him, but I quickly tired of spending so much time together.

The following week, Joe Cochran sent word that he had arrived at the Columbia College of Physicians and Surgeons. I immediately set out on foot to find his building, assuming it was only a few blocks away. To my chagrin, when I asked the information desk I was told, "The medical school is on West 168th Street, almost three miles away. You'll need to take the cable car."

We hadn't seen each other since April, and Joe seemed a bit startled when he first saw me. His reaction was likely due to my weight gain, but dear Joe didn't say a thing about it. I admired his face while he talked with fervor about his medical courses, his intelligent blue eyes shining with ardor and sincerity. I pictured him as the devoted missionary doctor that his father had been, risking his own life to save the lives of the poor Persian people. Yes, this was what I would always love about Joe.

"I'm so happy you're here, but you won't have time for socializing with such a course load," I said.

"I must keep my nose in my books, but we could meet Saturdays for lunch and go to the opera or the symphony," Joe replied.

"What about Broadway shows?"

"I know I'm a bit odd, but comedies and musicals don't interest me."

"But that is how people in New York entertain themselves."

"Maybe it was a mistake to take me to Oscar Wilde's 'Lady Windemere's Fan' when I visited you last Easter. A play about a suspected affair between a husband and a mother-in-law did not strike me as either comic or believable."

"But I do recall that you liked one of the lines in the play."

"Yes. 'We are all in the gutter, but some of us are looking at the stars.'"

"And what does that mean exactly?"

"Always believe in yourself and your future. Aim for the stars. That's what I intend to do."

"So do I."

Later that week, Frank returned and visited me at Whittier Hall. When I came to the parlor, he had helped himself to tea and was sitting rather upright and stiffly, and it made me apprehensive. *What would he say?*

"Most of the students are back at Teachers' College. Is it true at Union?" I asked.

"All but Stanley Hunter." Frank looked up at me with a strange smirk on his lips and a purposeful, penetrating stare. He raised his cup slightly above the saucer and swirled its contents. "He's not coming back this year, taking his church service charge at Bryn Mawr for the winter."

"Not coming back?" I exclaimed. "I had expected to see him any day."

Frank looked up again, scanning my face with a strange, almost malicious look in his eyes, silently watching me react. It was such a surprise that I couldn't speak for the longest time, trying to comprehend.

Finally, I found myself saying, "It will be a meaningful experience for him."

How could it be, with all my plans to return and win Stanley's heart?

After Frank left, I aimlessly walked the halls of Whittier with a dull emptiness inside me. It was as if nothing in the world mattered. That morning I had been anxiously awaiting my first glimpse of Stanley and was overtaken by a horrible longing for him. A deep loneliness settled into my heart like a cold stone. *This is the sort of loneliness that must drive people to become engaged, in spite of themselves.*

Frank came again for tea in the late afternoon, and I tried to chat about what I'd done over the summer. He said little, forcing me to carry the conversation. There were uncomfortable stretches of silence where I couldn't think of anything to say. As I rambled on, he scanned my face with calculating eyes.

After dinner at Whittier with the girls, I excused myself "to write some letters." Once I got to my room, I threw myself down on my bed and stared at the ceiling. *I'm so disappointed that Stanley won't be returning this year. All summer I dreamed of him and sang my Persian love song as I played "Kammenoi Ostroi." If only Stanley would ask me to marry him. I would accept without a question, and with a glad little gasp of relief I would sink into his arms.*

How silly I was. I didn't really know Stanley well enough for it to matter if I never saw him again. I really was not in love with Stanley. It was just a romantic infatuation. With Joe close by, I thought I would be able to lose my feelings for Stanley, but I simply could not get his handsome face out of my mind.

Will I ever see him again?

A few weeks later I sat in front of my window in Whittier Hall, staring out at the city. After Frank's first day back, when he visited twice, he stopped coming to see me without any explanation. Frank's behavior caused me such consternation. Why did he abandon me? Did he guess my feelings for Stanley? Guy and I were seeing each other before Frank got back. Was that it? It hurt so to lose both Frank and Stanley.

Frank always waited for me after Apostles class at Union, but for two weeks he wasn't there. I wanted to see him badly. *I miss Frank, nice Frank who I had grown to consider part of my thinking apparatus.*

Then one day after Dr. Ross's Apostles class, Frank was there, waiting outside the classroom.

"Hi, Frank," I said cheerfully. "Where have you been keeping yourself?"

"Busy as usual," he replied flatly, and then he was on his way. Gone. It happened this way for another two weeks. How strange he behaved. He planned for us to meet, then avoided talking at any length and escaped as if in terror. It was all so strange and unhappy.

"I thought you told me you that Frank and you were over," Madeline said, "but every day he waits for you after class. It's obvious to everyone."

"I know. I don't understand him. I don't know why he's doing it."

"Well, I happen to know that he's going out with Dorothy Dickinson."

"Oh? I don't know her."

"Are you going to the Union tea this afternoon?"

"Yes, of course."

"Well, I'm sure that she will be there with Frank. I'll introduce you." There was an emptiness in my stomach. *Frank was going out with another girl?* He was so inexplicable, and my jealousy was inexplicable too. I wanted to know Dorothy Dickinson and find out why Frank suddenly left me for her.

When I arrived at the Union tea parlor, the room was full of people, and I was discomfited by not being accompanied by Frank. I maneuvered around the crowd, running into groups involved in conversation and not being able to get a word in, just standing there trying to say something, trying to fit in, feeling like a fool. Finally, I caught sight of Madeline and made a beeline over to her.

"Oh good, you're here," Madeline said. "Frank and Dorothy are over there, close to the serving table. We'll go together, fetch some tea and cake, and accidently run into them as we leave."

Madeline made a circuitous route to the serving table along the side of the room opposite from where Frank and Dorothy were standing. Armed with tea and cake, we were ready to make a surprise attack.

"Hi, Dorothy, hello, Frank," Madeline said gaily as we came from behind them.

Dorothy turned first. She was a tall, athletically built woman with an aristocratic face and intense turquoise eyes behind her pince-nez. "Oh, good to see you, Madeline," she said, hesitating as she surveyed me.

"This is Agnes Wilson," Madeline said.

Frank turned and looked at us silently, fidgeting with the handle of his cup and pretending to be watching the crowd.

"Charmed. Dorothy Dickinson," she said, her eyes never leaving mine for half a minute.

"I'm a student at Teachers' College," I interjected. "I take classes at Union with Frank."

Frank turned toward me with an angry look in his eyes. "Yes, Agnes and I know each other."

Madeline giggled, and Dorothy lowered her eyebrows.

"Dr. Ross is over there," Frank said. "I must speak to him. Come with me." Frank took Dorothy's arm and abruptly started away.

Dorothy turned her head as they left and with an enchanting smile said, "See you around, Agnes."

"What do you think of Dorothy?" Madeline asked.

"I'm no competition to her. She's enchanting, enticing. Those turquoise eyes. She is the most handsome woman I've ever met."

"You're not supposed to fall in love with her. Well, she knows you now, if she didn't already. She'll make a point of finding you at Union later. You can count on it."

The next day after Apostles class, Frank was not outside the classroom but further down the hallway, looking toward the building entrance. As I approached, Dorothy Dickinson came briskly down the hallway toward him. "I thought you were meeting me out front," she said to Frank.

"Better to be away from the door with the rain," Frank replied.

"Oh hello, Agnes. A pleasure to see you again so soon." Then turning toward Frank, "Let's be off then."

"Hi …" I mustered as they were off down the hall and out the door. Oddly, every day after Apostles class for the next month, Frank and Dorothy met in the same spot in the hallway.

In mid-October, Madeline and I sat together at a table across the room from Frank and Dorothy at a Union tea. "I think Frank wants to make sure that people see them together, and especially you," Madeline said. "People talk about it."

"What do you mean?"

"Frank and Dorothy only seem to be together at social gatherings that you are sure to also attend. What's also obvious is the way you watch them."

"I'm very confused by Frank's behavior. I believed in his friendship and now I miss his companionship. He had become part of my thinking apparatus."

"Don't feel bad about the way he treats you. Men have a hard time letting a girl know when it's over in a gentle way. They always make a mess of it."

"But it's not over. We are still good friends."

"Oh, look. It's Dorothy. Oh, my goodness, she's coming over here."

"I don't know what to say."

"Dorothy dear, hello. Please join us," Madeline said.

"Hello, Madeline, Agnes. I told Frank that I was going to powder my nose, so I must be brief. I came to ask Agnes to lunch, so we can get to know each other. Friday, perhaps?"

"Why, yes. Friday would be fine."

"You're at Whittier Hall, if I'm not mistaken?"

"Why, yes, I am staying there."

"I'll pick you up at half past twelve. I'll be waiting in the parlor." Dorothy offered a radiant smile, then turned abruptly and was gone.

"What should I do?"

"Meet her in the parlor at twelve-fifteen. She's always early."

On Friday, I was nervous all morning and tried on a few different skirts before I settled on a dark-green one. It would match the bloodstone ring, which I chose to wear "for courage." *Such an odd thought, that I needed courage to protect myself from Dorothy Dickinson.*

Dorothy was waiting for me at Whittier Hall at twelve-fifteen, just as Madeline predicted. As I approached her, I felt my throat dry up and could hardly get a word out. A smile spread across her lips as she turned and saw me. I was still apprehensive.

"I know a café on 5th Avenue. It is a bit of a walk from here, far enough that students from Union won't be there, but it's a beautiful fall day."

Why doesn't she want Union students around?

We sat down on wooden chairs at a tiny round table with a white marble top. "I come here often for a café au lait, the best coffee in town," Dorothy said. "I highly recommend their quiches or the salade niçoise."

"Quiche Lorraine sounds good."

"Monsieur," Dorothy called to a passing server.

Que'est ce que vous prenez?" he asked.

"Nous voudrions une Salade Niçoise et une Quiche Lorraine, s'il vous plait."

"Tres Bien, Mademoiselle, et quelque chose a boire?"

"Oui, deux café au lait, s'il vous plait."

After ordering, Dorothy turned her attention to me, her splendid turquoise eyes studying my face up close. "I'm glad that you could join me. Frank talks about you all the time and says such wonderful things about you. I simply had to get a chance to know you."

"He does?"

"Yes, he's so taken by you."

"What do you mean?" My ears and cheeks were burning.

"Well, even when we're together I can tell he is looking around the crowd to see if you are there. And once he finds you, he's always tracking your every move."

"That's nonsense. I think he's found all that he wants in a woman like you and has no need for me."

"Not at all. Frank and I couldn't be more incompatible. I have a very objective, analytical mind. He, well, Frank is very emotional, an Irishman after all."

I laughed. "Being of Irish descent, I never would have put it that way. But, if you're incompatible, why do you go out with him?"

"He's amusing in short bursts. We really don't see each other much outside of Union social events. And you know why that is don't you?"

"No, why?"

"Because the only point in being seen with me is to make you jealous."

"Is that why Frank acts so strangely? Is it all a game to make me jealous?"

"Yes."

"Well, I'm not jealous. As it says in James 3:16, 'where jealousy and ambition exist, there will be disorder and every vile practice.' "

"I'll bet you that the next time I see Frank he finds a way to ask me about you."

"What shall we bet?"

"What about your ring? Bloodstone, isn't it? A common gem, not too expensive."

"Oh no, I couldn't," I gasped, "It means too much to me to ever give it away."

"I only wanted to see how you'd react. I'm sure it's one-of-a-kind, irreplaceable. How about something simple like a café au lait?"

The following week, we were back at the café, and I bought Dorothy her café au lait.

Despite all the trials with my relationship with Frank, one of the most wonderful things that came of it was getting to know splendid Dorothy Dickinson. Out of our perplexities and doubts, and through all the mess-ups of our dear mutual friend Frank, we came to find each other and developed a close, understanding friendship.

During the first months back at Teachers' College I was miserable after losing Stanley and then Frank. A wild restlessness came upon me, and I couldn't sleep. And when I did sleep, I had nightmares of Howard Baskerville, gunshots at the mission, and the cannon on top of the Arg. The stress was so great that sometimes walking in the sunlight I longed to sob my heart out. Why were these thoughts of the Persia Revolution haunting me again? Why did I feel such loss, such grief?

I had thought the solace of my friend Joe would sustain me, but we hardly saw each other. Out of desperation, I began to indulge in social gaiety with any boy who asked me. I went dancing and to theater, suppers—so many things that I couldn't always remember who took me to what. A lot of the plays and musicals were silly and frivolous, and improved my mood, but only temporarily.

When I look back on those months, I remember it as a time of repeated internal struggles. I was very selfish and thoughtless. I shudder when I think of how plainly one girl at Whittier put it, "You never cared enough to give of yourself or show you really cared for us."

One weekend I visited Marcia at her parents' house in New Rochelle. We took frequent walks along Long Island Sound and gossiped about our former Vassar classmates, their beaus and fiancés.

"Who are you spending time with these days?" Marcia asked.

"I go out with Guy and several others," I replied. "And of course I see Joe from time to time."

"Goodness," Marcia exclaimed, "Several different boys at once. Aren't you worried that people will talk?"

"No, they are only companions. There is no romance between us."

"Well, my advice to you is to decide who you really want to get to know and only be seen with two at the most. Otherwise, people will think you are ... well, quite different from a missionary's daughter."

Her words stung. I knew she was trying to say, that I was damaging my reputation by running around with so many different men. She was trying to point it out kindly, as my friend, but I felt ashamed of myself. Wasn't this what Father and Mother warned me about, and I ignored them?

I spent Christmas at home with the family strangely restless and depressed. Father had regained some strength and mobility, and he could sit up for hours writing book chapters and articles. He was happy and full of wit and humor. Seeing him made me feel ashamed of my melancholy. *Why can't I have the strength to rise above my limitations and pain like Father?*

Even Christmas Day I couldn't escape my pervasive desolation. Guy gave me a small leather purse, and Joe sent me a beautiful blue woolen scarf with matching mittens. Frank sent a queer letter, and nothing, not even a word to be heard, from Stanley. I couldn't even bear to play Anton Rubinstein's *Kammenoi Ostroi.*

Rose knew something was wrong because I was quieter than usual. She asked me questions to jolt me out of my doldrums, but it only made me feel worse.

"Aren't you excited about the vote on the Nineteenth Amendment next month?" Rose asked.

"The Nineteenth Amendment?" I responded.

Mother and Grandmother looked up from their knitting with alarm and disdain. "The right for women to vote," Grandmother snapped. "You must have your head in the clouds."

"No, I've heard of the Susan B. Anthony amendment," I said. "I was confused. I don't know the amendment numbers."

"Women have been trying to get it passed since 1878 when Susan B. Anthony first introduced it," Grandmother said. "She's dead now, but I want to be alive to vote. I've supported the suffrage movement for over thirty years. I wish you girls were more politically conscious."

"I agree," Mother said. "You spend too much time thinking about boys and not enough time on social matters of importance. You might not be so melancholy if you felt the passion of commitment to a cause in your heart."

Rose tried another avenue to help me out of my despair. "Let's go to Saltsburg and visit Anna and Sarah," she suggested. "Anna is four months pregnant, and Sarah's baby Wilson is one year old. It would be fun to see their little homes on the Kiski campus."

I enjoyed playing with baby Wilson and teasing Anna about her belly, but on the train back to Indiana the melancholy returned.

"I'm not ready for babies," I muttered, "the drooling, the diapers."

"Well, I would hope not, especially if you plan to return to Persia," Rose responded.

As we sped along the snow-covered Pennsylvania countryside, I thought about Stanley. *But if Stanley married me tomorrow, I'd be happy for him to give me babies.*

Rose and I sat together quietly in the parlor writing New Year's Resolutions as Father read the newspaper.

"What are you working on, Father?" I asked.

"It likely would not interest you. I'm writing about the migration of Muslims," he said, smiling wryly. "But then this article from *The New York Times* today might. The headline is 'Foes in Trenches Swap Pies for Wine—British and Germans Exchange Gifts During Christmas Truce on Firing Line." Rose and I looked up, our eyes wide open.

"They stopped fighting?" I exclaimed.

"Yes, but it is only a truce for Christmas."

"What does it say?" Rose asked.

"The troops on the Western Front stopped fighting and sang Christmas carols to each other on a moonlit Christmas Eve. The next day they shouted Merry Christmas to each other, exchanged gifts, and played soccer."

"Thank you, Father," I said, with tears in my eyes. "I feel so much better about the world."

On New Year's Day, I packed to return to New York, and I wanted to talk to Father again before taking the train the next day. I found him in his study, lost in thought, looking out the window.

"Father, are you busy?"

He turned and smiled. "Not too busy for my daughter. What is it?"

"I have been so miserable these last three months at school, and I don't know why."

"Have you looked into your heart? Have you looked to Him?"

"I haven't had much time with all my coursework to spend time in prayer and self-reflection."

"You must find the time to seek His guidance when you are in despair. How do you think I was able to rise above my misery and pain? 'I waited patiently for the Lord. He inclined to me and heard my cry. He drew me up from the desolate pit, out of the miry bog, and set my steps secure.' "

"Psalm 40:1-2," I said. "I've only been praying to pass my courses. I was in despair and I did not ask for His help."

"Foolish missionary girl," Father retorted.

When I went to bed, there was a Bible on my nightstand. Someone had placed the ribbon page marker at Psalm 143: "My spirit is overwhelmed within me; my heart within me is desolate. I stretch forth my hands unto thee; my soul thirsts for thee like a parched land. Make haste to answer me, O Lord: my spirit fails! Hide not thy face from me, lest I be like those who go down in the Pit. Let me hear in the morning of thy steadfast love, for in thee I put my trust. Teach me the way I should go, for to thee I lift up my soul."

"I love you, Father," I whispered. "Thank you."

Chapter 17

TEACHERS' COLLEGE, SPRING 1915

GRANDMOTHER LOANED ME A LITTLE BOOK OF POETRY by Emily Dickinson to read on the train back to New York. One poem, called "Time and Eternity," seemed to speak to me. The poem was about a little boat adrift as night approached. Amidst fierce gales, the little boat was thought to be ravaged and lost to the sea, but in the light of dawn the little boat was found afloat. It had "retrimmed its masts" and "redecked its sails."

"And I too will weather what life brings me," I said. "I will retrim my masts and redeck my sails, and speed onward with my life. I shall not drown in my melancholy."

My first night back in my dormitory room in Whittier I felt serene as I looked out my window on the lights of New York below. All the restlessness and misery I'd felt a month before had dissipated. One of the girls at Teachers' College, looked at me and said, "I like to look at you now with your happy misted gray eyes. Did something happen to you over Christmas?"

"I suppose it did," I could only answer. But what, I could not claim to know.

In the weeks that followed, sometimes I feared the "charm" would break, and the wild anger and vague restlessness would return, but it didn't, not even one day when Stanley came on a visit unannounced. He simply walked into our class at Union, and I spent three quarters of an hour hot and breathless, wondering if he would leave before seeing me. But he did see me and after class walked with me to Whittier. All the while my heart sang a strange little song.

"My plans for Paris were shattered on account of the war," I told him.

"I'm so sorry for your disappointment," he said. "I'm sure you'll make the most of it; you seem very resilient." If he only knew how glad I was for the change of events and a chance to see him again.

When Stanley told me he wouldn't be back in New York again until next fall, I decided to rekindle my hopes of going to Paris in the spring. In case the war ended, I was determined to graduate with my master's degree in February. It meant keeping the heavy course load that I had registered for in the fall. Before the end of semester, after working night and day on papers, I nearly broke down.

After I turned in my last paper, I met Dorothy Dickinson for lunch. "What a relief to be finished," I exclaimed. "I'm so happy."

"You're too cheerful," Dorothy replied, to my surprise. "I suppose you haven't been following the events of the world."

"No, what happened?"

"The Nineteenth Amendment," Dorothy replied. "Women's right to vote. The House rejected it."

"When did that happen?"

"January twelfth. It was close, 204 to 174. We'll try again. Please tell me you'll find time to support the cause."

"I will. For us, our mothers, and our grandmothers."

For a graduation present, Joe took me to the opera. He hired a carriage for the night, made reservations for dinner, and bought us excellent tickets to the Metropolitan Opera at Broadway and 40th Streets. We saw a new production of Verdi's "Il Travatore," conducted by Toscanini.

"I'm glad you were finally able to get away from your medical schoolbooks," I said.

"I'm at the top of my class," Joe replied. "You must be angry with me for not taking you out more. I'll be more sociable next semester now that I've proven myself."

"I'm not angry with you," I replied. "I have the dormitory girls to entertain me." Joe never knew that during his first semester at Columbia my social life was a hectic whirlwind with boys whose names I couldn't remember.

After a wonderful evening together, I was disappointed that Joe didn't stay and talk for any length of time. The other men I went out with wouldn't leave until I yawned once or twice. What was I to him? All of Joe's energy was focused on becoming a doctor and returning to Persia to follow in his father's footsteps. Did our life together matter much to him?

Our relationship did not fit my romantic notions of love. I was comfortable with Joe, and I truly admired him, but did I love him in the way a woman should love someone she wanted to spend her life with and raise a family? Could I ever love him that way?

Once a month, Joe and I went to a Metropolitan Opera matinee, including a memorable performance of "Tosca" with Geraldine Farrar. On Saturdays after lunch, we went to the Strand Theatre at 47th and Broadway to watch motion pictures, which were becoming popular in New York. We saw "Alice in Wonderland," starring Viola Savoy, and three movies starring Charlie Chaplin and Edna Purviance—"The Champion," "In the Park," and "The Tramp." Afterward, Joe and I tried to walk down Broadway like Charlie Chaplin's tramp. I laughed so hard I almost wet my pants. How I cherished our Saturday afternoons together.

Other than Joe, Guy was my only other companion. As usual, he kept me well supplied with flowers, which I wore pinned to my dress or in my hair. Others talked but I told them, "They're so beautiful it would be a waste not to wear them."

"People think that you and Guy will be engaged any day," Madeline said. "Is there any truth in that?"

"Nothing of the kind. We're just good friends. I'm sure it means nothing to him."

Then one day in March, Guy was waiting for me after class and wanted me to go for a walk in Riverside Park. It was chilly along the Hudson River, but the sun was bright, and yellow and blue crocuses were popping up between bare spots in the melting snow.

When we reached the river, Guy abruptly turned to me and said, "The Presbyterian Mission Board has assigned me a commission in Japan. I'll be leaving this summer, and I'd like you to come with me as my wife."

"This is so sudden," I gasped.

"We've been seeing each other for over a year," Guy continued. "I thought you would jump at the opportunity to be a missionary's wife. We could fulfill our dreams together."

I swallowed hard. "I'm afraid there has been a misunderstanding."

Guy looked perplexed. "I know this is very sudden, but please think it over, Agnes."

That night I wrote to Guy and explained that I wanted to keep our friendship, but I thought it would be best if we stopped seeing each other. He wrote back, pleading for me to reconsider. Then it all came out in the open when he started asking others frantically for advice.

"Everyone knows what is going on," Madeline said.

"He's been such a dear and unselfish friend," I responded. "I never understood what he felt for me. I never thought much of it."

The memories and guilt I had felt about Howard Baskerville came back to haunt me that evening. I found the bloodstone signet ring wrapped in a piece of Persian cloth in my jewelry box and slipped it on my ring finger. "Mrs. Jackson said that martyr's stone helps one face difficult choices. Six years ago, Howard proposed. I was only sixteen and didn't understand the potential danger of my flirtations. Now I have hurt Guy in much the same way. I vow that from now on I will be frank and honest with men."

Dorothy Dickinson invited me to spend Easter at their wonderful summer house, Kakro, in West Hampton Beach. I found her absolutely fascinating, marveling at her turquoise eyes glinting through her pince-nez glasses, her well-shaped eyebrows, and her full lips that seemed to kiss each word that came from her mouth. She was so much more sophisticated than I and had exquisite taste in clothes. At their home at 168 Clinton Street in Brooklyn Heights, she had a collection of over sixty stylish hats.

"My grandfather owns a hat company," she explained. "He wants me to wear them around town. He gets free advertising and I get free hats."

Dorothy's father, Dr. Robert Latou Dickinson, was a renowned gynecologist and a remarkable genre of a man. He was also multitalented: a doctor, an artist, and an outdoorsman. He illustrated the stages of gestation with life-size sculptures and wrote hiking guides.

Dorothy told me proudly, "Father is why I have such a scientific view of men and sex. He's provided me with the most thorough sex education a girl could have. To Father, sex is even appropriate dinner conversation." Seeing that my cheeks were scarlet, she added, "Of course, with you as a guest at the table, he will refrain."

"Thank goodness," I said with a sigh of relief.

"It's not romance, you know; sex, that is. It's nature, science from conception to the tying of the umbilical cord, which that too, the practice of tying it off, my dear father was the first to institute as practice."

"Did he?"

"And he supports 'family limitation,' or 'birth control,' as Margaret Sanger calls it."

"Margaret Sanger?"

"You haven't heard of her? Why she's the woman who tried mailing 'The Woman Rebel,' a newsletter promoting contraception. The obscenity laws prohibit it, and she's now in exile in England. Daddy visited her before she left and collected all seven newsletters. He supports her cause."

"The newsletters are on pregnancy termination?"

"No, she opposes pregnancy termination. She promotes methods for preventing pregnancy all together. Her motto is that a woman should be 'the absolute mistress of her own body.' "

"That's quite radical, isn't it?"

Dorothy shared with me Margaret Sanger's articles on birth control called "What Every Girl Should Know."

"You must be exposed to this," she said.

"But we can't buy contraception."

"Father believes that will change. He says it will be the most important step for women of this century."

"I marvel at all you know from your father. So much I have never been exposed to."

"We were brought up in different environments. You're a minister's daughter, and I'm a doctor's daughter."

One evening she said to me, "Frank told me that what upset him most about you is that you go out with practically anyone who asks you. I told him, that wasn't what bothered me; it was all the older men. Did you know that Frank is three years older than you?"

"Yes, you see we share the same birthday, September tenth. But you're right, I do have a tendency to be attracted to older men."

"I don't understand why. Do you want to marry your father?"

"No, I have always considered men my age to be 'boys' and older men to be 'real men.' "

"That's nonsense. Father says older men are desperate to find a wife and push younger women into family life before they've started a career."

"Perhaps he's right. Frank seems rather desperate."

"What about the fellow from Persia, the medical school student I met when I ran into the two of you in Central Park?"

"Joe? He has been a friend since childhood. I've known him for over fifteen years."

"I thought he was quite handsome on my first encounter; eyes that pull you into his mind. Why bother to look elsewhere? He's perfect for you."

I laughed. "I suddenly realized that you are so much like him. He's very serious and factual. He keeps his emotions inside. I'm so different, sentimental and romantic. Sometimes I think it will never work between us."

"Are you talking about Joe or me?" Dorothy said, teasing me.

"You see I've always wanted a man who knocked me off my feet, sending me head-over-heels in love. A fiery romance like in the romance novels."

"Agnes, my dear, I fear life is more practical than romance novels."

"I believe in passion, in romance. I fear that Joe will never have the passion I crave."

Dorothy laughed and shook her head. "Maybe that's why you like men who give you flowers. Well, don't wait your whole life for your prince on his white steed."

"Seriously, it concerns me that I won't find the right man."

"And I hope, my dear friend, that your heart does not let the right man walk away, when your brain knows he's the one."

All spring I worried about what I would do next year. With the war continuing and women banned from foreign travel, there was no possibility of going to Paris or returning to Persia. I considered looking for a teacher's position or trying to find work at Columbia University. I wanted to stay in New York since Joe would be there three more years at medical school, and if I moved somewhere else, I might never see Stanley Hunter again.

I'd be willing to scrub floors to be able to see you, glorious Stanley Hunter.

To my surprise after I returned from Easter vacation, Teachers' College offered me a position. It was not a job scrubbing floors, but a position running the Young Woman's Christian Association and various religious organizations in the Religious Education Department. When they offered me $1000 a year, I gladly accepted the job.

At first, my new position was not openly announced since there were complications with its final approval, but I told everyone that I was returning next year. It was a rather embarrassing mistake, as people gossiped that my return meant I was getting engaged. Finally, the last week of April, my new title was announced, "General Secretary of Religious Work," a position without a predecessor and without fully defined functions. With all the difficulties getting the various religious organizations to work peacefully together, I would have my hands full.

In the background the war continued. Italy had declared war on Austria-Hungary in April, and the scope of the war was expanding. Armies of the Allied and Central Powers were killing hundreds of thousands in the trenches. The British navy, led by Winston Churchill, tried to attack the Ottoman Empire at Gallipoli and lost half the British ships to Turkish mines.

In April, Germany violated the Hague Convention and started using chlorine gas. Then on May 7th a German U-boat sank a British ship, the RMS Lusitania, with 123 Americans on board.

"The paper says Alfred Vanderbilt was among those who perished," I said. "He gallantly gave his life vest to a female passenger even though he couldn't swim."

"Some are saying we should declare war on Germany because American lives were lost," Dorothy said. "But I don't agree. The RMS Lusitania was a British ship."

To our relief, and that of our other pacifist friends, President Wilson chose to remain neutral saying, "America is too proud to fight." On the other hand, former President Teddy Roosevelt thought it was an act of piracy that should be punished. His sentiment was shared by other Americans, who started vocalizing anti-German sentiments.

The last week of May, a strange thing happened; Frank suddenly lost his terror of me and called many times, wanting to come over.

"I have something I must say before you leave for the summer," he said on each occasion, but never came to the point of what he wanted to say. The last time Frank called to see me again, I responded, "But I'm going to a Decoration Day party at Marcia's in New Rochelle. It's a reunion of my Vassar dormitory friends."

Could he come out to see me? No.

Could he see me at Buzz's afterward? No, we could say goodbye at that moment.

He left for West Orange, New Jersey, and wrote a strange letter saying, "It would be best for me not to see you, as I cannot trust myself. It is not because of anyone else. I have gone through as hard an experience as any man could."

I really did not understand what he was trying to say, but I felt uneasy and annoyed. From Marcia's I sent him one of the frankest letters I had ever written, telling him all about my struggle to believe in his friendship after he stopped coming over without explanation. I told him how I had rejoiced over his friendship with Dorothy Dickinson, since it seemed that mine could not reach him.

When he received my letter, he called me at once and was quite broken up over it.

"I had thought that you did not care at all," he sobbed. "Please forgive me."

"I do forgive you, Frank," I replied, "but our relationship cannot go on this way."

In June, as soon as classes finished, I hurried to Vassar to attend Rose's graduation before going to the Silver Bay Conference. Rose looked lovely on Class Day, as I imagined she would. Father was there with Mother, and I watched his radiant face as Rose ascended the steps to take her diploma. Rose had never failed him or argued with him as I had. She always said and did what was "right."

If only I could do something to make Father proud of me too.

Mrs. Vanneman was at the commencement and sat with her youngest daughter, Irene, a freshman at Vassar. "Aimie and Dorothy graduated last year," Mrs. Vanneman said. "Aimie moved to Colorado and Dorothy to Detroit. Irene is the only one living with me now."

"Do you hear from Dr. Vanneman in Tabriz?" I asked.

"I haven't heard from him for a year," Mrs. Vanneman replied. "The mail does not go out and the telegraph is down. He's still in Tabriz as far as I know. We are all afraid that the Turkish army will invade, kill them, and destroy the mission."

"When I graduate from Vassar, I'm going to go back to Persia to find Father," Irene said.

"But Persia is neutral," I exclaimed. "They aren't at war. I'm shocked to hear that Tabriz is in danger of being invaded by the Turkish army."

The night boat from Poughkeepsie to Albany was a nostalgic voyage. Sitting on the bow I remembered how I met Joe five years ago at the train station after his brother's graduation from Williams. I looked forward to being at Silver Bay and listening to the speakers of the Presbyterian conference, but my mind was preoccupied. All I could think about was what might happen to the mission and our house in Tabriz if the Turkish army invaded. *What would happen to Dr. Vanneman, the Pittmans, and Elizabeth Coan?*

One night I dreamt I was back in Tabriz and the cannon on top of the Arg was firing continuously. There was thunderous pounding on the house door, but Mousa was not answering. Suddenly, soldiers burst in and came charging up the stairs toward my room. When I woke in a panic, I was drenched in sweat. Nightmares of our house in Tabriz being ransacked and destroyed disturbed my sleep for weeks afterward.

After Silver Bay, I stopped in Burlington, Vermont, to visit Margaret Darling, a friend from Teachers' College. Margaret warned me to keep my pacifist views to myself during our visit as her father, Judge Charles Darling, had been the Assistant Secretary of the Navy under Theodore Roosevelt.

"Above all, don't mention the Lusitania," she said.

Unfortunately, the first night at dinner Mr. Darling brought up the subject himself as we ate pecan pie. "If Lincoln had responded to the firing on Fort Sumter the way Wilson did to the Lusitania, we wouldn't have pecans today. What would you say to that, Miss Wilson?"

"I could go without pecans forever if they would stop this war," I responded. "It's a bloody and pointless stalemate."

Judge Darling's chin became firm as he clenched his jaw; his eyes narrowed as he stared at me. "You shall not express your opinions on the war again in this house, Miss Wilson. Is that clear?"

"Yes, sir," I responded and held back my overwhelming urge to stand up and salute him.

Margaret sighed and said, "Let's go outside and look at the stars. We'll sleep outdoors tonight."

The following days, Margaret and I fished and swam in Lake Champlain, and tramped in the Green Mountains in order to avoid any other political conversations with Judge Darling.

Next, I stopped in Proctor, Vermont, for a little glimpse of Kitten and her baby, Sinclair Jr. After Vassar, Kitten had married Sinclair Allen, and they lived in a white wood-clad house with dark-green shutters at 44 Oak Street. We sat on the sun porch with little Sinclair Jr. and watched the darling drool while we partook in tea and gingerbread. She seemed so happy with her cozy country home and little family. Her life was so different from mine, and so much easier.

On the train back to New York, I contemplated Kitten's existence and if I could be a housewife in a small town. *I think not.*

Staying briefly in New York before taking the train to Pennsylvania, I accepted an invitation to dinner with Frank. After ordering, he looked directly at me for a few minutes, then said, "I wrote to you every other day, and your letters to me were too few and far between. I didn't expect you to ignore me. How can you treat someone this way?"

"I was at a conference and visiting friends. What time did I have for correspondence?"

"Can I visit you in Indiana?"

"No," I said. "We can see each other in New York when I return." I was proud of myself for holding my ground.

"Let me at least take you to the train station this evening. I'll be in Orange, New Jersey next year when you return to New York. We'll only see each other now and then."

I accepted his offer for a ride to the station, but it was a relief to say, "Goodbye, Frank."

After a rough year at Columbia, it was comforting to be back with the family for the summer at 36 South 6th Street. Bobby was twelve and a handsome young man, with his charming smile and big blue eyes. His antics were a source of constant amusement, and Father thoroughly enjoyed his silliness. Bobby had a gang of four boys, and they set up a street stand on the corner of 6th and Gompers to make money for entertainment at the County Fair. They convinced a seven-year-old boy named Jimmy Stewart to play accordion while they sang, "A loaf of bread, a hunk of meat, and all the mustard you can eat."

Annie, at fifteen, had also blossomed into a pretty, curly, blond-haired girl and insisted on going to all the dances. Rose and I were busy serving as her chaperones throughout the summer.

"Any special man?" I asked her once.

"Goodness, no. If I get tired of one boy, I move on to another. A smile and a twinkle in my eye are all it takes to get the next one."

I decided to warn Annie about the dangers of flirtation since she was the same age as I was when Howard arrived at the mission. "You should be careful not to flirt with your male teachers," I said. "You might get yourself in trouble, like I did with Mr. Baskerville."

Annie looked at me with wide eyes. "Goodness sakes. I wouldn't think of flirting with old men."

In July, the family took a weekend trip to Northpoint for swimming, picnicking, and camping on Mahoning Creek. Mother cooked over a fire, and we gathered in a circle afterward to sing songs and tell stories. We stretched out on blankets on the ground and fell asleep under the stars just as we had when we went camping as a family on Mount Sahand outside of Tabriz fifteen years earlier.

Rose and I, lying next to each other, took turns pointing out constellations.

"I find myself wonderfully happy and serene here," I said. "I'm so thankful that I'm happy again."

Rose laughed. "Yes, we should be thankful for simple things."

Rose did not realize that for me, finding happiness again was not a simple thing. Just nine months before I was in a wretched mental state. I prayed that the downward mental spiral would never return.

Chapter 18

TEACHERS' COLLEGE, FALL 1915

ON SEPTEMBER 14ᵀᴴ, HELEN DULLES TELEPHONED THE house. Mother turned pale and put her hand to her heart as she listened. "I'm so sorry, Helen. Let us know when arrangements are made. Our love is with you." After she hung up the receiver, Mother started to sob.

"What happened?" I asked.

"Uncle Will collapsed during a walk along the shore on Fisher's Island," Mother said. "He died from heart failure, apparently he had a heart defect."

"He was only fifty-seven," Grandmother said.

"He took his last breaths with his head cradled in her lap," Mother added.

"I could return to New York a week early to attend the funeral service for the family," I offered.

On the train, I recollected my first months in America. Uncle Will met me on the dock when I first stepped ashore in New York. He bought me dresses for dances, gave me water-wings when he discovered I couldn't swim, and how patient he was teaching me to dance. Such a generous man he was. *My cousins Dorothy, Edith, Rhea, and Winslow will surely miss their father, as I will.*

I arrived at Columbia a week before fall semester, and they let me stay at Whitter Hall, even though it wasn't officially open. During summer vacation I had avoided thinking about the job I had accepted at Teachers' College, but now I was alone with my thoughts in an empty dormitory. I suddenly had pangs of panic. This was my very first job, and I had no idea what I was supposed to do. In addition, since the position was new, there was no one to teach me.

When I arrived at the office the first day, I was relieved to find two of my close friends, Margaret Darling and Dorothy Dickinson, working in the same office. The next day, my dormitory roommate arrived, Margaret Merriam from Newburyport, Massachusetts. "But I already have a close friend named Margaret," I exclaimed.

"Well, now you have two Margarets," she replied.

"Yes, I'll refer to you as 'my two Margarets,' " I said. "That will simplify things."

She insisted on helping me unpack my trunk before she attended to her own. Something about her put me at ease immediately.

"What's this?" she asked as she held up a silk-covered box. "It's stunning."

"It's a jewelry box from Persia," I responded. "I thought I'd misplaced it." She handed it to me, and I eagerly opened it. There it was, the bloodstone ring. "I thought I had lost this old ring."

"How precious," Margaret Merriam murmured. "Bloodstone is said to help balance the mind and body, to help overcome stress and anxiety."

"Is that so. Then I surely could have used its power to help balance my mind last year."

Margaret Merriam turned out to be a caring and level-headed girl, and, I dare say, one with a more mature attitude toward men than I. "I simply have no time for hurt relationships, love affairs, and crushes," she said.

"Goodness, I wish I had your solid foundation to deal with men," I replied.

With the demands of my new position, my social life was sparse, and I only saw Joe on the weekends. We went to numerous Charlie Chaplin movies, which Joe was so fond of, and once a month to a Sunday symphony or opera matinee. It was enough companionship to sustain me, but my heart felt empty.

On November 3rd, a letter from Father arrived: "The Presbyterian Mission Board was awarded over ten thousand dollars for Near East Relief and beseeched me to lead the Relief Effort, saying, 'You can make a dollar go farther than any other man.' Hundreds of thousands of Armenians have fled Turkey to the Caucasus to avoid massacre. Having recovered to some degree from my accident, my conscience could not let me say 'no' in the face of such great need. I'll be sailing in two weeks from the time you receive this letter."

After the news from Father came, Joe came to console me.

"The trip to the Caucasus will be physically demanding," I said, "let alone the relief work once he gets there. Father is no longer as strong as he was before the accident. I don't think he's up to it."

"What does your mother say?" Joe asked.

"Her letters are cheerful, with no hint of doubt about Father's decision to go. She wanted to go with him, but women and children are excluded from foreign travel due to the war."

"Will life be difficult for her without your father?"

"I don't know how she could live without Father after thirty-five years of marriage. She'll be left to care for my eighty-year-old grandmother, Bobby, and Annie alone."

Father's steamer for Bergen, Norway, left New York on November 18th. I took leave for the day from Teachers' College, and Rose came down from Watertown, New York, where she was teaching high school. We had many happy hours together walking in Central Park and at dinner with Aunt Annie, who came up from Baltimore. Rose and I watched Father board the steamer and waited until it disappeared on the vast ocean. We fell into each other's arms and sobbed. We were likely a pitiful sight for the other farewell bidders on the dock.

"I remember that when I left for America, Father recited Deuteronomy 31:6," I said. " 'Be strong and courageous; do not fear or be in dread, for it is the Lord your God who goes with you. He will not fail you or forsake you.' "

My heart was aching badly, thinking of the possibility of Father's ship being torpedoed by German U-boats and the hardships he would face during his long trek to the Armenian refugee camps in the Caucasus. Friends took me to entertainment in an outpouring of kindness, and I wore the bloodstone ring as Margaret Merriam suggested to overcome my anxiety. Of all of my friends, however, Joe understood me best. His father, Dr. Joseph Cochran, Sr., had died of typhoid ten years earlier while serving the people of Persia. He knew the dangers Father would face and my unspoken fears.

Each evening, Joe came to Whittier Hall to comfort me. We sat in the parlor for hours, reminiscing about our childhood until late in the evening. When he prepared to leave, he looked at me with weary eyes, and I suspected that he would likely be up for many hours afterward studying. At those moments, I had the urge to take his hand and pull him close to me, but I didn't. I wished I had. My dear Joe, so unselfish and so deserving of my love.

In my room at Whittier Hall, I was pulling the laces of my corset to dress for a dinner party at the Humes when I heard a knock on the door. "Mr. Fitt in the parlor to see you," said the voice of the dormitory receptionist.

"Yes, I'll come shortly." *Another surprise visit from Frank.*

Frank was sitting in the parlor reading *The Atlantic Monthly,* and his eyes met mine. He rose and gave me a delicate hug. "It has taken me so long to find a way to express myself," he said. "I've been thinking hard these past months since I moved to West Orange and I want to see you again." Frank looked deep into my eyes and grasped my wrists. I felt like an animal about to become prey.

"No, Frank. I can't go through that again," I responded.

"Please, Agnes. Hear what I have to say. I came all the way from West Orange to talk to you."

"This is not the time to talk. Mrs. Hume expects me at her house at five o'clock sharp and the car arrives in ten minutes. You should have told me you were coming." I stood up abruptly.

"Very well." Frank sighed and released my wrists. "I'll write to you and tell you what I intended to say to you in person."

I hurried up the stairs to get my coat. "Frank, Frank, Frank. Always impulsive. And later another of your confessional letters. Will this never end?"

Dr. Hume, a Professor of Religious History at Union Seminary, was known for translating the Upanishads from Sanskrit to English. He and his wife's home was decorated with intricate Indian tapestries in a rainbow of colors, brass bowls, and bronze statues of Hanuman, Ganesh, and Shiva that they had collected during their seven years as missionaries in India.

The Humes' home was the social center for missionaries on furlough and students of the religious organizations in New York. Laura Hume, in her mid-thirties, took a particular interest in the social life of the "reverends-to-be" from Union Seminary. She deftly maneuvered around her guests with a knowing smile on her lips, asking direct and embarrassing questions, and noting potential romantic interests with a calculating eye. I supposed she presumed it was her right as the hostess to do so.

When at dinner, Mrs. Hume asked me to sit next to her. I was delighted to find her little baby Jane in the bassinette beside me. When the baby started to babble, I touched her palm with my little finger, and she curled her tiny fingers around it.

"I've been meaning to ask you," Mrs. Hume said. "Do you know if Stanley Hunter is engaged?"

I swallowed hard and focused my attention on baby Jane as I answered, not wanting my gaze to meet Mrs. Hume's piercing eyes.

"I hear he is moving back to New York this fall to look for a position."

"Yes, I know that, but the girl he met at Bryn Mawr, are they engaged?"

Playing with baby Jane's hand helped me to keep my emotions under control. "Why, he hasn't mentioned an engagement to me, and I've seen him on several occasions this fall."

I was amused at myself, sitting calmly and talking quietly and off-handedly, while caressing a baby's hand and burning up inside.

After returning to Whittier Hall that night, I had a letter waiting from Frank that he had sent by courier. I opened it with trepidation, but there was only one page.

"Dear Agnes,

I will be brief in explanation of my behavior last year. You see, I never felt in a position to tell you how much I cared for you. I feel like a fool now, not being able to communicate my feelings and instead coming off as a cad. Not to be a burden on you in any way, but I want to continue to be close friends and to see each other when I'm in New York.

Most Sincerely,

Frank Fitt."

Even though there had been so much turmoil in our relationship, I finally realized that Frank would always have a place in my heart. He really had been a dear friend. As a reconciliation, I accepted his invitation to accompany him to a Union tea on his next visit.

"Dr. Ross is holding the tea in my honor," Frank said. "It's to congratulate me for being ordained and appointed as pastor in West Orange."

"Frank," a voice said directly behind me that made my heart stand still. I turned to come face-to face with Stanley Hunter.

"Well, what a surprise," Frank said. "Wonderful that you could come."

"I'm not far away," Stanley replied. "I accepted a position in Brooklyn as temporary pastor at the Church of Pilgrims."

"In Brooklyn?" I gasped, trying to conceal my elation. "You're back in New York City?"

Stanley laughed. "Back for six months, then to Pittsburgh. You'll see me at Union now and again."

Stanley spoke to me briefly and smiled his knee-numbing smile; he asked kindly about things, and then he was gone in his calm, great-purposed way.

After returning to my room, I sat on my bed thinking about Stanley. Did I ever enter his thoughts? Could he ever have feelings for me?

My roommate, Margaret Merriam, came in. "You look a bit dreamy," she said.

"Oh, Margaret, I've been keeping this in me so long and never told a soul before. There's a man that I've loved desperately for the past year and a half and he barely notices me."

"Do I know him?"

"No. His name is Stanley Hunter. He took me to a tea once, about a year ago."

"It sounds like an infatuation."

"Yes, a wonderful infatuation. I enjoy being in love, even if it is unrequited. It gives me a deep joy, pure affection, just thinking of him. Sometimes I wonder if he doesn't belong to me more than I could ever have him in reality."

"Agnes, dreaming of a man like this isn't healthy."

"Perhaps I shouldn't love him so if he belongs to someone else, but I know I never show my feelings for him overtly, of that I am sure."

Margaret was right. Thinking about Stanley for any length of time plagued me with perplexities, and I feared that the vague restlessness associated with my previous downward mental spiral would return. I couldn't allow myself to lapse into another state of depression.

I was surprised at myself for telling Margaret about my feelings for Stanley. The question was, would Margaret tell anyone else? Would Stanley somehow find out about my obsession with him?

Proverbs 16:28: a whisperer separates close friends.

I became worried to distraction that Margaret might tell someone, and I finally decided to confront her. When she came into the room, I took a deep breath and said, "Margaret, you are a dear friend, but I want you to know that I've never told anyone before about my feelings for Stanley, and I don't want anyone else to know."

She looked at me blankly. "Stanley?"

"Yes, I talked about him earlier this week."

She continued to look at me blankly, then shook her head. "I'm afraid girl talk goes in one ear and out the other, never residing very long in between."

I laughed. "Then I guess I shouldn't worry about you telling anyone."

"Your secret is safe with me, as long as you don't want me to remember it for you."

Quite a good, trustworthy sounding board, my dear Margaret Merriam, not a "whisperer."

December 18th was International Night at the Cosmopolitan Club at Lexington Avenue and 40th Street. Stanley helped organize the event, and from across the room I admired him as he walked around ensuring everything ran smoothly. A short man with straight, sandy-brown hair and large blue eyes approached and engaged me in conversation. When he first introduced himself, I didn't catch his name and was barely listening to him, but I found it convenient to have him there. He was short enough that I could watch Stanley over his shoulder. As he went on at length about a trip he had taken to New Hampshire, I nodded politely and smiled from time to time. He kept talking and talking.

Finally, Stanley came over, said hello to me, and introduced himself to my good conversationalist, whose name I caught the second time. It was Harold Osborne.

After a few minutes of polite conversation, Harold said, "I'll take my leave so the two of you can talk, but first I'd like to exchange calling cards."

After a quick exchange, Harold looked at me with his big boyish blue eyes and asked, "Could I call on you in a week or so?"

When I nodded "yes," his eyes lit up and his mouth broke into a smile that stretched the width of his face. Harold turned and vanished into the crowd.

I'm sure he'll call. What have I gotten myself into with Harold? Things are already so complicated.

"Impressive fellow," Stanley remarked.

"What do you mean?" I replied.

"He's one of Alexander Graham Bell's engineers. See, his card says 'Engineer, American Telephone & Telegraph Company.'"

Stanley and I had a chance to talk for some time. "People tell me that you are doing a fine job getting the leaders of the various religious organizations to work together. That's quite an accomplishment," he said.

I smiled coyly and looked up at him, making as much eye contact as I dared. "It has taken an extraordinary effort. I've been working like a Turk."

"A Turk?" Stanley laughed and smiled his radiant, knee-numbing smile.

"Yes, 'working like a Turk.' Haven't you ever heard the expression?"

"I can't say that I have. Is it Persian?"

"Why, no. It's an Irish expression my family and relatives use to describe hard work."

"Hmm, very well. I guess you have been 'working like a Turk,' and doing a good job of it. Now, I should make the rounds and say hello to everyone. Good to see you, Agnes."

And with that Stanley left me standing in the middle of the room, where I stood, not moving for a few minutes, trying to recover, my heart racing.

As usual, I ruined my chance to impress him.

Finally, I caught sight of Dorothy Dickinson, with a crowd around her as usual, and managed to slip in and stand there, half-listening to the conversation, as I watched Stanley again move his way around the room.

How foolish I am trying to persuade myself that I don't care about Stanley. I care about him more than anything.

At Christmas, Mother gave us little packages Father had wrapped before leaving for the Relief Effort. "He knew he would not be home for Christmas, so he bought each of you a gift before he left," Mother said. Rose, Annie, and I received gold necklaces, and Bobby a leather wallet. There were tears in our eyes.

"Now don't be sad. Father would not want you to be sad on Christmas day," Mother said.

With Father gone, the house was quiet and had an empty feeling. Occasionally, as I passed the door of Father's study, I thought I saw him in my peripheral vision, but when I turned to look, the "ghost" was gone.

At Christmas dinner, Bobby tried to take Father's place at the table, but Mother would not let anyone sit in Father's chair, and it remained empty and foreboding.

"I miss Father's affectionate humoring," Rose said.

"I'm sure Father needs his humor, camping out in the Caucasus in the snow with hundreds of thousands of Armenian refugees," I said.

Mother said a prayer for Father before we ate. "Dear Lord, strengthen and protect dear Samuel, your faithful servant."

"I hope Father is comfortable and safe," Annie said.

"Father's risking his life to bring relief to the fleeing Armenians," I said. "He's neither comfortable nor safe."

"He's so courageous in spite of his physical weakness," Rose added. "I worry about Father."

"I hope he does not suffer," Bobby said.

"Your father has always said: 'We rejoice in our suffering, knowing the suffering produces endurance, and endurance produces character, and character produces hope,'" Mother said.

"Romans 5:3-4," I said. "We should always keep hope in our hearts for Father's safe return."

Chapter 19

TEACHERS' COLLEGE, SPRING 1916

PREPARATIONS WERE IN FULL SWING FOR THE YWCA 15th Anniversary Jubilee when I returned to Teachers' College. Robert Speer's wife, Emma, was the president of the Y.W.C.A and gave the address at the banquet, along with New York Mayor Mitchell and former President Teddy Roosevelt. Afterward, I accepted the Speers' invitation to spend the weekend at their home in Englewood.

I arrived Saturday evening in the midst of a large dinner party for missionaries on furlough, and Dr. Speer met me at the door. "These are a few of the hundreds of Presbyterian missionaries I oversee in addition to your father. I've visited their missions in Persia, Japan, China, Korea, and South America. Let me introduce you."

"Agnes Wilson is an aspiring missionary," Dr. Speer bellowed. "Inspire her to join you in the field." They all crowded around me to tell missionary stories, which continued throughout the meal, each missionary trying to one-up the others by embellishing their stories.

At the end of the party, Mrs. Speer put her arm around my shoulder. "You were quite over-whelmed, weren't you? Someday you'll come back with your own stories to tell, I'm sure."

Over Sunday dinner, Dr. Speer talked to me about the different positions that would open up in the missions after the war was over.

"I know your heart is set on Tabriz, but the missions in northwestern Persia are simply out of the question. The fear is that the Turkish army will invade and ransack Urmia and Tabriz, as they are closest to the border. The mission in Tehran will be better protected with the Shah's army there."

"I don't trust the Shah's army," I said. "They murdered people in Tabriz during the Revolution."

"If you are in a rush to be in the field, then I would suggest China, Japan, or India. They are far from the fighting and easier to reach by the Pacific. I can look into it for you."

I looked down and replied, "Thank you for trying to help me, Dr. Speer, but I'll wait until there is a position in Persia. I couldn't imagine going anywhere else."

On Saturday, March 4, Dorothy Dickinson met me for lunch at the Oyster Bar in Grand Central Station, both of us craving their oyster stew.

"I joined the Women's Peace Party, the WPP," Dorothy said. "You should join as well. Jane Addams was elected chairwoman."

"Jane Addams?"

"She represented us at the Hague for the International Congress of Women for Permanent Peace. She thinks women should be involved in government, a real progressive."

"Oh, yes. I remember her name from a newspaper story on the Women's Suffrage Movement."

"Roosevelt calls her 'silly and base,' and the male reporters pick her speeches apart like straws of the haystack. It's not just her political leanings men oppose, she's quite open about her romantic relationships with other women."

"What?" I stopped with my spoon in mid-air, full to the brim with oysters.

"She has romantic relationships with women." Dorothy looked at me with her eyes squinting through her pince-nez. "Women do make that choice these days, as do men. Is this something new to you?"

"Yes, Dorothy. I'm so old-fashioned. It's my missionary upbringing."

"This has been going on since civilization began, and maybe before. But, to continue ..." Dorothy was looking down at the table. "I must have startled you. It looks like you lost one to the revolution." She pointed to the table next to me, where a large oyster had fallen off my spoon.

"The Bolsheviks got to it," I said, and we both laughed.

"In January, I heard Helen Keller speak at Carnegie Hall. She believes that Congress's War Preparedness Act is only meant to benefit manufacturers of munitions and war machines. I tend to agree with her."

"I would have liked to have seen Helen Keller."

"She was truly marvelous."

"With Father going through all the hardship of the Armenian Relief effort in the Caucasus, I'd like to work for one of the peace organizations, but I don't know which one to choose."

"Since you have a religious bent, F.O.R. might interest you. I joined with my parents' approval."

"You'll think this a foolish question," I said with embarrassment. "But what does F.O.R. stand for again?"

"It's the Federation of Reconciliation. The name is hard for people to remember; its name is from Corinthians, I believe."

"2 Corinthians 5:8," I said. "'All this is from God, who reconciled us to himself through Christ and gave us the ministry of reconciliation.'"

"You always amaze me, my dear Agnes, with your ability to recite the scriptures. It is quite a precious gift, but do try to use it with discretion." Dorothy smiled sweetly. "Now, back to F.O.R. When it started in New York last year, they named Norman Thomas as secretary, a Presbyterian minister and socialist at heart. They go farther than pacifists. They believe that to remove the 'seeds of war' from society and prevent it from happening again, social reform is necessary."

"How do I join?"

"They have an office on Lexington Avenue. I can take you there after lunch if you'd like."

"Yes, that would be a great help. I'm so lazy about doing these things on my own."

"Any contribution to the peace cause could help. The War Preparedness propaganda has become rather fierce. They work off public paranoia over rumors that German U-boats are venturing into our harbors."

"I've seen advertisements everywhere for the May 13th Preparedness Parade."

"Yes, the Parade will go from Bowling Green to Central Park. Father thinks it is a scam organized by politicians to demonstrate American support for the military buildup."

"We're sending munitions to the Allies, but Wilson keeps saying we're neutral. At least he has kept us out of the war. Roosevelt would have already had us fighting if he was still in office."

"Quite true, but I suppose you only like Wilson because you're related?" Dorothy couldn't hide that she was teasing me. Her raised eyebrows and smug smile gave her away.

"There's no record of any relationship. Possibly several hundred years ago in Ireland we had a common ancestor," I responded. "My Uncle Rob is quite convinced that no one in our family would have 'such naïve idealism,' but my Uncle Andy is convinced that Woodrow is his cousin. He even wrote to the White House and requested a special visit based on a supposed relationship. It makes for quite interesting arguments at family gatherings."

"Then I won't offend you if I tell you that Father calls Wilson a 'sham reformer' and Mother detests him because he opposes child labor laws."

"I see."

"Now that we've finished lunch, let's go down to 108 Lexington Avenue and visit nice Norman Thomas to sign you up with F.O.R., but I'll call first. I have a card." Dorothy opened her purse, an exquisite brown leather handbag with a floral design carved on both sides, with an intricate silver clasp. The contents were amazingly organized, and she quickly produced the card. "Madison Square 1240-5378," Dorothy told the operator.

After she hung up, Dorothy said, "Yes, the office is open, and Norman Thomas expects us."

We took the cable car to Lexington Avenue, then changed to the Lexington Avenue car and got off at 28th Street. On the way down Dorothy assured me, "There is no real commitment; it is only so they can contact you for events. Once you go to one, I think you will want to go to the others. You're a natural fit for the Fellowship cause."

When we got to the office, Norman Thomas greeted us. His face was stern, and a large forehead from premature balding emphasized the intenseness of his face. He shook my hand and held onto it for a full minute, looking at me with his ardent and piercing green eyes. "Thank you for joining. Here's our meeting schedule," he said as he handed me a pamphlet. "There's an F.O.R. conference in April that you might be interested in attending."

As Dorothy and I rode back, we talked excitedly about going to the conference together. When we hugged each other at the trolley station before going our separate ways, tears came to my eyes. "What is it?" Dorothy asked.

"A year ago, I was preoccupied with completing my master's degree and didn't have time to be involved with the peace movement. Now, with Father risking his life to save the Armenian refugees, I feel guilty not doing my part. You've helped me find a way to commit to the cause for world peace. It's what I've been looking for. I already feel closer to Father."

After the F.O.R. conference, I spent Easter vacation in Westhampton Beach with Dorothy Dickinson, staying at Kakro, the Dickinson's summer home. It was a lovely warm mid-April weekend, and perfect for long walks along the beach and talking together.

"You haven't spoken about any boys you've been seeing lately," I said.

"You are a dear friend and I suppose that I can confide in you," Dorothy said. "Five years ago, I met a young Scotsman visiting New York and we've been writing ever since. He graduated from Cambridge and, once the war is over, he plans to come to Columbia for graduate school."

"What's his name?"

"George Barbour. He's in the British military. I'm scared to death when I don't hear from him for three weeks at a time."

"It's rather romantic that you're waiting for him."

"With George in a bunker risking his life, going out for merriment with some care-free fellow doesn't appeal to me. I'd rather concentrate my energies on the peace effort and F.O.R."

"My social life has calmed down too, with Frank and Guy gone. Joe is my primary companion. Only there is someone else I dream about."

"Who might that be?" Dorothy raised her eyebrows in anticipation.

"Stanley Hunter."

"Frank's friend? I thought he moved to Pennsylvania."

"Yes. Two years ago, he went to Bryn Mawr, but in September he came back. He's a temporary pastor at a church in Brooklyn. I see him at Union functions."

"He didn't seem like the missionary type to me somehow; more like a very social preacher, attending teas and spreading warm feelings with that winning smile."

"So you noticed him too. I think he is so handsome. I can't take my eyes off him."

"But, I thought I heard that he was engaged. Has that changed?"

"I heard the rumor, but then there was no announcement."

"You don't seem to know him very well. Is it simply an infatuation?"

"I'm afraid so. I try to get his attention whenever I have the opportunity, but I don't think I cross his mind. The problem is that I can't get him out of my head."

"Agnes, take my advice. Forget him. You have plans to go abroad for missionary work. He doesn't fit that plan. What would you do if he did become interested in you, or even proposed?"

"I'd marry him." I surprised myself at how the words simply came out of my mouth.

Dorothy stopped abruptly and looked at me, her eyes wide and her mouth agape. "And give up your plans to return to Persia?"

I hesitated and sighed. "You're right. I'd have to make a choice then, and it would be hard to make. I'm so confused these days about what the future will bring. Sometimes I just long for a man to hold my hand and protect me from all the horror around us, and other times I hold resolutely to my plans for missionary work with no thought of marriage. This war has ruined everything—my chance to study in Paris, to return to Persia, everything." Tears welled in my eyes.

Dorothy stood in front of me and put her hands on my shoulders, caressing them slowly. "I worry about my George every day. There is always the chance he'll be killed in the midst of the fighting. Our relationship is long-distance, but it's not an infatuation. It is quite real."

My cousin Edith Dulles's wedding was Decoration Day. Aunt Helen held the ceremony and reception in the Ballroom at the Hotel Gotham, and Reverend Allen Dulles performed the service. I was thrilled when Allen Dulles, Jr. appeared and sat at my table.

"It's been two years since I've seen you," I said.

"I'm in Washington working for the State Department," Allen said. "I'll soon be sent to Vienna for diplomatic service."

"Isn't it dangerous with the war?"

"We've been warned that hostilities may force us to relocate to Switzerland."

"I'd like to be on my way back to Persia soon. Would you write me and let me know your recommendations for safe travel?"

"Of course. I'd blame myself for the rest of my life if something happened to you."

"You once protected me from gypsies in Paris, and now the war in Europe."

At the end of May, I received a letter from Father: "I had planned to go to eastern Turkey to secure an encampment for the Armenians, but I found that the Allies and Central Power armies were still fighting there. I've decided instead to go to Tabriz to obtain wheat seed. The Armenians will need it when it is safe for them to return and sow their fields."

The next letter I received from Father came in early June: "The new train from Julfa to Tabriz took only three hours. Three years ago, on our trip to America, the eighty-mile trip took us three days by horseback. Throngs of friends met me at the train station in Tabriz—Muslims, Europeans, and Armenians. This week I was invited to a banquet at the Armenian Club to talk about my Relief work. I was honored as a 'savior of their people.' It's hard to believe, after years of hard work in the face of prejudice and opposition by the Armenians, I'm now a bit of a hero."

I felt such pride and happiness, picturing Father back at the mission in Tabriz where he'd spent thirty-six years of his life. He was with Dr. Vanneman, the Pittmans, and all of his old friends.

On June 21st, I left for the Silver Bay Conference with the atrocities of the world, the war, and the massacre of Armenians weighing on my heart with unusual intensity. The conference organizers gave no opportunity for discussing the war, even though people expressed interest. I tried to induce one of the organizers, Miss Burner, to give time for a discussion hour on peace issues, but she simply responded, "Politics are outside the scope of our discussions. It is not on the agenda, and I will not introduce it."

"It's hypocrisy not to find it relevant to a religious conference," I responded, to her surprise. "Just like the rest of America, you choose to ignore the war and its atrocities."

"The church has retracted its open opposition to the war to avoid retaliation from the government," she retorted. "It's dangerous to profess pacifist views."

Those ten days at Silver Bay it panged my conscience that I had been ineffectual in galvanizing the crowd to address the war, the killing, and suffering. "Have I done enough?" I asked myself over and over. A deep sorrow filled on my heart, an unbearable weight of despair.

The climax of the conference was Saturday, July 1st, and the joy and gaiety of the final dinner reception seemed too inappropriate to attend. Instead I skipped supper and fled into the woods.

Oh, those wonderful woods, how I clung to the tall white birches and wept and prayed as one can only do in such heart-searching moments. It seemed as if the trees cared, and the red lilies that grew underneath them cared. I found myself picking a glorious bunch of red lilies, and it comforted me to remember how I picked flowers as a young child in Tabriz with Father by my side. "The flowers are beautiful, but don't pick them all," he'd say. "Leave some for the angels."

In the gathering darkness, out in the stillness with the trees, peace slowly came to me. It was the most spiritual night I had at Silver Bay.

Returning to the conference hall, I gave the red lilies to Miss Burner.

After Silver Bay, I returned to New York, planning to spend a week helping with summer school registration. First thing Monday morning, when I ran into the office, I found a telegram from Mother: "A cable came from Tabriz saying: 'Dr. Wilson in hospital—Typhoid.'"

My heart just sank. *How could it be?* Before leaving America, Father had been inoculated against typhoid fever. In spite of his precaution, he'd contracted the disease.

It wasn't an hour before the second telegram from Mother came.

As I pieced together the events of the past week, I realized that while I cried in the forest at Silver Bay, out in Persia the great bright morning was dawning on the last day of Father's life. It all seemed so strange, so inexplicable, that I knew nothing of it at all. Father had been called from his earthly mission in Persia to some other higher service.

I stood holding the telegram like a statue of ice, feeling as though I could crack apart at any instance. "Oh, Lord, it cannot be."

I left the office and walked to the river where I could sit on a bench and be alone. Shaking my head, I kicked the dirt with the toe of my shoe. "And dust returns to earth as it was, and the spirit returns to God who gave it," I whispered. "Ecclesiastes 12:7."

Father, how could you leave me without another word? I need you more than anything now, even more so than when I was a child.

Tears streamed down my face. I sobbed uncontrollably and gasped for breath. I don't know how long I sat there. I knew I was missed in the office, but I couldn't make myself return. Suddenly, I felt two hands gently touch my shoulders and turned to find Joe standing behind me.

"Dorothy found the telegram on your desk and phoned me," he said. "I knew where to find you, on your favorite bench by the river." He sat down and held me and stroked my hair. I tried to speak but I only choked on my tears. "Don't try to talk," he said.

Finally, I took a deep breath in and exhaled. "He never forgave me," I whispered.

"Agnes, whatever it was I'm quite sure your father forgave you in his heart, if he did not find the words. Even I know that the Bible preaches forgiveness. 'Forgive as the Lord forgave you.' "

"Colossians 3:13. But I'll never know for sure."

Joe put his hand under my chin and lifted my face. He pressed his lips against my forehead. Through my tears I could see his gentle concerned eyes. "Agnes, dear, your mother needs you by her side. I'll help you back to Whittier to pack and then take you to the station."

The evening train was the first I could take to Philadelphia. The next morning, when I arrived at the Indiana station, Uncle Harry was there to meet me and held me in his arms. "At such times, how wonderfully sustaining is the love of family and relatives," he said.

Rose and Aunt Jennie were already with Mother, who looked as if she hadn't slept for days.

"He spent those last months of heroic service at the front, bringing relief and hope to thousands of homeless ones," I said. "I'm glad it could have been there among the people for whom he had given so much of his life."

"He did not count the cost as God's soldier and we must not," Mother replied.

"Dear Mother," Rose said, "how you must have longed to be near him, the dear tender husband and father to whom his family meant so much."

"Distance never separated us," Mother replied.

The sweet sympathy letters from friends were an inexplicable comfort. Even Frank wrote a beautiful letter saying, "the vision of his task did not shut out this vision of his loved ones in those last days, of that we may be sure."

Two weeks later, we received a letter from Dr. Vanneman at the mission in Tabriz. He wrote: "The funeral was held in the mission church where he had preached, and in the three languages he had used there, Azeri, Armenian, and English. Addresses were made at the cemetery by his associates, former pupils, and representative Armenians. The Armenian church held a special ceremony for him, and a number of the Armenian newspapers devoted the entire edition to his memory.

"He was laid to rest at sunset of a cloudless summer day. His grave was heaped high with Persian flowers, and a stone was placed at his head with the inscription from Matthew 10:39: 'He that loseth his life for thy sake shall find it.' "

On August 24th, we celebrated Mother's 55th birthday together with Robert and Mary Labaree, her friends from the mission in Urmia. Aunt Jennie asked Jimmy Stewart to bring his accordion and when she brought in the cake, we all sang "Happy Birthday" to Mother.

"Robert, tell us the news from Persia," Mother requested.

"I have sad stories and happy ones. Which would you like to hear first?"

"The sad ones, ending with a happy note."

"On March 24th, the Russian soldiers left, and the Turkish troops attacked and occupied Tabriz. Most of them stayed on, hoping the American flag above the mission would protect them, but eventually evacuated. Will Vanneman and Fred Jessup decided to remain. They, of course, were the last ones to see Sam alive in the hospital."

"Now the good news," Mother said.

"The good news is gossip about a new missionary couple."

"Who?" Mother asked. "Tell us."

"Elizabeth Coan and Howard Richards, a social worker in Tabriz."

"Elizabeth Coan is engaged?" I exclaimed.

"Yes, and we know all about you and Joe Cochran, Jr.," Mrs. Labaree said. She paused when I appeared startled. "We're so happy that you continue to be close friends."

I was relieved. I thought she was going to say, "that you and Joe are a couple too."

Mother remained in mourning the rest of the summer. The letters from Persia kept coming in a ceaseless tribute of deep devotion and gratitude to Father. Even the old Armenian priests and the others who worked against him so long wrote in appreciation, saying, "He was one whom truly gave his life to our people."

Mother spent much of her time reading and responding to the mounds of sympathy letters that came from around the world. She also kept another stack of letters on a table next to her parlor chair, the letters that Father had written to her while in the Caucasus and Tabriz. She often read these in the evenings, tears coming to her eyes, and muttering "Oh, Sam," under her breath. When it was late, either Rose or I would pat her hand and say, "Mother, you should go to bed. You're tired."

On August 26th, all the Wilson relatives congregated for Father's memorial service in Indiana. Robert Labaree gave an address, and Uncle Rob read an excerpt from a letter he had received from the Tabriz Mission: "It is difficult to express our appreciation of Dr. Wilson as a Christian scholar, educator, financier and planner of mission work. If one thing more than another stands as his monument it is his life work in the Tabriz Boys' Memorial School. Receiving it in the spring of

1884, a tiny seedling from the hands of the original founder, under his care and devoted supervision it expanded to a great tree, an institution from which have gone forth many pupils who were there brought into contact with the Word of God and its ideals, which they could have never obtained elsewhere."

"It will always be hard to live up to Father's example of perseverance and righteousness," Rose said. "We can only try."

"I sought most of all to return to Persia with Father," I said. "Now I can only return with his spirit in my heart."

After the service, Uncle Rob pulled me aside, saying, "The letter from the Tabriz Mission I received is long and has much more information. Some of it took me very much by surprise. I don't have it with me, only that excerpt I copied to read. The next time you visit us in Princeton, I'd like you to read it yourself. Your Father would want you to know."

As he finished those last words, Uncle Dick came up and grabbed his arm, saying, "Rob we need to go, or you'll miss your train."

The rest of summer went by quickly in the delirium of grief. It was almost gone before I realized that this might be the last summer together with my family. The following summer I hoped to be on my way to Persia.

Chapter 20

TEACHERS' COLLEGE, FALL & WINTER 1916

BUZZ MET ME ON THE TRAIN PLATFORM IN NEW YORK, and Mr. and Mrs. Howson were waiting in their car. "I'm excited to have you staying with us until you find your own apartment," Buzz said. "It will be like old times, when you first came to New York."

"As a staff member, I decided that it was no longer appropriate for me to be living in the dormitory with the students," I said, "but I'm apprehensive about living alone for the first time."

After looking around for several days, I found an apartment at 37 Madison Avenue, with a front room facing Madison Square Park. The location was an easy commute to Teachers' College: a brief walk to the Broadway Station on 28th Street, a car change at west 42nd Street, then directly to Columbia University.

The apartment was clean and full of light. Although sparse, it was homey and a welcome retreat at the end of the day. It surprised me that I wasn't lonely in the evenings without the dormitory girls around to gossip. Instead, I looked forward to my quiet apartment, a place for my mind to rest. *I must be getting old.*

Joe was busy with his medical studies, and I was occupied with my obligations as Secretary of the Religious Organizations, but we saw each other on weekends. Our first weekend together, we went to two Charlie Chaplin movies that were released that summer: "The Vagabond," about a left-handed violinist who saves a girl from gypsies, and "One A.M.," a solo performance by Charlie, a drunk who tips over about every thirty seconds. We saw four other Chaplin films that fall, including "The Rink," where Charlie is a waiter on roller skates. It was our favorite and we had to go back and see it three times. Joe also bought Sunday matinee tickets to the New York Philharmonic, including an all-Beethoven program with the "Erocia" Symphony, the "Leonore" Overture, and the "Emperor" Concerto, with Josef Hoffman on piano.

At the end of some entertaining afternoon or evening, Joe would hug me and sometimes gently kiss my forehead or my cheek, but always with an emotional aloofness, like embracing a sister. I desperately wanted to have those dreamy romantic yearnings for Joe that I had for Stanley, but I couldn't conjure up the same feelings. Was it because I'd known Joe since I was a child and felt maybe too comfortable with him? I decided that it was more like the love for a brother that I felt for Joe.

On weeknights, Joe worked in the hospital, and I occasionally accepted Harold Osborne's invitation to take me to a Broadway show. We went to musicals mostly: "The Girl from Brazil," "Betty," and "The Century Girl." Harold was five years older than I and an electrical engineer at the A.T. &T. Although he had a serious scientific bent, he was silly at the same time. He loved to tell jokes and laughed heartily at his own, even if they were not very funny.

Harold was quite a pleasant companion, but persistent. If he had tickets on a night that I said, "I am engaged," he'd change the tickets rather than ask someone else. "I bought the tickets thinking that you would especially like to go," he said.

The other source of entertainment in the fall of 1916 was the presidential election. President Wilson, with the motto "He kept us out of the war," ran against Justice Hughes.

"I hope Wilson is re-elected," I told Dorothy. "He now supports women's suffrage."

Most of New England and the Midwest voted for Hughes, and early election results favored him to win, but when the final votes came in from the West, it was a cliffhanger. Finally, California, a state expected to go to Hughes, went to Wilson instead.

Dorothy Dickinson and I celebrated. "We'll finally be able to vote," I said. "It's a victory for women as well."

"It's a good start," Dorothy said. "But we still have battles to fight. Margaret Sanger opened the first birth-control clinic in America in Brooklyn. Then a week later, she was arrested for breaking the state law prohibiting distribution of contraceptives."

I shook my head in disgust. You'd think with the threat of war hanging over us that they wouldn't bother policing such things as contraceptives. We can't vote to choose a president, and we can't choose whether we want children and when. Will change for us women ever come?"

In December, the newspapers reported that the battles of Verdun and Somme on the Western Front had finally come to an end, with over 500,000 dead on each side. The British had employed tanks, a new war technology consisting of big metal beasts that rolled on metal tape. Half of them had mechanical problems and never made it to the front, but they won anyway. In the aftermath, newspaper stories told of attacks with arsenic, chlorine and phosgene gas, villages blasted into oblivion, millions of unexploded shells and casualties littering fields, and trenches submerged in blood and crammed with dead bodies gnawed by rats.

"What happened to the vision of God in Isaiah 2:4?" I asked. "'They shall beat their swords into plowshares and their spears into pruning hooks; nations shall not lift up sword against nations, neither shall they learn war anymore.' Why can't people live in peace?"

Before Christmas, I made plans to visit Uncle Rob and his family in Princeton. The letter from the mission in Tabriz piqued my curiosity as did Uncle's last words at Father's service: "Your father would want you to know." *Know what? What did it say?*

Then I received a letter from Mother saying she was anxious for Rose and me to come home: "I need to tell you something urgently."

"What did Mother need to tell us that couldn't wait?" I said.

Reluctantly, I took the first train to Indiana instead. When I arrived, the house was cheery with the smell of fresh pine needles, cinnamon sticks, and apple pie. Bobby had selected the tree and Annie had decorated it before Rose and I arrived. Mother and Grandmother seemed in good health and greeted us affectionately as usual, but Uncle Foster was sick and stayed in his room.

The surprise announcement came our first night at dinner.

"Uncle Foster is going to a sanitarium in California in the spring," Grandmother said. "His consumption has become worse."

"So far away?" Rose said.

"He'll be going to Las Encinas Sanitarium in Pasadena," Mother said. "They say that the air in Southern California can cure tuberculosis."

Rose and I nodded that we understood. *And?*

"I want to be close to Foster rather than stay in Indiana," Grandmother said.

"And the lease will be up on this house then," Mother added.

"Where will you live then?" Rose asked.

"I thought it best if the rest of the family moved to California as well."

Rose and I looked at each other anxiously.

"How will you move everything?" Rose asked.

"We'll manage somehow," Mother responded. "Where there is a will, there is a way."

"I'll resign from my teaching job in New York and help you move out to California," Rose said. "I'm sure I can find another job there."

Mother looked at me and smiled. "I don't expect you to come as well, Agnes. But with you in New York, I'm afraid it means we won't see you very often."

"Only on my summer vacation," I said. "I'm sure it takes at least a week to get to California by train." I felt as though my family was abandoning me and held each moment for the rest of Christmas vacation precious.

Otherwise Christmas was full of the usual cheer. Aunt Agnes invited the local relatives over for a thirty-pound turkey with all the fixings, and the presents were many. I received a fine leather shoulder bag from Joe, the kind the Suffragettes wear, and a dark-brown fur muff from Harold.

"What kind of fur do you think it is, Mother?" I asked.

"It looks like mink. Very elegant, and definitely expensive."

"I think it's squirrel," Bobby said.

"Who's Harold?" Annie asked.

"Yes, I'd like to know too," Grandmother remarked.

"Why, he is an electrical engineer, a friend who works at American Telephone and Telegraph," I said shyly, realizing that I had never mentioned him to the family.

"How did you meet someone from the telephone company?" Mother asked.

"At International Night at the Cosmopolitan Club."

"Joe will be finished with medical school in a year and a half," Grandmother added. "I'm hoping that the two of you tie the knot and keep the missionary blood in the family."

"Poor Agnes has always had trouble brushing men aside that don't really interest her," Mother interjected. "We will talk about it later. Rose and Agnes, come and help me with the pies for Christmas dinner."

"Why does Grandmother keep after me about Joe?" I asked Mother when we were safely in the kitchen.

"She would like nothing better than to see you marry Joe, and I happen to agree with her. But if you are truly in love with someone else, then it's your happiness that most concerns me."

I breathed a sigh of relief. At least Mother understood that I could have a choice in the matter.

A few days passed. Then one afternoon, Rose took the children ice skating and Grandmother was napping. I sat alone in the parlor reading when Mother came in and stood in front of me with the dreaded "I want to talk to you" stare.

"I want to talk to you about the Christmas present from Harold."

"Yes?"

"That's quite an expensive muff that he gave you."

"Harold earns a good salary at A.T.&T."

"Are you accepting presents from him because you intend to marry him?"

"Why, no."

"Then why did he give you such an expensive present? He must think you are inclined to accept a proposal."

"We're only good friends."

"Only good friends? You continue to encourage men without sincere intentions. It's selfish and cruel what you are doing. It's exactly what you did to Howard Baskerville."

I looked at Mother in horror as she continued her tirade. "I've never told you this before, but you're old enough now. After you left Persia, the other missionaries and Howard's students talked about you. They said Howard was in a mad rage after his proposal was rejected and that you were to blame for his decision to join the Nationalist army."

"Me? It was Father who denied him."

"Nonsense. If Father gave Howard his permission, you would have turned him down yourself. Isn't it true?"

"Yes, I would have said 'no.' I didn't want to marry Howard."

"I think Harold is another Howard Baskerville. You are leading him on, and it's selfish and cruel."

"I didn't think ..."

"Well, think. Think like an adult, not like a sixteen-year-old. And what have you told Joe about Harold?"

"Joe doesn't pay attention to who I see. He's busy with medical school."

"Joe doesn't know, does he?"

"No, why should I ..."

"You're not honest in your relationships. It's not right or becoming of a Christian woman."

Just then, Grandmother came in carrying her knitting basket. "What's not becoming?"

"Oh ... a dress I was considering. Mother thinks it's too short; it shows the calves."

Mother was glaring at me.

"Never knew my Annie to be conservative about dress before," Grandmother said, smiling slyly.

"I'll fetch tea since you are up," Mother said and abruptly left the parlor, leaving me alone with Grandmother.

"You've become very argumentative, Agnes. That's what is unbecoming."

"Young women express their opinions these days."

"But you shouldn't argue with your Mother. She only wants the best for you. Surely you must know that."

"I do."

"She's concerned because you seem to make questionable choices, whether it be dresses, or men." Grandmother looked down at her knitting and started humming to herself until tea arrived.

How do I feel about Harold anyway?

Shortly after Christmas I received a note from Dr. Speer asking me to meet him at his office in the Presbyterian Building at 156 Fifth Avenue. I shivered as I walked to the cable car station on Broadway, partly from nervous anticipation. When I arrived shortly after one o'clock, I could see there was another man in his office, so I politely stood outside the door to wait.

"Agnes, come in, come in," Dr. Speer erupted enthusiastically when he noticed me. "I want you to meet my friend, Reverend Samuel Jordon from the mission in Tehran."

"Of course, you don't remember me," Reverend Jordan said, "but I stayed at your home in Tabriz in 1898. My wife, Mary, and I were on our way to Tehran to teach at the Boys' School."

"No, I'm afraid I don't remember. I was only six then."

"Come sit down, Agnes," Dr. Speer said. "We have a proposal for you. Why don't you go first, Sam?"

"We're looking for someone to head our new Girls' School at the mission in Tehran. Robert compiled a list of candidates for me, and we've started our interview process. You are our first candidate for the principal of the school."

I was overcome with surprise and couldn't get a single word out. How strange it was to walk right into an interview.

Dr. Speer laughed. "She's in shock, Sam. It's a unique thing in mission history to send a woman to Persia as the principal of a school. I told him you were the best candidate for the position."

"And it's yours if you want it," Reverend Jordan said.

"Want it? It has been my dream to go back to Persia," I exclaimed.

"Then it's settled?"

"Let me write Mother first."

"I called her this morning," Dr. Speer said. "She told me that she wouldn't want anything better for you. It was quite a task to get her to promise me not to tell you first."

"Then there is nothing to stand in my way. I accept wholeheartedly."

"We will arrange a meeting in the next week or so with the others that we select as teachers," Rev. Jordan said. "We will be speaking again soon. Congratulations."

My cheeks were burning with surprise and excitement, and I couldn't feel the cold as I stumbled back to the cable car. Suddenly I had an entirely different path to follow, and I could not instantly comprehend the ramifications.

The Presbyterian Board held a meeting two weeks later and decided that Laura Lynch and Rachel Schwab would go with me to Tehran. They moved us into the same office so we could plan for the trip together, and in a short time we became close friends.

"I vow that none of us will ever be separated by marriage," I said. "Marriage is an unimportant part of our lives."

"That should be easy for me," Laura said. "After my broken engagement I'm completely disillusioned with men."

"And I'm not at all attracted to men," Rachel added.

"The three of us will embrace our mission to educate the women of Persia," I said. "I've known these women since I was a child in Tabriz and have witnessed their plight. It's been my dream to return someday and help them."

In February, Stanley came to visit the Theological Seminary, and I saw him at the Union tea. We had a chance to talk for some time, and I told him all about my plans to go back to Persia and become a principal of the Girls' School in Tehran. "This may be our last chance to see each other," I said.

"Let me walk you to the cable car station," Stanley offered, "so we can say goodbye."

"This February is bitter cold," I said as we walked.

"Not as bitter cold as my heart feels right now," Stanley said.

Is he referring to the sadness he feels in his heart because I'm leaving?

"I had a great embittering disappointment come into my life over Christmas," he continued. "I asked a girl in Philadelphia to marry me, and she rejected my proposal."

Who was she that could not love Stanley? "Perhaps it was a blessing in disguise," I said. "Surely someone more deserving will come along."

"Somehow I cannot feel happy or thoughtful over it."

He was so open and sincere that I suddenly found myself telling him everything he meant to me. Well, a modest version at least.

"I have all my trust and hope in you," I said. "I have put some of the deepest energy of my soul into prayer for all the joy and inspiring companionship someone could make to your life, someone who would make your life still fuller."

Am I really saying this? Who would ever have thought of such a thing?

"You have?" Stanley looked at me with eager wonder. "It surprises me is that you feel this way. We never saw much of each other."

"I know. I always wished that we'd had more time together."

"All of this time at the Seminary, I thought of you as a shining distant mountain peak with a life pressed so full of friends and plans that it needed nothing more."

"I do care for you," I said, looking deep into his blue eyes. "I hope you understand that."

Stanley's eyes became wide. He didn't say anything at first and then swallowed hard. "But we can be real friends, can't we?"

"I could certainly be nothing less, Stanley," I responded. And those were my last words before he said goodbye and hurried off.

When I got to my apartment and shut the door behind me, tears started rolling down my cheeks. The bouts of crying continued all evening until I was exhausted and went to bed. *Those were our last words?* I supposed that most people thought of me as Stanley did, full of plans and friends, and not as lonely and longing as I truly was. Our judgement of people is usually about as accurate.

I flipped through my photograph album. There it was, a photograph taken of me at Christmas while thinking of Stanley. I looked purposely and gladly into the future, one that could not include Stanley, but would never be wholly without him. It showed on my face so completely how much Stanley had brought into my life without knowing it. If only I could always look and be like that person in that picture.

Chapter 21

Teachers' College, Spring 1917

On Monday, January 22ND, President Wilson spoke to a joint session of Congress. The newspaper called it the "Peace Without Victory" speech. I read the article aloud to Dorothy Dickinson during our tea break.

"Wilson said, 'Victory would mean peace forced upon a loser, a victor's terms imposed upon the vanquished. It would be accepted in humiliation, under duress, at an intolerable sacrifice, and would leave a sting, a resentment, a bitter memory upon which terms of peace would rest, not permanently, but only as upon quicksand.'"

"I can understand why Wilson thinks peace would be fragile if the terms of peace cause resentment," Dorothy said, "but I simply can't imagine another war like this in our lifetime."

"But how can Wilson call for the terms of peace when we aren't actively engaged in the war?"

"Wilson does have a voice after all. Two years ago, he convinced Germany to discontinue torpedoing merchant vessels after the sinking of the Lusitania."

On February 1st, Germany again resumed unrestricted submarine warfare. After an emergency session in Congress, Wilson announced that diplomatic relations with Germany were severed. The break with

Germany cast a shadow across America and involvement in the war appeared imminent.

The second week of February, I took the train to Vermont to visit my former Vassar classmate Kitten. It promised to be a restful weekend in the quaint town of Proctor, away from the news in Washington. To my dismay, Kitten's husband, Sinclair, practiced at the rifle range every evening. "I'm preparing in case I need to protect my family," he said.

"He's afraid that the Germans will invade America," Kitten explained. "With our lovely babies, the war means something very real to him."

A few days after I returned to New York, the newly organized Emergency Peace Federation suddenly announced that Washington's birthday would be "University Day" in Congress. College students and faculty were invited to attend the hearings before the Committees of House and Senate on American involvement in the Great War. With two hours' notice, twelve of us from Columbia assembled at the midnight train for Washington, D.C., and the next morning we were lobbying our senators. Joe called on Senators Clapp and Nelson from Minnesota to urge for noninvolvement in the war, and Dorothy challenged New York Senators O'Gorman and Wadsworth on their positions and worked on them in her persuasive way. I went hand-in-hand with my coworker from Pennsylvania, Ted Martin, to confront Boies Penrose to vote for peace.

On my return from Washington, Harold met me at the train station and took me to lunch at the Hotel Nassau in Long Beach. By coincidence the hotel was next door to Castles by the Sea, a dance hall where Irene and Vernon Castle performed.

"How I'd love to see the Castles dance," I said. "Let's stop by the ticket office after lunch and ask if they are performing today."

Harold was reluctant but consented to oblige me and bought tickets for the matinee. "Let's take a walk down the boardwalk while we wait for the doors to open," he said. "It's a bit brisk but a walk will do us good."

The wind was bitter cold, and I was glad that I remembered to bring the mink muff that Harold had given to me. Harold was about to reach for my hand when he saw my hands in the muff. "Well, that gift was a mistake," he said. "Now I can't hold your hand as I wanted to." I laughed and extended a warm hand.

"I've wanted to tell you something for several weeks and thought this would be the right occasion," he said. "You see, your friendship has come to mean a lot to me. I know that I am not the only man you see, but my feelings for you are serious. I want you to think about us and consider whether you could feel the same way about me some day." Harold's cheeks had turned quite pink, and his big blue eyes were soft like a small child begging for ice cream.

"Harold, I do enjoy your company and good humor, but we can only be good friends. It can't be otherwise with my plans for Persia. Certainly, you must understand that would be a serious complication for our relationship."

"We will talk about it again after you have had more time to think about it."

I didn't think he heard me so I said firmly, "I will be returning to Persia."

We paced along the boardwalk above the white, wind-swept sands until the doors to Castles by the Sea opened. I was certainly happy to get out of the cold wind and avoid any further opportunity for Harold to continue the conversation about our relationship. Irene and Vernon Castle danced the one-step and foxtrot splendidly, and the maxixe was exquisite. I talked about nothing else all the way back to the city.

A few months would pass, but the subject of our relationship would come up again and again. Harold was careful not to press me too much, and really was quite patient and sweet—not at all like Guy or Frank had been. I had no desire to push him away. In fact, I was strangely attached to him.

"Have you thought more about our relationship?" Harold asked as we walked home from a show one night.

Finally, after a long pause, I said, "Eight years ago, a young man named Howard Baskerville and I were to be married in Tabriz. He was shot in the back by a sniper, and I have not been able to open my heart to another man since."

"Oh, Agnes, I had no idea. You must have been in shock."

"Well, now you know."

I smiled to myself. Harold fell for it so completely. Although I felt disgusted with myself for making up such an excuse, my little lie stopped the uncomfortable questions about my feelings, at least for a while. Soon it became apparent that he felt there was some hope, despite my plans to go to Persia. Why didn't I simply tell him that we could only be friends?

On March 1st, a telegram was intercepted from the German foreign secretary, Arthur Zimmerman, inviting Mexico to join the war as its ally against the United States. In return, Germany promised to help Mexico recover its "lost territories": New Mexico, Arizona, and Texas. Then, on April 1st, Germans torpedoed the U.S. steamer Aztec and 28 crew members drowned. President Wilson saw no other choice and on April 2nd asked Congress for a declaration of war on Germany.

Our F.O.R group sent letters and telegraphs to representatives of the House and Senate, but our efforts were in vain. On Friday, at twelve minutes after three in the morning, the tally was reported: the House of Representatives voted 373 to 50 to declare war on Germany, and the Senate passed the declaration 82 to 6.

Despondent, I asked to leave the office early and Dorothy joined me for a walk in Central Park. It was a beautiful spring day, with crocuses and daffodils blooming, which seemed so strange in the midst of this horrible war we were now a part of. After a long silence, Dorothy said, "We couldn't fight it anymore. After Germany sent that invitation to Mexico, and then torpedoed the Aztec, you couldn't hand out pacifist literature on the streets. The pro-war fanatics were out in full force."

"Our representatives in Congress did not listen to us. And why should they listen to women when we can't vote?" I replied.

"Father knew I'd be a bit down, so he called this morning to tell me that our first woman in Congress, Jeanette Rankin, voted 'no' on the declaration. She heard us."

We turned to each other and hugged, and just let the tears pour down our cheeks.

Laura, Rachel, and I were perplexed. "What will the war mean for our plans to go to Persia?" Laura asked.

"Allen Dulles sent a cablegram from Switzerland saying travel through Europe and Russia is impossible," I said. "He advises that we go via the Pacific."

"Let's push forward and leave before something else gets in our way," Rachel urged.

We clung to our plans in spite of all odds and continued to make purchases for the trip to Persia, ignoring all of the warnings.

As America prepared to join the war, Teachers' College grew insistent on my staying another year and withdrew the posting for my successor. "It's too dangerous for you to go until the war is over," Dean Russell said.

Our families and friends also pleaded for us to wait.

"Surely you could not go to Persia now," Mother pleaded. "I'd be worried sick about you."

Then, all in one week, a miracle happened. Love came into Laura's life and claimed her wholly. The quiet hours working together with

Roger Albright had brought them into a relationship. Roger's devotion and tenderness filled Laura's adoring heart, and her unsought love just blossomed into a rare and precious flower. She shared her joy with wistful yearnings for me, urging Harold, Joe, or some other.

Rachel took it hard and just gave in as though it was the ultimate defeat of our plans. "This is it; we'll never go now," she moaned.

I tried to console her. "Putting off our trip to Persia is difficult, but worse is the thought of giving it up completely. I won't give up my hopes of going."

I feared all our rainbow-colored dreams of service in Persia would be broken forever, but I remained committed to going forward, if not with Rachel and Laura, then alone.

By April, Uncle Foster, Grandmother, and my family had moved to Pasadena. For Easter break, the Labarees invited Joe and me to Doylestown, Pennsylvania, where they had rented a large house while on furlough. As a guest pastor at the local church, Reverend Labaree led the Easter service, which he infused with missionary wisdom and humor. After Easter dinner, we sat together in the Labaree's parlor.

"I read your account of the Christian massacre in Salmas, Persia, in *The New York Times*. It was horrifying," Joe said.

"When the Czar was dethroned, the Russian soldiers withdrew, and the Turks and Kurds rushed in. A great number of Christians fled. Those that remained were protected by Muslim friends, but the Turkish soldiers sought them out. They were captured and bound together, eyes were torn out, limbs severed, parts of bodies flayed."

"How horrible," I exclaimed.

"There is worse to tell. After the men of the village were killed, the women were given over to their captors. None were spared."

Joe and I looked at each other in astonishment. I felt a sinking feeling in the pit of my stomach.

On the train back to New York, I said, "I don't know what to do. I've been preparing to return to Persia for the past six months."

"Wait and return with me," Joe said.

"But that's three years away. I can't wait that long."

"You heard what Dr. Labaree said. It's not safe to go now."

"But Elizabeth Coan is there. So are the Pittmans, Dr. Jessup and Dr. Vanneman."

"Elizabeth wrote that all but Dr. Vanneman and Dr. Jessup have fled three hundred miles south to Hamadan."

"With August approaching, I'll need to decide if I will make the trip to Persia," I said.

The decision weighed heavy on my heart for days, and finally I called on Dr. Speer. As I rode the cable car to his office at Fifth Avenue and 20th Street, my head was busy with internal conversations. *What would I say to him?*

Dr. Speer greeted me from his desk and studied my face. "I'm sure you've been thinking very hard about your proposed trip to Persia given the current situation," he said. "Let's go over the pros and cons together." He cleared his throat and continued. "Persia is neutral in this war, but the Russians and Turkish forces cross the northwest borders as they find it convenient. In their wake, marauding cavalcades of Kurds descend on the Persians. The missionaries have had to intercede to prevent entire villages from being massacred by Kurdish raiders."

"What about Tehran?" I asked.

"At present, Tehran is far enough south to avoid the conflict," Dr. Speer continued. "The problem is that you would have to go by way of the Pacific. Once you reach the Persian Gulf, the nearest port is six hundred miles from Tehran. It would be too dangerous for a woman to travel through Persia alone. You would need to wait until a caravan of Americans or Europeans has room for you. It could be a six-month journey. On the other hand, if you wait until the war is over, your journey by way of the Atlantic would only take six weeks."

"What about the position at the Girls' School?" I asked.

"The position in Tehran will be on hold indefinitely until you arrive. There is no hurry on the part of the Mission Board."

"Thank you, Dr. Speer."

"Let God's wisdom guide you in your decision."

After hearing what Dr. Speer had to say, I faired it alone at the Cathedral of St. John the Divine where I was met by Dean Robbins.

"I need somewhere to be alone with my thoughts," I said.

"What's your name, Miss?" Dean Robbins asked.

"Agnes Wilson."

"An Irish name. St. Columba is the patron of Ireland. I'll show you to his chapel."

The chapel was brilliantly bright with light even on that cloudy day and empty except for a tiny wooden bench. Three large stained-glass windows commanded the space, one behind the altar and two on either side. The glass panel design was delicately intricate and compact, full of knots and links. My eyes were drawn to the carefully placed colors, the blue, red, and gold flowers and braids. It was a maze of tiny pieces of glass, like my own thoughts, a maze of logic and emotions.

I focused my eyes on one of the panels containing five circles, each connected by flower-embedded braids. I assigned each circle a choice. "The top circle represents sailing, to go to Persia alone in August. The second circle stands for waiting, to stay in New York for three years and go to Persia with Joe when he finishes his medical studies. The third circle stands for postponing, to reevaluate my choices and make a decision when the Great War ends. The fourth circle represents abandoning, giving up my missionary position in Tehran and continuing indefinitely in my position at Columbia. And the fifth circle represents moving, leaving New York and moving to Pasadena with Mother and my dear family."

My eyes became moist with tears. *If I go to Persia, then who knows when I'll see my family again? Oh, how I wish Father was here to advise me; he would know what the real danger is.*

Sitting alone on the little wooden bench, I focused on each circle, following the links and braids from top to bottom, weighing the pros and cons of each choice. Finally, my eyes rested on the top circle of the stained-glass panel, sailing to Persia alone in August.

This would be my fastest way to return to Persia. But what would my life be like without Father? My long-held dream was to be in Persia again with him. What would it mean to me with him not there, but in a grave?

I imagined myself sitting alone in an adobe-brick house at the mission in Tehran, without Father and without my family. It was a lonely image. *Is that what I want?*

I knelt and prayed. "Dear God, help me to make this decision. It may lead me to happiness or endless sorrow. 'Your word is a lamp to my feet and a light to my path.' Psalm 119:105."

Suddenly the sun broke through the clouds and illuminated the yellow flower in the third circle of the stain-glass pane. *Postponing. I won't sail in August. Instead I'll postpone my trip until the Great War ends and then reevaluate my choices.*

Despite my misgivings and utter disappointment, I accepted my decision with a resigned sigh. *But when will this dreadful war end? When will I be able to return to Persia?*

It was starting to get dark outside, and it seemed that the sun was setting on my life-long dream.

That night in May, Harold asked me to go horseback riding in Central Park. He chose a tall white steed and I chose a chestnut mare.

As we rode slowly side-by-side, I said, "I have an announcement to make. I've decided to delay my trip to Persia due to the war."

Harold smiled widely. "I'm so happy you came to that decision. I hope you forget about going altogether. Perhaps you can think again about our relationship."

"My decision did not take you into consideration. It hurts me to say so, but my staying makes no difference between us. It is impossible."

"Impossible? How can you say that? Don't you enjoy being with me?"

"Of course I do, but a serious relationship between us is still impossible."

Impossible. From then on Harold struggled against that word. At the end of a perfect day together, such as a canoe ride at Bear Mountain or a walk in Riverside Park, he brought it up time after time. He wanted to discuss what "impossible" meant until he was sometimes hard to manage.

I hated myself for telling Harold that Howard Baskerville was the reason, but if that wasn't the reason, what was it? Harold was a fine man, with his taste for food, music, and art, his love of poetry, and his endless thoughtfulness. Perhaps it was because we didn't have quite enough in common. He thought very conservatively in every respect, whereas I was a liberal, a progressive. I believed in F.O.R and social reform, while he didn't agree with either. Not having the same values, now that could lead to serious problems in marriage.

A life with Harold offered me money and a gay life in New York. But would a life like that satisfy me? I needed to serve humanity, just as my parents had. *My missionary work in Persia—I just won't give that up.*

Billy Sunday's evangelist revival was a welcome diversion from the war. He was a former outfielder for the Chicago White Stockings who left baseball for the Christian ministry. His make-shift tent tabernacle on Broadway and 168th Street seated 18,000. The stuffy tent had an unpleasant, stale, musty odor, and we sat on hard wooden bleachers, packed like sardines in a can.

Billy Sunday's delivery was shockingly unorthodox. He charged around on the platform, dropped to his knees on occasion, flopped on a chair one minute and then jumped up on it, shaking his fist, shouting, then laughing. He certainly put a lot of energy into his performances.

Billy Sunday spoke on the current state of Christianity: "Lord save us from off-handed, flabby-cheeked, brittle-boned, weak-kneed, thin-skinned, pliable, plastic, spineless, effeminate, ossified, three-karat Christianity. Religion needs a baptism of horse sense."

I laughed so hard that my sides ached, and others nearby gave me angry looks.

"You should leave if you can't sit quietly," the woman sitting next to me whispered.

But it was too late, Billy Sunday pointed at us in the front row and said, "Look into the preaching of Jesus and you will find it was aimed straight at the sinners in the front seats."

"I'm not a sinner," I shouted back, which caused quite a stir.

"Better leave now," the woman next to me whispered. "Please."

The people in my front seat row stood up to let me pass. Then, as I headed up the aisle, Billy Sunday continued, "Better die an old maid, sister, than marry the wrong man."

I was relieved to be out the exit and take a deep breath in of the fresh air. *Did Billy Sunday just curse me?* A shiver traveled down my spine.

On May 30th and 31st, the first Conference on Democracy and Terms of Peace was held in Madison Square Garden. The conference was organized as a reaction to Woodrow Wilson's decision to enter the war in April, with the aim of "aiding our government in bringing to ourselves and the world a speedy, righteous and lasting peace." Teachers' College requested that I attend with my coworker, Ted Martin.

There was a large crowd of socialists, pacifists, radicals of all sorts, and other political factions attracted by Norman Thomas's presence. Police were on every corner, ready with riot guns to arrest anyone disruptive. Inside the theater the constant din of the crowd filled the place with sporadic yelling, cheering, and booing. I was swept away by the conflict of the debates, the different points of view, and the energy of the affair, and it helped me to survive the many hours in the bleachers with Ted. The stale air and smell of sweat made one feel faint.

I did not know Ted very well. He dutifully accepted my companionship at this affair as an obligation of his employment. When he came with our group to Washington, D.C., to lobby against the war, our social interactions were limited. At the office, he was always cordial to me but seemed a bit aloof. Nonetheless, he invited me to join him for lunch and dinner during the meetings.

We walked silently and sternly hand-in-hand past the police surrounding the Gardens and found a restaurant nearby. I had never thought Ted to be much of a talker, but he surprised me by dominating the conversation, focusing primarily on a breakdown of the pros and cons of the debates. The second day at lunch I was feeling more comfortable with Ted and ventured to interject some more personal questions into our conversation.

"Where are you from?" I asked. "I can't quite decipher your accent."

"I'm originally from Manti, Utah. Where are you from?"

"I was born in Persia, in Tabriz. I thought everyone knew that."

"Oh, yes. The missionary's daughter, the 'Princess of Persia.' I remember hearing that. They say you weren't really exposed to men until you came to Teachers' College, going directly to Vassar when you arrived here."

I was taken aback. "Sadly, that's somewhat true, but I was almost engaged at sixteen."

Ted raised his eyebrows and responded with a softer tone. "That I did not hear. I suppose everyone doesn't really know your past that well. How people talk." He started to busy himself with his food.

"What do they say?" I managed to ask, "About me?"

Ted looked up from his food. "Do you really want to know?" He shook his head. "Maybe I'd be doing you a favor, but I'd rather not." He started to eat again.

"I want to know."

"Well," Ted started, then swallowed hard. "The men at Union have the opinion that you are only looking for an escort for entertainment and don't want to develop a meaningful relationship. One week you're going to the theater with Frank, the next to dinner with Guy, then to a show with Harold, or the symphony with Joe."

"What's wrong with that? We are just having a good time together."

"At this time in life, usually men and women go out with each other to develop a relationship, to potentially get engaged and married," Ted responded with a smug tone in his voice.

"Marriage is not something I am sure will happen for me, not in the near future," I answered. "I hope to go back to Persia for missionary work."

"If you were serious about returning to Persia, then you shouldn't be taking advantage of men's invitations. They could be asking out other women who really are available. Did you ever think that others might see you as using these men just to entertain yourself?"

"No, they are friends. They know and accept that I plan to go back to Persia."

"Really, think about it." Ted was becoming more animated. "You weren't honest about your feelings with Guy. After spending a year taking you places, he found out that you lacked feelings for him."

"I try to be plain about my intentions," I mumbled.

"You have a sixteen-year-old approach to men that's not suitable for a woman in their mid-twenties. Spending time with men with no intention of developing a serious relationship is what high school girls do. After hearing about how you treated Guy, I decided to avoid you."

"I noticed." I was becoming quite irritated. *Ted is preaching at me like Billy Sunday.*

"Not only that, but these friends of yours will abandon you and look for a real relationship."

"They are free to go out with other women whenever they like."

"You know, Agnes," Ted kept on, "someday you will wake up and realize that you too need more than mere friendship with men."

For the rest of the afternoon, we spoke little, but Ted's blunt words played over and over in my head.

Chapter 22

SUMMER 1917

THE LAST DAY OF SECOND SEMESTER I EAGERLY BOARDED the train to Princeton to attend my cousin George Stewart's graduation. Since his family lived in Pasadena and couldn't attend, I felt it my duty to go, but I also had another motive. I was staying with Uncle Rob and Aunt Ellen and would finally have a chance to read the letter Uncle received from Tabriz after Father's death. *What did it say that Father would want me to know?*

When I arrived at the Princeton station, Uncle Rob and Aunt Ellen were waiting on the platform. "My dear niece, how happy I am to see you," Uncle Rob said as he enveloped me in his arms. I could tell by the stale, acrid smell of his shirt that he had been wearing it several days.

A smile spread across my face as I noticed that Uncle's trousers were secured by safety pins to his suspenders. "Uncle Rob, you hold your pants up with safety pins?" I asked.

Aunt Ellen shook her head with a sad smile. "Rob has become so disheveled in his attire these days. I don't know what to do about it."

"I look like an old professor and that's what I am," Uncle Rob retorted.

Disheveled or not, I loved my Uncle Rob. He reminded me so of Father.

It was a short drive to 93 Stockton Place, the fine, red-brick, three-story house where six children had been raised, and only one daughter remained, sixteen-year-old Julia. Aunt Ellen ushered us into the parlor for tea, and we chatted for some time. Finally, I said, "Uncle Rob, I hoped to read the letter you received from the mission in Tabriz."

"Of course. It's in my study," Uncle Rob said. He sat down at his desk and unfolded a several-page letter. He looked at the floor for a minute, deep in contemplation, and then he looked up. "I told you after your Father's service that I needed to tell you something."

"Yes, I remember."

"The mission doctor in Tabriz, Dr. Vanneman, sent this letter after your father's death via the Presbyterian Mission Board. It's long, and I will let you read the entire letter alone. First I should read to you a few passages that might cause you some concern so we might discuss them together.

"The letter starts: 'The members of the Tabriz Station desire to put on record their deep sense of loss and bereavement sustained by us in the death of the Rev. Samuel Graham Wilson, D.D., which took place at Tabriz, July 2, 1916.' Now I'll skip ahead, 'Though his furlough unavoidably extended itself to over three years, we regard it as one of the most fruitful portions of his missionary life. When he wrote us he was ready to return to his field, we rejoiced greatly at the prospect of having with us once more one of his experience, large acquaintance with the country and people, ripe in intellect and judgement, free to devote himself of the literary and evangelistic work of which Persia stands in great need. While we eagerly awaited for news of his sailing, the Armenian and Syrian Relief Committee in New York requested Dr. Wilson to act as their agent on the ground in the distribution of relief funds and in planning for the future support of the fugitives. With the consent of the Board of Foreign Missions and this station, he accepted the appointment.' "

My head was reeling. "Over three years' furlough?" I exclaimed. "He wrote the mission that he was ready to return to the field? But Father resigned from his post at the mission three years before his death."

"No, Agnes. Your father never resigned. He understood that you wanted to return to Tabriz and work at the mission with him. He wanted you to fulfill your dream and felt it his duty to make that possible. Your happiness meant so much to him."

"Father sacrificed his health for me?"

"You were not the only reason. Your Father also had his own self-interest in mind. He was very bored and restless in America. It was so hard for him after the train accident that left him an invalid. As he wrote me once, 'The easy life I have here in America is suffocating me.' He had spent over thirty years in Tabriz and it was his home, it was in his blood, and he wanted to return and finish his work there. He had arranged to leave for Persia in October 1915. Then the call to go to the Caucasus for Armenian Relief work came. It was an opportunity for him to go without causing attention to the true purpose of his journey—to return to his mission work in Tabriz."

"He left Mother and the family in America, with no plan to return until his next furlough?"

"Annie has your Grandmother and two teenage children to take care of. Your father knew what this meant. Even if the war ended, she would not be able to join him with those responsibilities."

"I don't understand," I said, overcome with disbelief. "When Rose and I saw him off, he said that he would be back after he completed his work for the Near East Relief. Mother surely would have told us if he had decided differently."

"No, she ..." Uncle Rob came closer and put his arms around me and held me for some time. It felt like Father was hugging me. Although my uncle's embrace was comforting, it caused me to gasp and sob.

Then a tear fell on my forehead and Uncle Rob cleared his throat. "I don't think Sam told her."

"I must tell her then."

With his hands on my shoulders, Uncle Robert gently pushed me away at arms' length and looked into my face. His glasses were misted, obscuring the intensity of his stare. "Would you want to break her heart again?"

On May 18th, Congress passed the Selective Service Act. All men between the ages of 18 to 30 years were required to register on June 5th and get their "number." Those in the clergy were exempt, so many of my friends from Union, including Stanley and Frank, were not at risk. Harold would turn thirty on August 1st, so he would likely not be required to go to Europe, but Joe was only twenty-four. Congress also quickly passed the Espionage Act on June 15th that called for fining or imprisoning spies and informants of sensitive information, and anyone who "willfully obstructed the recruiting or enlisting to the military." This was effective in scaring off many of the anti-war activities against the Selective Service Act. The draft loomed over everyone's silent and subdued conscience.

After I returned from Princeton, I spent a week with Buzz at her home in New York making bridesmaid dresses for Marcia's wedding. The fabric was a lovely gold taffeta with red and blue accents. The bridesmaids were Mary, Buzz, and me; Marcia's classmates and former double-alley roommates from Vassar. Marcia's and Malcolm's wedding was on Saturday, June 23rd, in New Rochelle.

Anna came on the train from Kiski for the wedding, leaving her baby Betsy and two-year-old Jack Jr. with Aunt Bessie. She talked in a hushed voice when Marcia was not in earshot. "With the dreaded draft number selection coming in four weeks, I can't sleep from fear that Jack's number will be selected."

"What if Malcolm is drafted?" Buzz said.

"Surely this must be in the back of Marcia's mind as she takes her vows," Mary added.

"Weddings are supposed to be so full of hope for the future," I said. "It is so fearful with so many friends and relatives who have to register."

Marcia was beautiful in her white satin gown with flowing tulle, and the bodice and sleeves trimmed with pearls. As she and Malcolm each said, "as long as we both shall live," I thought about how the war could shatter this beautiful start to their happy lives together.

After the wedding, Mr. Howson drove Buzz and me back to New York, and I rushed to finish packing my bags for the midnight train to Los Angeles. Just as I was leaving with Joe for the station, flowers arrived from Harold. I was so rushed and embarrassed that I hurried off, bringing the card and flowers with me.

Before I boarded the train, Joe held me in his arms for a long time with a sad look in his eyes. "I may not be here when you get back," he said.

"What?" I exclaimed in confusion.

"The draft," he replied. "They pick draft numbers in three weeks. They say a few weeks later the men with the first numbers will go to France."

The harsh reality of his words, they hit me like a blow to my head. "I hadn't even thought..."

"I'll write to you when I know."

On the long hot journey across the country by train, Harold's daily letters were called out at the train station stops. So as not to encourage his persistence, I decided it was better not to respond. The train stops became fewer and the stations smaller as we travelled farther West. If Harold was still writing letters, they never made it to these rural stations, and it was a relief not being followed by them anymore.

Dorothy Dickinson's gift for the journey was H. G. Wells' book *God, the Invisible King*. In his book, Wells professes that God is not Nature, nor the Creator, but the "finite" God of the human heart. He sees the world through our eyes and stands and walks next to us. Rather than allowing Him to guide our feet, we submit to His will and understanding. He is the perfect companion for our loneliness, the perfect strength for our weakness, the perfect love for our selfishness. I found this conception of God appealing. *God is riding on the empty seat next to me and I do not feel alone.*

As the miles rolled along, I prepared for my summer's work travelling around California and asking for donations for the Armenian Relief effort. And when I was tired of reading and writing, I gazed out the window for hours at a time. Oh, those fearful, burning Western deserts; my heart ached for the poor people living there. At night I dreamed of them, all in their gray, dusty, sack-like clothes, tired women with faces aged by the sun and blond hair gray with dust, children with dirty faces and without shoes, men thin and sinewy from too little to eat and constant toil. Carcasses of horses that died in the fields, lying baking in the sun, cows with huge ribs bulging on their sides.

America's rural poor were no different from those of Persia, and the horror of the poor was no less horrific. At night I dreamed of a great weary procession of poor people trudging across the sands and I was with them.

Uncle Dick and Aunt Clara drove up from Santa Ana with two-year-old Andrew and met me at the train station in Los Angeles. I was so weary after the long train ride I simply fell into Uncle Dick's arms. Father's youngest brother always kept up with the latest developments and had a new electric-starting Cadillac rather than one that had to be cranked.

"I'm enjoying the palm trees," I shouted to Aunt Clara from the back seat as we sped east to Pasadena. "It's so different from the East Coast. What's that mountain range to the north?"

"San Gabriel Mountains. The one toward the front is Mt. Wilson."

Then Uncle Dick turned south, and after two more turns stopped in front of a two-story yellow house.

"Here?" I asked. But my question was answered by the rush of family out the front door—Mother, Grandmother, Rose, Annie, Bobby, and even feeble Uncle Foster. 177 South Mentor Avenue, Pasadena, California, my new home for the summer.

It was a sweet home, with porches in front and back and the artistic placement of climbing rose bushes on either side of the steps. Rose and Mother had fixed it up so daintily, and everything was to set off by Uncle Foster's vivid paintings. Annie was quite a young lady of sixteen, thoughtless, sweet, wholesome, and romping, always engineering good times, always surrounded by young men, dreaming great dreams. Bobby declared, "She drafts in the boys, a new one every time she feels the need." I nicknamed her "our great big beautiful doll."

The house was well situated near Las Encinas Sanitorium where Uncle Foster was being treated for his tuberculosis. He was weaker and thinner than before, but as cheerful as ever. Every day Grandmother visited him, and on special occasions, like today, he came to the house. Although I despaired at having my family so far away, the possibility that the Southern California air would cure Uncle Foster certainly warranted the move.

After tea, I sat with Mother in the parlor.

"After Father's accident, I always wondered what your feelings were about being trapped here in America," I said.

"It wasn't what your father and I had planned," Mother said, "but in 1913 when he had his train accident, the children were only ten and thirteen. The bonus was that they could go to school in America while he recovered."

"When Father got better had you planned to return?"

"Your father's progress was slow, and we decided it was best to resign. Of course, I miss Persia. When Sam built our house at the mission, I blessed it saying, 'For now I have chosen and consecrated this house that my name may be there forever.'"

"2 Chronicles 7:16," I said. "Is your heart still there like mine?"

"My heart will be there for all time. There is still a room in that house with all of our belongings. I'd like to touch those things again, many were wedding presents. But I can revisit those things in my memories. Returning to the mission now wouldn't be the same without Sam, and I have no desire to return without him." Tears came to her eyes and I touched her hand.

"No, it would never be the same without Father."

Later in our room Rose told me, "Mother has hard times adjusting to life without Father. She gets queer ideas that are difficult to dislodge."

"What do you mean?" I asked. "She seems still bright and determined."

"After Father died, she was surprised to receive a letter from the Presbyterian Board. They asked her if she planned to retire or withdraw from mission service and gave her the option to return. They said Father never officially resigned in 1913. This caused her much confusion."

I told Rose about visiting Uncle Rob and the sympathy letter from the mission.

"Do you think we should tell Mother?" Rose asked.

"We should never do anything to dull her appreciation of life or her love for Father," I answered.

On July 2nd, the one-year anniversary of Father's death, we had a short remembrance in the parlor. Mother placed a vase of roses from her garden under a life-sized picture of Father. Rose promised me an outdoor activity with our cousin George Stewart the next day "to free our minds of melancholy."

"Which would you prefer, the mountains or the ocean?" she asked.

"The mountains," I answered. "Up in the mountains I'll remember hiking with Father and try to come to terms with his death."

"I haven't come to terms yet either," Rose said.

It was different for me than for Rose. Father died without saying that he forgave me for the disgrace I had caused him at the mission with Howard. A wound that never healed.

Shortly after sunrise, George parked his truck in front of the house and honked his horn. Tootle-tootle. Out he sprang, tall, loping and gangly, with straight dark hair falling over one eye and his glasses cock-eyed on his nose.

"Are you Wilson girls ready?" he asked.

"I'm always ready," Rose replied. "Old Agnes is ready too."

"Old Agnes?" I replied as Rose and George laughed. "I'm only two years older than you."

"Hop in the truck," George said. "Mount Wilson isn't hard, but it isn't easy either. We'll take it slow for your sake, Old Agnes."

"George is quite the nature lover," Rose said. "He took me hiking whenever he was home from Princeton. We hiked together in Yosemite too."

I sighed. "I'm looking forward to being in the wilderness."

"It's not really what you'd call the wilderness," George retorted. "Mount Wilson has been popular with hikers since Pacific Electric brought the 'Red Cars' to Sierra Madre. A few days ago, there was a regular parade up the mountain when they drove up the five-ton mirror to the observatory."

"Observatory?"

"Yes, and I must admit that if it wasn't for that 100-inch telescope, which I desperately want to see, I'd be taking you to the wilderness to get acquainted with a grizzly bear."

"Will we be able to see the planets and the stars through the telescope?"

"No, it won't be working yet, if ever. A fellow named Hale had the mirror made in France and it came back with bubbles. Too much champagne is my guess. But it's so clear up there that you can view the heavens with your naked eye."

"You said we'd be camping, but where, on the summit?"

George laughed. "No, no. You and Rose will stay at Orchard Camp Mountain Resort."

"A mountain resort?" I exclaimed.

"It's not really a resort," explained Rose. "We'll rent a tent, and George will wander out in the wilderness to sleep under the stars."

At the base of Mount Wilson, Rose and George donned backpacks, and George handed me a shoulder bag with a canteen. "We'll fill our canteens in the creek at First Water," he said.

The trail climbed steadily upward, hugging the side of the canyon, and it was hot on the sunny, exposed slope. I felt dizzy and anxious for a drink of water, but too proud to admit my thirst and fatigue. When I heard rushing water and saw the creek ahead, a sudden surge of energy propelled me forward. We had reached First Water. How I relished the taste of the cold water on my lips and tongue.

"Fill your canteen," George instructed. "It's not far to Orchard Camp, but you need to drink when you can. There won't be opportunities for water on the final ascent."

Orchard Camp, the "mountain resort," consisted of a main building, a few cabins, and a dance pavilion. Horse-pack groups had filled the outdoor tables and small children raced around an ancient oak tree. Rose and I rented a tent at the main building, and George quickly assembled it with surprising adeptness.

"Our Princeton English major is also apparently an engineer," I jested.

"One must always be ready in case civilization ceases to be," he responded. "Now ladies, we mustn't tarry. To the summit?"

"To the summit," Rose and I chimed in unison.

We left the shaded glen of Orchard Camp and began the steep climb. With each turn new vistas opened, the cities below and the shining ocean in the distance. My heartbeat thundered in my head and my breathing was heavy.

Father would have loved being here in the mountains. When we hiked together though, I don't remember being so breathless. Getting older, I guess, almost twenty-five.

After another half mile of climbing, the light started to darken in my peripheral vision, and I heard a buzzing in my ears as if I was carrying a beehive on top of my head. Then clamminess swept through my body. "I'll sit down for a minute," I called ahead to George and Rose.

They stopped abruptly and retraced their steps. "What's wrong? You look as white as snow," Rose said.

"Drink some water," I heard George saying above a loud crackling and popping in my ears.

The last thing I remember was my vision going dark. When I came to, I was on the ground and could make out through blurred vision the faces of Rose and George bending over me.

"You've been out a few minutes," George said. "Fortunately, your head didn't hit a rock when you collapsed."

"Are you okay?" Rose asked.

"Yes, I think so," I replied and smiled up at her. "Father visited me."

"What?" Rose exclaimed.

"I had a vision of Father, with a yellow glow around his head. He smiled and laughed and said, 'You aren't dying, Agnes. So get back on your feet.'"

"You're delirious," Rose said, shaking her head.

"If you can sit up, rest your head on your knees," George instructed.

As I moved with hesitation, I noticed Rose and George exchange worried glances. Rose sat down next to me and stroked my hair. My vision slowly became clearer.

"I felt very close to Father when I saw his vision," I whispered.

"That's sweet," Rose whispered back.

"We'll go back down to Orchard Camp when you're ready," George said.

"No," I pleaded. "I want to reach the top."

George seemed reluctant, but I managed to help myself to my feet with Rose's help and take a few steps forward.

"Stay behind her as we go up," George instructed Rose. "And Agnes, if you feel at all dizzy, sit down immediately."

As we proceeded slowly up the mountain, my breath stabilized, and the cold clamminess dissipated. My body felt warm again and sweat beaded my brow. I kept each foot moving ahead—left, right, left, right—watching my boots carry me forward.

After some time, Rose said, "Look up. The view is spectacular from here."

And there it was, the most beautiful vista I had ever seen. The hills in the late afternoon sun were shades of deep green, blue, and purple, the deep blue ocean stretched far into the horizon. Wispy clouds hovered above, almost close enough to touch.

"We're on the top of the world," I cried. "Almost in heaven."

"Shhh," George hissed. "There's something spiritual about being on top of a mountain. The awe in the wonder and beauty of nature brings speechlessness to me. Listen to the wind."

After several moments of silence, I turned to Rose and whispered in her ear, "I feel so close to Father, to God." My voice broke and tears streamed down my face.

"Stop it," Rose said as she hugged me. "You'll make me cry too." But it was too late.

"I'm going to the observatory," George said in a soft voice. "I'll be back soon."

After the tears stopped flowing, we wiped our eyes. "Look at us," Rose said. "We both look pitiful." We gasped and laughed.

"I feel like a hundred-pound weight has been lifted off my chest," I said.

We sat on a rock, and Rose opened her backpack and gave me an apple. We ate apples and watched the sun go down in silence.

Just as the sun hit the horizon, we heard the crunch of granite under George's boots. "Mr. Hale wouldn't let anyone get close to his precious mirror, bubbles and all," he said as he sat down with us.

"The view is magnificent," I said. "Thank you for bringing me. It has done me much good."

"I consider it my duty to take every able Wilson on this journey, to summit their namesake," George said. "Let's look for Saturn." George proceeded to lead us on a tour of the summer planets and constellations.

When he finished, Rose said "George's knowledge and love of nature are exceptional."

"I love the sky, the mountains," George replied. "People come and go, but earth abides."

"Ecclesiastes 1: 4," I replied, "or something close to it."

"Father used to show us the constellations," Rose murmured. She put her arm around my shoulder and squeezed me. Her warm body was comforting in the cool mountain air.

"Yes, I remember," I responded as a nostalgic smile spread across my lips.

"Are you ready to go down the mountain?" George asked. "I have lanterns for each of us. The batteries should last the night."

It was an anxious, exhilarating trip down the steep mountain trail, trying to keep from falling off the precipice into the coal-black abyss. When we reached a switchback, George motioned for us to stop. "A rattler." George stomped his boots for a few minutes, then turned and said, "She's gone. The first one surprises, the second one angers, the third gets bitten."

"I would have gotten the strike," Rose gasped.

"You always sacrifice yourself for others, dear Rose," I said. "How I wish I could only be like you in some small way."

After descending another hour, I was relieved to see lights below dancing between the trees. It was Orchard Camp, filled with tents and glowing lanterns. George rustled off into the spruce trees to find a place to sleep, and Rose and I bundled up with the covers in our tent.

As we lay there, I turned to Rose and said, "Something feels different now, as though the burden of grief has left my soul."

"Maybe Father really did visit you on the mountain," Rose murmured, half asleep.

Soon after I turned off my lantern, I too fell asleep, a deep sleep with many dreams. The only one I remembered vividly was my vision of Father, smiling and laughing. I was roused by the morning light and lay quietly, remembering my vision. I felt Father's deep love and felt in my heart that he had forgiven me.

On July 21st, the blind-folded Secretary of War, Newton Baker, picked a capsule from a glass bowl with the first draft number: 258. The draft hit hard in many cases, but Americans solemnly acquiesced because of the Espionage Act. News quickly followed of the repercussions the draft had on friends and family. Marcia's husband, Malcom, and Kitten's husband, Sinclair, had been spared. Cousin Lad's number was picked last, and his wife Edna fainted upon hearing the news. My cousin Dorothy Dulles wrote that James Bourne, her fiancé, was drafted, and they decided to marry before he was sent to Europe. Cousin George Stewart hadn't waited for the draft and enlisted. Then a letter from Anna came. Sarah's husband, James, was spared but Jack had been drafted. "In two months, I'll be alone with Betsy and Jack Jr.," Anna wrote.

"Anna alone with two small children?" I gasped.

A week later, I received a letter from Joe. I could tell when I held the envelope that was a short letter, so unlike Joe: "Please forgive the brevity of this note to you, but I wanted to let you know right away. Both my brother Andrew and I were selected in the first group of the draft. Andrew will go next month, but I've decided to resist the draft. This may mean that I will go to prison, but I cannot go to war with a fair conscience."

His words just took my breath away. He wrote so bravely about refusing to serve and preferring to go to prison. His brothers Clement and Harrison thought he was obliged to serve and gave him no sympathy. They thought that I was responsible for Joe's decision, calling my pacifist views a "pernicious influence."

For weeks later I had a knot of dread in my stomach, worrying about Joe. *What would happen to him?*

Chapter 23

FALL 1917

AT THE END OF JULY, ROSE AND I ACCOMPANIED
Mother to a tea at the Pasadena Presbyterian Church. Mrs. Wishard,
Mother's neighbor, organized the event and passed out pamphlets for
the Southern California Presbyterian Conference.

"Alamitos Bay in Long Beach is a delightful venue," Mrs. Wishard
said. "It's right on the ocean, with seagulls and pelicans right outside
the meeting-room windows. The classes cover a gamut of topics, but
this year the emphasis is on African missionary work and religion
in Russia."

"Would you girls like to go?" Mother asked. Rose and I nodded
enthusiastically. "Then it's settled. You have two recruits."

Although lectures were stimulating, we most enjoyed dodging the
waves as we walked barefoot along the beach, sinking our toes into
the cold wet sand. During one of our walks Rose said, "You seem very
dreamy. Are you in love?"

"I'm so transparent. For the past three years I've been infatuated
with a man named Stanley Hunter."

"How did you meet him?" Rose asked.

"I discovered him in one of my classes at Union Seminary. He's a pastor in Pittsburgh now and I only see him occasionally when he visits New York."

"Does he know how you feel about him?" Rose asked. "It doesn't do any good to just dream about someone." *Rose is so practical.*

"He does, in a way" I said. "I had fully intended on telling him all he meant to me before I left for Persia, but I'm not sure he understood. His last words were: "We can be real friends, can't we?""

"Oh. That doesn't sound very promising."

Saturday evening at the conference, Rose and I sat at an empty table so we could talk about how concerned we were about Uncle Foster's tuberculosis, not really dinner conversation to share with strangers. During dessert, a group of older ladies sat down at our table and hailed a waiter for coffee. As they engaged in idle chatter, Rose and I quietly ate our dessert, pretending not to listen.

"We're being very rude to ignore you, young ladies," one woman said, looking at Rose and me. "I'm Mrs. Hunter, the wife of the minster who will speak tonight. We just arrived from Riverside."

I stopped cold, my fork in mid-air on its way to my mouth.

"Rose and Agnes Wilson," Rose replied awkwardly when I didn't immediately respond.

In the front of the room a minister was standing near the lectern. He was the perfect image of Stanley, say thirty years from now, a tall, strong, deep-browed man. Yes, it was his father, William Armstrong Hunter, and she was his stepmother, Elizabeth. I remembered Stanley telling me that he visited his parents in California. Why hadn't the name Hunter in the program caused a buzzer to go off in my brain?

One of the ladies at the table was talking about their church in Riverside, saying proudly, "Our minister's three sons are preachers too, wonderful young men, one in New York, one in Pittsburgh, and the youngest is now in Cairo. Such a family."

I couldn't hold myself back any longer. "Mrs. Hunter, I don't mean to intrude on your conversation but I'm from Columbia University. I know your son Stanley. We were in classes together at Union Seminary."

"Oh," she exclaimed. "Then I must tell you, Stanley will be here on Sunday. He is to give the sermon." I almost fell over in my chair.

"I'll have a chance to meet Stanley," Rose whispered. "I can hardly wait."

Fate, providence ... what is it that brings such things together by coincidence? That two people from far ends of the country should be brought together with no prearrangements or foreknowledge. I could barely sleep that night with anticipation of seeing Stanley the next day.

At Sunday service, Stanley gave a beautiful and lofty sermon. He looked like the epitome of everything a good pastor should be, handsome and stately. Everyone loved the sermon or him; I could not tell which. I was overwhelmed with joy, just seeing and hearing him, and a rush of exhilaration and giddiness swept through me. But, all the joy of seeing him did not blind me to the fact that I did not agree with the way he clothed the war with lofty idealism.

Afterward, I was quite frank with my criticism. "You've drifted far away from your F.O.R. faith," I told him.

Stanley smiled his charming, knee-weakening smile. "Just changing with the times."

He was eager to learn my opinion about possible Armenian Relief work that his church could support. As I told him about the opportunities I knew of, I intently surveyed his face, his eyes, his lips. I wanted to capture a picture of him to embed in my memory. The next day he was gone, back to Pittsburgh, and we returned to Pasadena.

On the automobile ride back to Pasadena, I felt thrills and chills run through me as I thought of him. Maybe there was a chance that Stanley and I would get together after all. *But hadn't he said he would call me if he was in Los Angeles this summer? Why didn't he call?*

Rose was excited to have first heard me tell her about my feelings for Stanley, and then for him to suddenly appear.

"He is rather handsome," Rose said, "but he seems more like an actor than a minister."

"Promise to keep Stanley a secret," I told her. "Mother has never heard me mention him."

"Your secret is safe with me," Rose replied. *Dear staunch Rose.*

Later that week, I wrote to Stanley about the points in his sermon that troubled me, particularly the phrases from the scriptures that he used to embellish the war effort. "One shouldn't associate the Bible with the war," I said.

I really hoped to elicit a response from Stanley and a dialogue between us, but he did not respond while I was in Pasadena.

On the train from California to New York, I sat across from a man in the dining car. He was staring out the window, but I ventured an introduction anyway. "Hello, I'm Agnes."

The man was blond with brilliant green eyes, and he barely managed a smile. "I'm Edward, pleased to meet you."

"You look concerned," I said. "These are hard times."

"I've been drafted and I'm a conscientious objector. I'm facing prison."

"My dearest friend is resisting the draft too."

"I've heard that they torture conscientious objectors in prison and that some die from the torture."

I shuddered. "Here's my work address at Columbia University. Write to me from prison and tell me everything. I'll see if I can help." I saw the anguish in the man's face. It made me long to be brave and fight for the rights of the conscientious objectors. The remainder of the journey I worried about Joe. Would he suffer in prison? I imagined him chained to a wall, half-naked, with gashes and bruises on his arms and his legs.

When I returned to New York, there was a letter from Joe waiting for me and I hastily tore it open: "A waiver was passed that exempts medical students from the draft due to the shortage of doctors," he wrote. "I'm safe as long as I'm a medical student, but when I've finished my training I'm required to serve."

I felt a great load lifted. Joe would not have to go to prison for resisting the draft. If the war was over before he finished medical school, he would not have to risk his life as a soldier either.

Since we shared the same birthday, September 10th, Frank Fitt never forgot to send me a card. This year, sending me birthday wishes wasn't his only intent: "Harriet Bradley and I were engaged August 15th. The wedding is planned for next year on the same day. Her father, Brigadier General Alfred Bradley, wants a big wedding for his daughter. It will take a year to plan. Of course, since I'm not in charge of invitations, I don't know if you'll be invited."

I knew Harriet since she was in my class at Vassar and came to our F.O.R meetings. Their engagement was not a surprise since during this past year Frank came to see Harriet on every occasion that he was in New York. Strangely enough, it made me jealous and I hated to admit it.

Harold called me to see if I'd like to go to a show. "I have a terrible cold," I replied, "and don't feel like talking to anyone."

Well, it wasn't the cold at all. I finally received a letter from Stanley. Initially, I held the letter in my hands, caressing it as though I was touching his hands. Finally, I opened it. *So brief, not even one page?*

Dear Agnes,

I wanted to tell you myself before it is formally announced in the newspaper. I'm engaged to Elizabeth Pierce, a woman from Pittsburgh I have come to know. I remembered how you prayed that this would come to me. You are such a dear friend.

We plan to have the wedding the first day of spring for good luck. Hopefully, you can meet my dear Elizabeth someday.

Your dear friend, Stanley

My mind went blank for a few minutes. *Elizabeth Pierce.* Six months before, Stanley told me that when he first proposed to her, she said 'no' and it broke his heart. Now she would be part of his life forever.

Would I ever love anyone else as much as I have Stanley? Not that I mean to stop loving him, not the way I love him now. My love cannot cease while he lives.

Each time I started to write back to Stanley, I stopped and tore up what I had written. Finally I wrote: "Dear Stanley, I have indeed always prayed for the best and richest life for you. I am glad that God brought so deep an experience into your life. I wish you the best as always.

Your dear friend, Agnes."

Over the next days, weeks, and months there was a deep emptiness inside me, a cavernous pit of loneliness. Only the business of work kept me from feeling directionless, with my future so indefinite. Stanley Hunter was out of my grasp.

Or was he? Engagements are broken off unexpectedly, aren't they? Maybe Elizabeth Pierce will change her mind.

Joe had a tough clinical schedule his last year of medical school, often being assigned night shifts in the hospital. Despite his busy medical school schedule, he always made sure we had time together on the weekends. Knowing I loved the New York Philharmonic, he purchased matinee tickets for the 1917-1918 season. Some were memorable per-formances in Carnegie Hall, such as Guiomar Novaes's performance of Chopin's piano concerto in F minor.

When Aunt Helen invited me for Thanksgiving at the Gotham Hotel with my cousins Dorothy and Rhea Dulles, she asked me to invite a guest "to assist in devouring the turkey." I asked Joe to come and he happily accepted.

The Broadway cable car to 57th Street was stuffy and crammed full of people going to holiday dinner, and the short walk in the brisk fall air to the Gotham Hotel at 700 5th Avenue was such a relief. The recep-tionist called Aunt Helen's apartment. While we waited in the Gotham Hotel lobby, we admired the marble floors and walls, the enormous crystal chandelier, and the large Persian rug.

"Is the rug from Salmas?" Joe asked.

"No, it's from Tabriz. The geometrical patterns give it away," I replied with a smile.

"Smug Tabrizian."

Aunt Helen sent Rhea to take us up to the apartment. He was a freshman at Princeton, a slender young man of seventeen, with daz-zling blue eyes and bushy eyebrows. Joe and Rhea took immediately to each other and were happy in male comradery amidst three women. Joe started off telling Williams fraternity stories, some that included my performance of Berkshire's Purple Queen. He kept us laughing throughout the meal. Later, Aunt Helen turned to me and said, "Oh, Agnes, Joe is quite the catch. Such a handsome young man and such a witty and intelligent fellow."

I just smiled without replying. Referring the Joe as a "catch" seemed inappropriate given we were friends since childhood. Were we destined to be married someday? That is a question I could not answer.

Just before Christmas, Joe and I went to the Youth Concert of the Philharmonic where they played a whole concert of Christmas music. We exchanged presents, and to our surprise we both gave each other gloves and scarves. Mine were fine black woolen ones. "Simple, but from the warmth in my heart," Joe said.

Things were always simple with Joe. Nothing he ever gave me was ostentatious, only practical.

Harold and I continued to go to shows together, but I insisted on going weekday nights. Wanting to avoid uncomfortable discussions about our "impossible" relationship, I could use the convenient excuse, "I need to get up for work early tomorrow." We did have pleasant times together, and it was a treat to be able to go to so many fine restaurants, which he could afford with his high-paying job at A.T.&T.

One evening as we walked to the theater he said, "Agnes, I want to ask you a favor."

"I'm afraid that depends what it is."

"I think you can do this, but it might take some effort as you'll need to break a habit."

"What is it?"

"Could you call me 'Hal' instead of 'Harold'?"

"Hal?"

"Yes, I prefer it. Hal is more endearing."

"Hal. I'm not sure I like Hal. I thought it was the nickname for Henry. In 'King Henry IV' Shakespeare called Henry, the king's son, 'Hal.' "

"Yes, that's why I like it, but the nickname is also rightly used for Harold."

"Very well. Hal, then."

"Do you have a nickname?"

"It was 'Aggie' to the younger children in my family. Agnes is the name I prefer."

"Agnes," Hal said with emphasis. "It's getting cold and we need to keep our hands warm. Since I can only hold one at a time as we walk, please give me your favorite hand." After we'd walked several blocks, Hal said, "Let's walk on the other side of the street so I can hold your other hand and continue to walk on the street side, as is customary for men to do."

We repeated this ritual every four blocks as we continued our walk through the streets of the city. At the end of the evening, my sides hurt from laughing. "Hal," I said, "your childlike silliness is one of your most endearing qualities."

After finishing work the last day before Christmas vacation, I was giddy with excitement when I checked my mail and found a letter from Stanley. I held my breath as I opened it. It wasn't a Christmas card as I expected but an invitation to his wedding, March 21st.

If only he knew how cruel it is to send me a wedding invitation instead of Christmas wishes. I couldn't possibly go. I'd be a wretched mess seeing him marry Elizabeth Pierce.

I held the elegant card with both hands quivering in disbelief, tears in my eyes. Then I screamed and ripped it to shreds.

For Christmas I was going to Saltsburg to stay with Anna and keep her company since Jack was at Camp Greene in North Carolina. Hal insisted on coming to the train station with me, and as I was about to board, he slipped a little package into my hand saying, "Don't open it until Christmas."

Of course, I didn't wait until Christmas to open it. I tore the package open even before the train reached Philadelphia. It was a shell cameo brooch, a bust of Virgin Mary set in 14k gold and surrounded by split pearls. I couldn't even imagine how much it cost, but it seemed excessive. *What should I think of such a gift?*

I stayed at the Daub's cozy house on the Kiski campus with Anna, two-year-old Jack Jr., and baby Betsy.

"Jack is going to France in the spring," Anna said. "He'll be a captain in the Third Infantry."

"You must be proud of him," I replied.

Beneath Anna's feigned Christmas cheer her dread and loneliness were apparent. It was sad to see these adorable children without a father in their little broken home.

"You wrote that you won't be going to Persia," Anna said. "I can imagine it isn't at all safe to go, with the war."

"So many begged me to change my plans and wait until the war was over—Mother, friends, Teachers' College. There was word from Persia that the Kurds are killing Christians in Salmas, near one the missions."

"I've never understood why you wanted to go back and be a missionary or go to teach at a Girls' School in Persia. Life is so much better here in America. I've never had any urge to travel or live elsewhere."

"Most of us from the mission feel the need to return someday. It's hard for others to understand that Persia is our home."

"Do you think that you will ever get married?" Anna asked.

"When that will happen is a big question with all the uncertainty in the world," I replied.

Will it ever happen to me? Will I ever get married?

As I held little Betsy in my arms, I thought about marriage and having my own children. It was the first time, there at Anna's, that I had ever really considered in a positive light the possibility of living a life like hers. Anna had all the things that were meaningful to her—her babies and the joy of motherhood.

As I thought about having children and a family, strangely I thought of Hal as their gentle father. With Stanley getting married, I could no longer dream of him. But why Hal? Why not Joe?

It was there at Kiski that I realized the slow quiet victory of Hal's relentless persistence. Somehow the seeds of his love had become lodged in my unresponsive heart and, unknown to me, had taken root. I did not realize how deep the roots had grown till the flower of love just began to blossom and fill my thoughts with its fragrance.

My love for Hal was as yet a fragile thing. It certainly was nothing of the "swept off one's feet" feeling. But the opportunity to go to Persia seemed so distant in the future.

Where was my place anyway, in Persia or with Hal?

Chapter 24

WINTER/SPRING 1918

IN JANUARY, WHEN I RETURNED TO NEW YORK, I STRUG-gled with the revelation of my feelings for Hal. Since coming to America, I'd dreamed of returning to Persia, and I'd spent the past five years preparing for missionary work. Prestigious people in the missionary field, including Robert Speer, had gone out of their way to help me achieve my goal. Would people view me as selfish and unreliable to suddenly give up my devotion to missionary service? The constant internal debate with myself, the roundabout of indecision, the tug-of-war on my heart, wore me down to a point of exhaustion.

The week of January 3rd I went to the Student Volunteer Conference in Northfield, Massachusetts. There were eighteen from Columbia University going to the conference, including Dorothy Dickinson and Joe. I hoped that by immersing myself in the missionary spirit again I'd come away with a final decision about my future.

Harry Ward's talk on "Christianizing Community Life" was particularly inspiring:

"There is much need for Christianizing our communities through providing education and decent housing and improving labor conditions here in America," he said. "You need not go abroad to be a missionary."

Why, of course.

There was nothing to keep me from doing missionary work here in America, not even the horrible war. I could take up action on social issues, such as access to education for all children, improvement of housing and working conditions. There was surely enough to be done right here in America.

On Sunday, Hal joined me in Northfield, much to the astonishment of the others from Columbia. Joe ran into us during a meeting break. "Harold, what a surprise. Have you decided to devote your engineering skills to the missionary effort? The developing countries are in desperate need of good telegraph and telephone service."

"I like your suggestion about helping developing countries with communication, but my reason for attending isn't so noble," Hal replied. "This week I was in Boston for work, and I've always wanted to see Mount Hermon School."

Just then bells sounded announcing the start of the next session, and Joe drifted back toward a meeting room.

"People are naturally curious as to why you are here at the conference," I told Hal.

"The only reason is to be with you," Hal replied.

The rest of the day Hal and I attended meetings, and in the evening we walked back to the Inn over the white fields of snow. The sky was clear and moonless, with thousands of brilliantly shining stars. My heart was too full to speak, and I did not.

A week later in New York I told Hal about my new-found love for him, about my indecision and conflict.

"I do believe that I love you, Hal, but there are other things that I need to consider—my commitments to the Student Volunteers and my ambitions to return to Persia as a missionary."

"You must remember the dangers involved if you return to Persia. These days missionaries are killed by foreign soldiers as well as disease," Hal said. "Your life will be so different than the one you now know in New York. Imagine not being able to hear the symphony or see a Broadway show."

Our conversations continued that way for some long weeks, and I listened and thought about what Hal said, but I remained unconvinced that a life in New York was what I wanted.

Then, one Sunday after a walk in Central Park, Hal turned to me with his lips pressed hard together in determination. "Agnes, I think what I am about to say may help you finally make a decision." He took a deep breath. "One thing that troubles me a little is my family's history of mental illness. My brother had a nervous breakdown and was committed to a mental hospital. I wonder whether it would be wrong to knowingly have children who might be born prone to insanity."

"A serious question indeed," I responded.

"If you want to say 'no' on that account, I certainly would understand. We can always continue to be good friends."

It was rather a hard thing for him to tell me, but so honest.

"Is there any way to know with more certainty?" I asked.

"Why, yes, we can be evaluated by a psychiatrist. I know a Dr. Kenyon who could perform an assessment, but we would need to go to Davenport for the evaluation questionnaire, about an hour west of Albany."

That Friday, Hal and I took the train to Davenport and in a small office filled out questionnaires about our families' mental-health history. It reminded me of the pressure of taking the Vassar entrance exams, and I wore the bloodstone signet ring for courage. Again, the results of this examination could change my life.

We spent the night at the Worchester Inn before returning to New York, and I couldn't sleep a wink. My thoughts kept churning in my head, and I tossed and turned all night.

I hope it will be all right. I do love him.

When the papers came back, I took them to Dr. Kenyon right away.

"It is a perfectly satisfactory bill of health for both of you," she said. "That is, if this is the right man for you."

"And he is," I found myself answering. So I really told her first.

I could hardly believe it—all my thoughts of what could never be, what I thought was "impossible," actually happened. There just was no explanation except Hal's kindness and thoughtfulness, and above all his relentless persistence. At that moment, I felt a deep love for Hal, and a warming glow spread from my heart to the top of my head. "This must be God's will," I said. " 'You make known to me the path of life; in your presence there is fullness of joy; at your right hand are pleasures forevermore.' Psalm 16:11."

"Do I need to ask your mother's permission?" Hal asked.

"I'll write to her and see what she says," I replied.

It was a long letter explaining that Hal and I had become closer over the past year, and that I finally decided to say "yes" to his proposal of marriage; that is, unless she objected.

The letter from Mother came mid-March on lovely blue stationary, wishing me all her love and saying, "It has always been for you to choose."

Mother made two requests: first, that I have the wedding at their home in Pasadena, and second, to "please be kind when you tell Joe." Those last words made my heart drop into my stomach. Oh, how I dreaded telling Joe.

Hal consented to having the wedding in Pasadena, even though his family would not be able to make the trip from Boston.

"A small family wedding is all I want," I said. "August is a good time, with many of my relatives on summer vacation. Let's say August 14th."

"Then August 14th it is," Hal replied and squeezed my hand. He seemed very happy. My guess was that he was surprised I was making my commitment to getting married so concrete. In reality, August 14th was the day before Frank's wedding to Harriet. My last sweet revenge.

For some time, I did not tell anyone around New York except my closest friends, Dorothy Dickinson and "my two Margarets."

I met Dorothy for lunch in the Columbia cafeteria. "I have something I want to tell you," I said. "It's not something I will tell many people right away, so I'm asking you not to tell a soul."

Dorothy looked up and squinted at me through her pince-nez, her eyebrows lifted high. "Please tell me."

"I'm engaged."

"Goodness, what a surprise. I had wondered if you and Joe might get married after he graduates in June. I'm so hap—"

"No, it's Harold."

"Harold?" Dorothy's jaw dropped. "I never thought he had a chance."

"He has been very persuasive and persistent, and finally captured my heart. I realized that I was in love with him over Christmas."

"Agnes, I can hardly believe what I'm hearing. What about your plans for Persia?"

"When the war is over, the mission in Persia will not be the same."

"But Joe still plans to be off for Persia in a few years. I'd assumed you would go with him."

"Yes, that was a possibility before, but I've fallen in love with Hal."

Dorothy was silent for a few minutes, digesting my words, looking down at her plate. She appeared to have tears in her eyes.

"I'm sorry. I get so emotional," she said. "I have always had this vision of you and Joe on fine Persian horses riding down a dusty road in Tabriz, the perfect missionary couple. But, how silly of me. I must congratulate you."

Somehow, I could not bring myself to tell Joe quite yet. It would be such a hard conversation, with all his assumptions and expectations about my returning to Persia with him. However, after I'd told Dorothy and Margaret Darling about my engagement, I realized I'd created a complication. They went to the same F.O.R. meetings that Joe attended, and I had to ask them to promise not to tell him.

"I already fear that reappointment to my position at Teachers' College may be in jeopardy," I told them. "My radical pacifist views created friction with my pro-war colleagues. Now they might not renew the position if they know I'm getting married. I don't want anyone else to know, at least until things get settled for next year, not even Joe."

"Why are you waiting to tell Joe?" Margaret Darling asked, incredulous. "He wouldn't have any reason to tell Dean Russell. Is he your fallback in case you break off your engagement with Harold?"

"I don't think it is right not telling Joe," Dorothy said. "If you weren't my best friend, I'd tell him myself." How the looks in their eyes made me feel like a vile creature.

"I know it isn't right," I replied, "but it wouldn't be a good time for him to hear such shocking news. He's busy finishing his medical studies and needs to concentrate. I would hate to disrupt his mental composure now. After he graduates, that's when I'll tell him."

Even though I decided to marry Hal, I needed to prove to myself that marriage would not mean that I couldn't have a career. Haphazard volunteer activities, like many other married women take up, simply would not satisfy me. I needed my own work. After the wedding, I fully intended on coming back to my job at Teachers' College, if my appointment was renewed.

Another reason I was eager to continue my position was the opportunity to lead the new Student Democracy program. Initiated as a result of the Northfield Student Volunteer Conference in January, its mission was to offer citizens a chance to help build a New World after peace and to "Christianize Community Life" under the principles of Harry Ward. It had swept in six to seven hundred interested students and faculty at Columbia University alone.

In my position, I would be able to promote education for all children, influencing teachers, who would in turn influence our country's rising thought. This would be my opportunity to contribute to social reform. As part of the movement to "Christianize Community Life," I could perform missionary work in America.

When Dean Russell called me to his office, I detected a stern tone in his voice and my stomach seized, but he was only being succinct and businesslike as usual. "With the growing impossibility of your going out to Persia this coming year, we'd like to extend your appointment along with more help from an assistant," he said. "You have a week to consider the offer."

"I don't need a week," I responded. "I've already discussed this with my fiancée, and he supports my decision to continue my work here."

"Fiancée?" Dean Russell replied. "Goodness, Agnes, congratulations. But I must admit I never thought you were the marrying type. I thought you were destined to become a missionary."

"The Student Democracy program will allow me to be a missionary in America," I said proudly.

When I told Hal that I accepted the position, he responded, "My only stipulation is that you mustn't work too hard. I want you to be strong and rested. There will be added responsibilities if we soon have a little child in our new home."

Children? Good grief, I hadn't thought about having children so soon.

"I feel that it would be better not to have a child in the first year. We will only have started building our life together in our little Morningside apartment. Besides, it would not be fair to bring a helpless little life into this world of fright and horror with this war. Such distress would wring a baby's little heart."

"But I love children. When the war is over, will you change your mind?"

"Yes. I want at least four."

"Good. We'll plan for four then."

I felt I knew so little about having children, but it seemed to me that it should be thoughtfully planned, not something a girl should leap into haphazardly. I was glad Dorothy Dickinson introduced me to Margaret Sanger's "family limitation" concepts. That information would come in useful.

Being on the Executive Committee of the Woman's Peace Party brought me in contact with interesting radicals and I moved, more or less, in socialist circles. At one memorable meeting, Jane Addams, Norman Thomas, and Crystal Eastman sat at the same table with me. I can remember Crystal saying, "It's our job to maintain something over here that will be worth coming back to when the weary war is over."

"The moral erosion will be great," Norman said. "It is idle to think they'll find liberty, walking serenely among the corpses of the dead and the agonies of the dying."

"Indifference is indeed harder to fight than hostility," Jane added.

"We must fight indifference if we want democracy and freedom to live," Norman responded.

"And democracy and freedom shall live," I managed to say. "I stake my life on it. Such emotion this war has wrought on my soul."

Tears streamed down my face as they stood and chanted, "Democracy and freedom shall live."

On May 16th, Congress passed the Sedition Act making it a crime to speak against the war. It was an effort to stop the pacifist movement. Hal became very alarmed and warned me that I should be careful what meetings I attended.

"The Act is aimed at socialists, pacifists, and other anti-war activists," Hal said. "If you go to Women's Peace Party meetings, you might be arrested."

"That's silly," I had replied. "The First Amendment protects the right of free speech and assembly."

"There has been a serious change in our democratic rights," Hal said in a stern voice. "Attorney General Mitchel Palmer is intent on stifling the spread of dissent against the war effort at any cost."

"Will people be too scared to hold the peace group meetings?"

A few weeks later, the presidential candidate for the Socialist Party, Eugene Debs, was arrested in Canton, Ohio, for giving an anti-war speech, and panic spread through the peace groups.

"The Secret Service is investigating F.O.R. because they find the words 'fellowship' and 'reconciliation' to be sinister," Jane Addams told us.

"We should be safe having our small private meetings at our homes," I told our Columbia F.O.R group, "but perhaps we should avoid the larger meetings."

"I'll miss seeing Norman Thomas," Dorothy moaned.

"The Student Volunteer meetings shouldn't be objectionable to the government," I said. "It has nothing to do with the war."

"Some of the speakers who talk about social reform, like Harry Ward, might be considered controversial," Dorothy said. "The Secret Service might raid the next meeting."

I continued attending the local Student Volunteer meetings but decided not to go to the conference in Northfield.

The walls were closing in on my little life, almost imperceptibly. I felt like a wild animal trapped in a cage that kept getting smaller and smaller.

After the initial elation following my decision to marry Hal, a strange apprehension swept over me and I had difficulty sleeping. I lay in bed at night trying to imagine what married life would be like. Unsettling to me was a strange little fear in my heart about becoming Hal's wife, the fear of not being adequate. While I was confident in developing the spiritual side of our love, I was uncertain if I would be able to understand or satisfy Hal wholly on the purely physical side of our relationship.

The physical side of marriage was hard for me to grasp. I loved the joyous sense of life's energy while running in the wind or feeling the soft lapping waters against my body in the lake. But I didn't understand my sensual side other than being physically present, tasting and enjoying it.

"Ever since I had my first kiss from a man, I found that I don't care for it," I told Hal. "For that reason, it doesn't mean much for you to kiss me."

Hal was clearly surprised, but simply responded, "It means something to me to kiss you, so I will continue to do it unless you object."

I pondered why my first kiss, the kiss Howard Baskerville gave me, had permanently imprinted a dislike for kissing. It seemed that it was associated with all the pain that it had caused me; making Father angry, being sent away to America.

Hal knew I had loved once before, but he thought it was long ago with Howard Baskerville in Persia. I wondered if I should be fully open and honest and tell Hal about my feelings for Stanley Hunter. My love for Stanley was built on a glorious romantic fantasy, a lovely creation from the pain and loneliness in my heart. I found pleasure in the sheer experience of dreaming about a handsome man with a radiant face. It was the kind of love that young women have, pure romantic love, born of the stars. That "Stanley" still lived in my heart, but Stanley Hunter, the man, I never really knew at all. Hal, the man of flesh and blood, was not a distant angel of light, but the close dear friend whose life I chose to share. In the end I decided not to tell Hal about Stanley.

Although Hal knew that Joe and I were close friends since child-hood, he never realized that there was more to our relationship than that. My love for Joe would be everlasting. He was part of my soul, but it was not the same romantic love I felt for Hal. I had made my choice, but Joe would never leave my heart. Hal did not express jealousy about my relationships with other men, but I decided not to tell him about my feelings for Joe either.

With Hal's permission, I continued to go out with Joe, to our reg-ular weekend lunches and to the symphony. Those last three concerts with Joe are etched in my memory. On January 24th we heard Bach's "Brandenburg Concerto No. 2," Schubert's "Unfinished Symphony," and Dvorak's "Cello Concerto," with Pablo Casals as soloist. On February 28th there was an All Wagner concert, and on March 16th, the last concert of the season, they played Elgar's "Symphony No. 1" and Chopin's "Piano Concerto," with Josef Hofmann as soloist.

During intermission, Joe turned to me and said, "I have to remind myself that when we go back to Persia, we won't hear music like this, even if we have a gramophone. We must embed this in our hearing memories." Then he took my hand and squeezed it. When the lights dimmed, I let the tears roll down my cheeks.

When Hal gave me a diamond engagement ring, I could no longer put off telling Joe about my decision to marry Hal. *What if he noticed the ring before I told him?*

I invited Joe to lunch to celebrate his graduation from medical school and bought a blue silk scarf tie as a present. I could imagine it highlighting the color of his eyes.

Before Joe arrived at my apartment, I carefully tucked the engagement ring into my jewelry box. We took the cable car all the way down Broadway and walked to Delmonico's on Beaver Street for lunch. We both had Delmonico's signature steak, mine "au poivre" and Joe's "Oscar," along with creamed spinach and potatoes garnished with bacon and cheese. For dessert we ordered Baked Alaska to share.

Joe seemed incredibly happy and was talking away about his plans as we sipped coffee.

"I'll spend the next year and a half in residency at Columbia Hospital, then the Presbyterian Board has agreed to offer me a medical missionary position. The letter came earlier this week."

"Where will they send you?"

"They want to send me to Persia, of course, either Urmia or Tabriz, but I'll have to wait until next year to be officially assigned. Do you care either way?"

The waiter had just arrived with our Baked Alaska, and I gasped at the sight of the ice cream and meringue delight.

"What a big piece. I'll gain at least five pounds from this meal."

"You'll still be beautiful," Joe said and took a bite. "But you didn't answer my question. Do you care if we go to Urmia, or do you want to return to Tabriz?"

I stopped eating and swallowed hard.

"Joe ..." I just froze.

Joe looked at me intently, with his spoon raised in mid-air.

"Joe, I'm engaged. I'm engaged to Harold. We're going to get married."

The color of Joe's face paled and his lower lip quivered. There was a long silence. Finally, he sighed and said, "I don't know what to say."

"Joe, I always want to be your dear friend."

"I thought six months ago that you were going ahead of me to Persia. After a few years at the Girls' School in Tehran, I assumed that you would join me wherever I was assigned."

"The war ruined my cherished plans, and it changed my mind about returning to Persia."

"I can't even find words to describe how I feel. I had always thought that we ..."

"Joe, I'm sorry. I never meant to hurt you."

Our Baked Alaska melted into a miserable soup. Joe struggled to keep from crying. And I hurried the waiter with our check.

"It's my treat," I said as I reached for the leather purse Joe had given me.

It was excruciating trying to make conversation on the long cable-car ride back. I talked about how I planned to continue at Teachers' College in September and to continue to go to F.O.R meetings. It was nervous chatter from the fear and dread that was pent up inside me for days not knowing how to tell Joe.

Finally, he reached for the top of my hand and held his hand there to silence me. He let out a deep breath and turned toward me. His eyes were sad and glazed with tears, and his glasses had fogged up around the edges.

"I'll always love you, Agnes. If ever you need me, I will be there for you."

I had Joe come in before he took the cable car home and gave him his graduation present. Afterward, from my sitting room window, I watched him slowly walk through Madison Square Park to the 23rd Street Station. When he reached it, he turned and looked back toward my apartment. He just stood there for several minutes, like a marble statue. Then the cable car came, he turned and boarded, and he was gone.

The rest of the afternoon I couldn't concentrate on the book I was reading. I lay down on my bed and stared at the cracks in the plaster on the ceiling. Like the ceiling, my life had been full of fissures in logical thinking and bad choices. I thought of how much time I'd wasted swooning over Stanley Hunter, and I found myself saying, "It's all because of you, Stanley Hunter. I wish I'd never met you."

Being in no mood for company, I called Hal and told him I wasn't feeling well and preferred not to go out as planned. He was disappointed, but more concerned about my health and suspected nothing.

I opened my jewelry box and took out my diamond engagement ring, then the bloodstone ring that Howard Baskerville had given me nine years earlier. I slipped Hal's ring onto my left ring finger and Howard's on the right hand. How different they were. I loved Hal's diamond ring, with its simple gold setting and stone with many facets. As I moved my hand in the sunlight, Hal's ring radiated all the colors of the rainbow. It was decadent, a precious, costly thing that I could never wear in the streets of Persia.

On my right hand, I wore the antique bloodstone signet ring with the engraved Lamassu.

"Oh, Lamassu, the winged man-bull, the deity of Persepolis. I abducted you from Persia and perhaps I was wrong to do so, but you were a small piece of Persia that I could take with me and hold dear to my heart. You gave me the courage to take the Vassar entrance exams, protected me from comets, relieved my anxiety in tense social situations, and helped to make magical moments. All my friends admired you. If I returned to Persia, I would take you back with me. I'd take you home. Surely you would have protected me in the streets of Persia, as you protected your other wearers for perhaps hundreds of years. But I won't be returning to Persia. My decision is final now that I've told Joe. I will be marrying Hal and live in New York."

How final it all suddenly seemed. Or was it?

Chapter 25

SUMMER 1918

I₸ WASN'T UNTIL I WAS ON THE TRAIN FROM NEW YORK to Los Angeles that I started to panic about the wedding. The journey, which a year earlier had been so long and dreary, sped by, my mind pre-occupied with all the preparations that needed to be done.

I want my wedding to be perfect, a storybook wedding, like one you'd read about at the end of a romance novel.

When I arrived, I was surprised to find that Mother, Rose, and Annie were nearly finished with the wedding dress. "The dress" was an orgy of family affection; Annie put in tucks, Mother blind stitching, and Rose, our artist, added an exquisite bead design to the bodice.

"It's a work of art in white charmeuse and crepe," I exclaimed.

"Annie's been practicing Mendelssohn's 'Wedding March' all summer," Mother said. "Even the postman asked who was getting married."

"I told her long ago that if she learned to play it well enough, I'd do my part and get married," I said.

"I did learn to play it well enough," Annie exclaimed. "Now you're obligated to do your part."

"I'll try," I replied. "But I can't promise anything until the groom arrives."

Although I tried to relax, I continually questioned myself. Was I right in marrying Hal? I had nightmares, like that day long ago when Howard Baskerville asked Father for my hand in marriage. With my ear again at the keyhole of my Father's study, I heard him telling Hal, "No. It's impossible." I woke up disorientated, not knowing if I was to be married or not.

As I was making a list of people to send wedding announcements, I wondered if I should send one to Joe. I remembered how it stung when Stanley sent me his and decided it would be kinder not to. On the other hand, I took great joy in sending my wedding announcement to Frank earlier than the rest. It was sweet revenge for not being invited to his wedding to let him know that I was getting married a day before he married Harriet.

A few weeks later, a letter from Hal arrived. He was concerned about several things: the 16th Amendment, with its new income-tax measures, the state of his mother's health, and, most of all, the government's decision to take over A.T.& T. He wrote: "I wonder if you realize all that is involved, my dear Agnes. This makes things even more uncertain. Will I have a job after the government takes over A.T.& T? How will the new income taxes affect our household budget? And with all this in mind, do you think we should put off the wedding? I feel myself that it is wise enough to go ahead but wanted you to be sure. Think about it and cable me if you think we should wait."

"Oh, no," I shrieked in horror. "After all the preparations, how could he even suggest we should wait?"

I replied, saying: "Hal, come to Pasadena as planned. Alexander Bell has already agreed to let you have the time off. You could meet my family, at the very least. They have been dying to meet you. When you get here, we can talk about the issues you mention and decide then whether to go through with it or not."

The Great War added so many perplexities to our lives. Hal may have never felt sure about my commitment to our marriage and may have doubted if I would even go through with the wedding. Perhaps he even thought that when the war ended, I would suddenly change my mind and go to Persia after all.

What was exceptional about Hal was despite all the uncertainties he seemed so self-assured that things would somehow work out. Even in the midst of all that pressed so heavily upon my heart, Hal's calm and balanced perspective always helped to keep me sane. Without him close by, there were moments when my mind sought its own irrational direction and I panicked. When my self-doubts arose, I always brought myself back to one thought: *Soon he will be here and hold me in his arms.*

Finally, the day came when Hal's train was arriving from New York. The hours before he arrived dragged by and I grew irritable. The porch swing squeaked as Annie and Bobby swung back and forth. Mother clattered plates and pans as she bustled around the kitchen. Grandmother's rocking chair creaked as she knitted in the parlor and whistled a hymn off-key. It all put me on edge. *Would they like Hal?* Surely Grandmother would compare him to Joe, whom I knew she would much prefer to see me marry.

The time came for the train to arrive, and Uncle George and Aunt Ella took me down to La Grande Station in order "to identify him in the line-up." And there he was, Hal, ready to please the family in a smart gray suit and a light-blue scarf tie. We hugged and hurried to the car with his suitcase.

Mother was the first to embrace him. "Welcome to our family, Harold," she said.

"Hal," I whispered. "He likes to be called Hal."

"Oh, yes. Welcome, Hal," Mother said.

That evening in the backyard, Annie held a benefit play for the Red Cross. She'd trained the neighborhood children to entertain us. As I collected donations, Hal quickly stepped in and helped hang lanterns and place chairs. The play was a godsend as it distracted Grandmother, who had been watching Hal like a hawk since he arrived.

Later, I talked with Hal over his concerns over A.T. & T. being taken over by the government.

"In July, Congress passed a joint resolution giving the Postmaster General the right to take over wire communications," Hal said. "We don't know what this will mean to our positions."

"Regardless of what happens at A.T. & T. I will go on working," I said. "We can live simply and face hard times together."

"I don't think it would be fair to rely on your salary. I'd feel like a cadger."

"You wouldn't be a beggar to your wife. Besides, I want to be married as planned. I've put myself into it so. With everything ready it would be a fearful disappointment to the family if we called it off."

"And a disappointment to us as well," Hal said.

So, we decided to proceed with the wedding despite our doubts about the future. My family never knew about our concerns or that we almost called it off.

Rose and Annie decorated the house with California flowers and banked the fireplace with green ferns, blue plumbago, and rose asters. For the service in the parlor, they created an arch of pink roses and blue plumbago under which Hal and I were to stand. And for the festive wedding meal, they hung lanterns on the porch.

Mother invited forty guests to the wedding, mostly local friends and relatives. Father's sisters Aunt Ella and Aunt Agnes were there with their families. Cousin Lad came with his wife, Edna, and my cousin George Stewart, just arrived home from his army base, added a uniform to the wedding party.

Rose was my maid of honor, and Hal asked a former M.I.T classmate who lived close by to be his best man. I had begged Uncle Rob to perform the ceremony, as he had for my cousins in Pennsylvania, but he couldn't make the trip from Princeton. Instead Reverend James McNaughton, a former missionary in Turkey, agreed to perform the wedding service. In Father's place, Uncle Foster made a special visit from Las Encinas Sanitarium to "give away the bride."

At seven o'clock, I went upstairs to dress. Before putting on my wedding dress I stood for a moment and admired it. The dress was absolutely lovely, a monument to my family's fond affection.

When Mother came to see if I needed help, I was already dressed and preening in front of the standing mirror. "Ay bari bakh," I said in Azeri. ("Look at me.")

Mother laughed. "You're as lovely as you could be."

Annie burst into the room with a startled look on her face. "There aren't any open orange rose blossoms for your veil."

"But it's a Wilson tradition for the bride to wear a wreath of orange roses," I moaned, and tears welled up in my eyes.

"Goodness," Mother said. "I know it's a disappointment, but I'm sure there are white roses in bloom. Annie, please pick some white ones from the climbing roses on the trellis." When Annie left, Mother turned to me and said, "Since your bouquet is white roses and ice white baby's breath, the replacement will be quite acceptable."

"But I wanted everything to be perfect, like Anna's wedding."

"Yes, dear, I want everything to be perfect for your wedding day too."

Suddenly I gasped and started to sob. Mother put her arms around me. "What are you feeling dear?" she asked.

"I don't know. It's as if I'm in a daze. I'm scared, Mother."

"Do you love Hal?"

"I love Hal with all my heart and soul."

"Then what are you afraid of?"

"Not having Father's blessing."

Mother started to cry too and enveloped me in her arms. She wiped the tears from my eyes, and I wiped the tears from her cheeks.

"Aren't we a pair," Mother finally said. "Your father is here. I can feel him in my heart. And he blesses your union in marriage with Hal, just as the Father above does. 'There is no fear in love, but perfect love casts out fear.' "

"1 John 4:18."

"Father and God trust that you have made the right choice."

It was a simple "war wedding," with no display of gifts or great hilarity. Bobby stood at the door, all resplendent in new white trousers, and greeted the guests as they arrived. In the parlor, the guests assembled in a semicircle holding onto loops of rose and blue tulle. Annie, dressed in a ruffled pink organza dress, sat down at the piano and played Mendelssohn's "Wedding March." Rose preceded me down the stairs wearing a white net dress, threaded with blue ribbons and red rose buds, and carried an armful of roses and larkspur.

Hal and Uncle Foster walked in from the porch, which was my cue to proceed down the stairs. Thrills and chills ran through my body. I could feel my heart beating against my chest. I paused to take a breath and survey the wedding party, and my hand clasping the rail went numb.

Is it really happening? Am I really getting married?

Relieved upon reaching the bottom of the stairs, I latched onto Uncle Foster's arm, and he led me to the arch of pink roses and blue plumbago under which Hal was standing and smiling.

Dr. McNaughton married us, and we said our vows unprompted, not quite by the book, but what we wrote for ourselves—"I, Agnes, take thee Harold to be my wedded husband, to have and to hold from this time forth, in sickness and in health, for richer, for poorer, for better, for worse, to love, to honor and cherish, so long as we both shall live, and there do I pledge thee my troth." After which, with our rings, we said, each in turn, "With this ring I thee wed, in the name of the Father, and of the Son, and of the Holy Ghost."

Right through I kept my eyes on Hal's, and we spoke to one another from our hearts. It was only after we turned toward the crowd that I felt anxious, with Grandmother staring at us and Mother crying.

The minute it was over, Grandmother exclaimed, "Well, you both look rightly sweet."

Uncle Foster whispered in my ear, "Except for you, your Grandmother is the most beautiful woman here. She shines with the radiance of heaven in her face." Little did he know that soon she would pass there.

Sitting at the bridal table, Harold took my hand and whispered, "I never thought I would be such a lucky man."

As I ascended the stairs to dress for the train, the girls lined up below and I threw the bouquet. When Annie caught it, she squealed with excitement. "I'll be the next one to get married."

"You can only marry one of your boys," I replied. "And don't wait too long to decide which one it should be."

"But how do I decide?" she asked, scowling with consternation.

"That's a good question," I replied.

"Indeed it is," Mother added.

I dressed in a beige silk suit and feathered hat. As I looked in the mirror and adjusted the hat, I said, "Well, Agnes, you're married, for better or for worse, and deep in my heart, it feels right."

In a whirl of confetti, we rolled off in Lad's car for Los Angeles to catch the eleven-thirty train to Modesto. Two blocks away, we stopped briefly for Lad to remove a pair of shoes that Bobby had tied to the rear fender. With unexpected traffic, it took us nearly half an hour to reach the Central Train Station, twelve miles away. I fretted as Hal caressed my hand.

"We're going to miss the train," I moaned. "I wanted everything to be perfect for our honeymoon." When we arrived, the South Pacific train was still there, and I breathed a sigh of relief.

Sitting in our stateroom on our way to Modesto, the last lights of Los Angeles disappeared behind us. I sighed and said, "To think of it, we are actually married. I can hardly believe it."

"It still seems like a dream," Hal said as he took my hand, "but a nice dream. Even nicer when you remember that it almost did not happen."

"You asked me once if I knew what love is."

"And do you know now?"

"Yes. As it says in 1 Corinthians 13:4-7, 'Love is patient, love is kind. It does not envy, it does not boast, it is not proud. It is not rude, it is not self-seeking, it is not easily angered, it keeps no account of wrongs.' This is a perfect description of you, Hal."

Early the next morning the sunlight woke me. At first, I was alarmed to find a man sleeping in the bunk above me. *It's Hal, remember? You're married, husband and wife.*

Hal came down from the upper bunk and sat beside me. He kissed me lightly on the cheek, dressed, and went in search of a newspaper. It was not till our first night at the Happy Valley Inn in Yosemite that he came and stayed with me. I was not at all scared as I had been afraid that I would be, but I found it strange that one could become so intimate in so short a time.

'And man and wife were both naked and were not ashamed.' Genesis 2:25.

Our first day at Yosemite, we climbed the Yosemite Falls trail to get our bearings. The next day we hiked nineteen miles, stopping at Vernal and Nevada Falls, where we picnicked on a slab of granite over five thousand feet above the valley floor. Great trees towered overhead, and we drank the clear icy water from a tumbling stream. The next segment of our hike was a long ascent to Glacier Point, with sweeping views of towering Half Dome and massive El Capitan. To my amazement, on the sheer height of the cliff was a hotel.

"The Glacier Point Hotel was just completed this year," Hal said. "Great views, but too expensive for our budget."

We reached the Happy Valley Inn at nightfall, tired and blistered, and watched the moon rise behind the black shadow of a cliff. Suddenly, the valley, the winding river, and Half Dome were flooded with brilliant moonlight. We stood spellbound as a deer stepped out of the dark woods and its shadowy shape moved down to the stream to drink.

"It's magical here," I whispered.

Our last day at Yosemite was a quiet and restful Sunday. We read Fosdick's *The Meaning of Faith* to each other under the trees and wrote letters on the cliffs above the Happy Isles. Despite blisters, we walked eight miles for our last picnic supper beside Mirror Lake, with Half Dome reflected in the water, changing colors with the sunset.

"I wish we could stay here forever," I murmured.

"Yes, I wish that too," Hal responded. "But I don't think Mr. Bell would be happy if I used his new transcontinental telephone line to let him know I wasn't coming back to work."

From San Francisco we caught the train back to the East Coast, traveling through the wooded Sierras, across solemn stretches of the desert, and skirting the blue waters of the Great Salt Lake. The train ascended the Rockies to Tennessee Pass at 10,000 feet, descended through the towering walls of Royal Gorge, and suddenly we were in the plains of Kansas, with wheat and corn fields as far as the eye could see.

I read a passage from Fosdick to Hal. "I would rather live in a world where my life is surrounded by mystery than live in a world so small that my mind could comprehend it."

Hal took my hand and squeezed it. "There will always be something I can't comprehend about you," he said, "but that's what I love about you. You will always hold me spellbound by your mystery."

We reached New York and took possession of our new apartment at 160 Claremont Avenue. It had a kitchen with a dining area, a bathroom, and a bedroom in the back. A long hallway connected the other rooms to a sitting room with a large window facing the river, providing a sunny airiness and wondrous changing views of the Hudson River. "Our home together," I said wistfully.

Dorothy Dickinson welcomed me back and filled me in on the gossip. "On August 15th, Frank and Harriet were married, the day after you and Hal. He was upset that you beat him to it."

"Really?" I asked.

"Actually, he was highly amused at receiving the announcement of your wedding before it happened. He was sorry that he couldn't say congratulations in person. He and Harriet moved to Highland Park, Illinois, where he is now the minister of the Presbyterian Church."

"Frank moved so far away?" I exclaimed. "Will I ever see him again?"

A package arrived from the post office containing the mail that had come in my absence. There were several letters from Anna: "In April, Jack sailed with the Third Division of the American Expeditionary Forces. In July they met the Germans at the Marne River. It was their first day of combat and they won the battle. They call his Division the 'Rock of the Marne.' I'm so proud of Jack."

Having just come back from our peaceful honeymoon, it was unpleasant being reminded of the war. I could only reply that I was happy that Jack was alive and well, and I hoped for his safe return.

Although I hated everything about the war, there was an unexpected development from the war restrictions that suddenly affected all women in a revolutionary sense—the ban on corsets. The steel used for corsets was diverted to the manufacture of guns and warships. After the ban was announced, women did not dare be seen in public wearing a corset. At the time, we were simply shocked to be stripped of a customary undergarment. We did not realize that the war would result in one in the most important steps forward in the liberation of women.

Soon after we arrived in New York, a telegram came from Hal's sister in Boston: "Mother very ill." It was the Spanish flu. Then, only a month after our wedding, Grandmother became sick, and after a day's illness passed away on September 11th. As I read the telegram from Mother, Hal put his arm around me.

"I can't imagine home in Pasadena without Grandmother," I sobbed. "How happy I am she could be at our wedding and you had a chance to win her over."

After my chest stopped heaving, Hal kissed my forehead and said, "Grief is made bearable only because in the end, life must go on." And life did go on, but only tenuously.

Later that month the entire Port of New York was under quarantine when a steamer with sick passengers and sailors docked. As the epidemic spread across New York, the libraries stopped lending out books, and mail delivery and garbage removal became irregular. People avoided shaking hands, and street cleaners wore masks. City regulations were passed banning spitting, and Boy Scouts stood on corners and handed out cards to violators saying, "You are in violation of the Sanitary Code."

Desperate to find out what Joe knew about the epidemic, I invited him to meet me for lunch. It took him a few days to respond, but he did. "I'm working in a makeshift emergency room treating flu patients. I can't be away for long."

I arrived at a café near the hospital before Joe did and chose a small table in the back by a window. I wondered how Joe would greet me. We hadn't spoken for months, since I told him that Hal and I were getting married.

Joe entered without much delay and a gentle smile lit up his face. "I was running late and ran all the way here," he gasped. "How are you?"

"Well and hoping to stay that way."

While Joe took some time to peruse the menu, I had a chance to look at him unabashedly. My tall stern Joe, the epitome of devotion and commitment to the medical profession, helping people no matter what the risk to himself. How Joe reminded me of my Father and his devotion to the people of Persia, gallant and courageous.

Once the waiter took our orders and left, Joe turned to me with clear blue eyes full of intensity. "It's a vicious flu. People die of cyanosis, bluing of the skin from lack of oxygen. Pneumonia sets in very quickly, and they cough up foamy blood from their lungs, some bleeding from their nose, their ears and even their eyes. The strange thing is that people from twenty-five to forty years old are dying, not just the elderly."

"Why do the health officials keep insisting there is no reason to worry?"

"The death rates from the flu in the army camps are very high," Joe whispered. "More soldiers are dying in France from the flu than from bullets. Officials are afraid to speak out and appear that they are not fully supporting the war effort because of the Sedition Act."

"Will people continue to die from this?'

"It will eventually pass, like all influenza epidemics. Until then, if you feel at all ill, promise me that you'll contact me. I'll send home nursing to you."

"I will, Joe. You are a dear friend."

As I walked home, I shuddered at the thought of the flu patients Joe described, and I remembered what Father taught me about fear. "It is the Lord who goes before you; he will not leave you or forsake you. Do not fear or be dismayed." Deuteronomy 31:8.

Soon afterward the "ambulance" drivers started to appear; men driving horse-drawn carts down the residential streets. "Bring your dead," they called as they slowly proceeded down each street and heaped dead bodies on their carts. The flu continued its savage path of mortality until the next year, leaving over 20,000 dead in New York City.

Despite our precautions, Hal and I both became ill. Hal had a mild case and returned to work after a week. My illness was more severe and required home nursing, which Joe arranged.

I lay in bed for three weeks and, in a feverish state, had recurring nightmares of the seven bowls of God's wrath in Revelation 16:1-17.

Seven angels blew their trumpets, and each poured a different wrath on the earth:

The first angel poured fire and burnt a third of the earth's trees and vegetation. The second poured blood into the sea and destroyed a third of the sea life. The third angel poisoned a third of the fresh water, killing all the people and animals that drank it. The fourth angel cast a third of the world into darkness. The fifth angel opened a bottomless pit, unleashing a swarm of locusts that bit humans like scorpions. The sixth angel brought an army of two hundred million on horses that killed a third of mankind.

Just before the seventh angel blew its trumpet, I awoke from my nightmare, soaking with sweat. "The seventh angel brought the Spanish flu," I muttered to the nurse. "God is punishing humankind for the war."

Chapter 26

FALL 1918-1920

DURING OUR FIRST SIX MONTHS TOGETHER, I MAR-
veled at my daily discovery of things about my husband that were previously unknown to me. When we first returned to New York, Hal
was eager to go to the "HMS Pinafore" and the "Pirates of Penzance"
at the Park Theater. Later, he surprised me when he revealed that he
knew all the lyrics. For several days following the performances, he sang
them to me, occasionally accompanied by marching or dance steps. It
warmed my heart to see my husband, the electrical engineer and serious
inventor, take life lightly.

I knew that he had a sense of humor before we were married, but I'd
only experienced the tip of the iceberg. One beautiful fall afternoon we
were strolling along Riverside Park, and Hal held my right hand as he
walked next to me. Suddenly, I felt a gentle kick on my derriere. When
I looked behind me there was nobody there. As we strolled along, there
was another kick. I looked at Hal and he was grinning from ear to ear.
He had found a way to swing his right foot back behind me and kick
me as we walked. He did it again, saying "Oops."

He really could be quite silly, and I loved that part of him. No, I
loved every part of him.

On November 11, 1918, they announced the end of the Great War. "Oh, Peace," I sighed, "so marvelous to come at last."

Everyone in New York went wild, and Hal and I couldn't resist going down to Times Square to help swell the excited happy mob and cheer with the crowds. Throngs of people filled the streets, some climbing up on anything they could—lampposts, statues, and car roofs. It was the sight and sound of full celebration; wild sirens, horns and whistles, and confetti pouring from windows until bits of paper covered the sidewalks two feet deep.

The end of the war also brought back our "doughboys," who we had prayed would be spared in the fighting. Among them was Anna's husband, Jack, my cousin Dorothy's husband, Jim, and Joe's brother Andrew. Many of those drafted were not sent to Europe, including my cousin George Stewart, and, of course, Joe, who was saved by the medical student exemption.

The Paris Peace Conference was held in the Hall of Mirrors at Versailles in April 1919. The terms of peace were settled by the "Big Four"—President Wilson, British Prime Minister David Lloyd George, France's Prime Minister Georges Clemenceau, and Vittrio Orlando of Italy. A photo of the Big Four on the front page of the newspaper showed Wilson towering above the others, with his tall stature.

"Wilson had his 'Fourteen Points' translated into German and pamphlets dropped by plane to convince them to end the war," Hal said.

"It was both ingenious and effective," I commented. "He ought to win the Nobel Prize."

"But I'm afraid not everyone approves of his Fourteen Points," Hal said. "Clemenceau commented sarcastically, 'Le bon Dieu n'en avait que dix!' "

"Yes, the good Lord only had ten commandments," I retorted. "Fourteen might be excessive."

During the peace discussions, Wilson became ill with the flu and was too weak and delirious to argue his terms. The French Prime Minister saw his chance to dictate the "War Guilt Clause" and demanded German reparation for damages and the return of Alsace-Lorraine to France.

"Germany can't possibly pay the 269 billion marks asked for reparations," Hal commented. "Peace will be tenuous at best with this treaty."

"But Wilson's League of Nations will negotiate future international disagreements and ensure world peace," I said. "The world will never suffer another war like this again."

One evening at dinner Hal announced, "The Chief Engineer at A.T.& T., Bancroft Gherardi, will be away for the summer. We have the opportunity to occupy his house in Short Hills while he's gone. Would you enjoy a summer in the countryside?"

"That would be wonderful, only it would mean that we would need to learn the joys of commuting," I replied.

Practically overnight we rented our Morningside apartment and moved into the lovely Gherardi estate, which had a backyard and covered garden house. With plenty of room for overnight guests, relatives and friends from Vassar and Teachers' College thronged the estate every weekend. The most memorable social event was a reunion with the Cochran and Coan families. I looked forward to the opportunity to have Joe with us, hoping to make him feel comfortable visiting me again. My plan worked, and Joe also visited several times that summer alone. On hot summer afternoons, we sat on the porch swing together and talked like old times. Joe spoke about plays and symphony concerts he'd gone to in New York, but never mentioned who he took with him.

Dorothy Dickinson told me that one weekend she saw Joe walking with a girl who she did not recognize. "I was on the other side of the street," Dorothy said. "They turned the corner and were gone by the time I'd crossed over. I was so disappointed not being able to find out who she was."

"Joe's finishing his clinical residency this year and will be going to Persia," I said. "I hope he's not going alone."

Between January 1918 and June 1919, Congress voted five times on the Nineteenth Amendment for women's suffrage. For two years, the National Women's Party picketed the White House and challenged the Southern members of Congress who opposed it. Finally, on May 19, 1919, besieged President Wilson called a special session of Congress to come to a final vote: the Anthony Amendment passed the House 304 to 89 and the Senate 56 to 25.

Dorothy Dickinson called as soon as the results were announced. "Agnes, darling, we'll be able to vote in the 1920 election," she said. "That is, if the states ratify the amendment in time."

"Such wonderful news," I replied. "If only it hadn't taken fifty years to be passed by Congress."

"Yes, but it happened, so we need to rejoice."

"But, my ..." I started to gasp and cry.

"Why are you crying?" Dorothy asked.

"Grandmother never had a chance to rejoice," I said. "She never got a chance to vote."

In the summer of 1919, Rose received an assignment as a volunteer for Near East Relief work in Constantinople. With one week's notice, she took the first train from Los Angeles to New York. While she traveled, I hurried to sew clothes that she would take on her trip, and when she arrived, we spent three rushed days filling her trunk to the brim. I was so proud of Rose and a bit envious.

Later, when I read her letters from Constantinople, I took vicarious joy in her adventures. "I'm running a shop selling embroidery made by Armenian refugees," she wrote. "Yesterday a tall handsome young American man came in, and today when he returned, he asked me to dinner. I said 'yes,' but after he left I realized that we had not been introduced. Fortunately, before we left for dinner he told me his name, Dr. Edward Dodd."

Rose referred to the handsome young doctor as Dr. Dodd in her first letters, but his name quickly became "Ned." Her next letters were filled with their activities together.

"Ned was stationed in Urmia for the Relief Effort," she wrote, "but he came to Tabriz and led the restoration of the mission hospital. He was in our house at the mission. Can you believe it?"

I almost fainted with surprise when I opened her next letter: "Ned and I are engaged. The wedding will take place when we return to America."

"Oh, Rose. I'm so happy for you," I replied.

When we returned to our Morningside apartment in the fall, Dorothy Dickinson asked me to lunch at the Oyster Bar in Grand Central Station. "Agnes, dear, you've put on a bit of weight. A baby perhaps?"

"Sadly, no, it is just my tendency to gain and the fact that I no longer wear a corset. But now that the world is at peace, Hal and I are considering children."

"Peace is wonderful," Dorothy said and gave a little sigh. "I have something I've been dying to tell you, a bit of a surprise."

"What is it?"

"I'm engaged to George Barbour, my Scotsman." Dorothy extended her hand with a shining diamond engagement ring for me to admire. "He's finishing graduate school at Columbia."

"Oh, Dorothy, I'm so happy for you. When do you plan to have the wedding?"

"We think in May would be best, a small family wedding. But that's not the only news." Dorothy looked at me with mischievous eyes, daring me to guess.

"What?"

"We're going to China to live. George has been offered a position as Professor of Geology at Yenching University in Peking. I've applied for a position in their Religious Education Department."

"It will be quite an adventure living in China."

"I told you when it came to a husband, I wanted a more adventurous one, and I found him."

"I'm immensely happy for you, but I will miss you terribly."

"Thank you, dear friend." Dorothy opened her mouth and hesitated, then looked at me intensely with her turquoise eyes and smiled. "The other gossip you probably already know, but in case you don't, I should tell you. Joe and Bernice are getting married next spring."

"Bernice?"

"Bernice Gregg. Joe brought her several times to our weekly F.O.R. meetings this summer. She's a wholesome beauty, if ever I saw one. No wonder Joe fell head-over-heels for her. They're leaving for Persia right after the wedding."

I was speechless. *Why didn't Joe tell me?*

Dorothy cocked her head and smiled again. "I was right to tell you," she said and touched my hand lightly as my eyes became moist.

"There is joy in my heart," I said. "Yet I'm sad that my closest friends are traveling to the far edges of the globe without me."

I truly missed Dorothy Dickinson Barbour, my beautiful friend, with her keen rational logic, her sharp wit, and frank, caring advice. She wrote me long letters from China about their travels and experiences, and her husband's geological finds. "They called the ancient skeleton they dug up 'Peking Man,' " she wrote. "Quite unimaginative, I think."

"My two Margarets" also moved farther away. Margaret Darling married John Roberts and moved to Toronto, and Margaret Merriam and her husband, Talcott Fischer, transferred to San Francisco. Fortunately, Marcia and Malcolm continued to live in New Rochelle, and Buzz Howson and Mary Phillips remained single in New York. Otherwise, I would have been hopelessly lonely without old friends nearby. Hal, fond of arranging romance, introduced Mary to his colleague, James Pilliod, from A.T.&T., and, well, things went as planned.

Joe and Bernice had a small family wedding in Storm Lake, Iowa, where Bernice's family lived. I wanted to send Joe something special to remember our friendship, something dear to my heart. *But what?*

The things that I treasured most were those I'd brought with me to America from Persia ten years earlier—my book of poetry by Hafez, a copper bowl, a scarf, and the bloodstone ring that Howard Baskerville had given me. The ring was a man's signet to be worn on his little finger and Joe had always admired it. I decided that it was the perfect gift for him.

It will protect him, as it protected me.

On the day that I told Joe that I was marrying Hal, I'd tucked the ring away in my jewelry box, wrapped in the scarf, and I hadn't worn it since. After unwrapping the ring, I held the scarf to my nose. "Incense. It still smells like the bazaar." Memories of Tabriz came rushing back and tears spilled down my cheeks. One last time I touched the winged bull-man deity engraved on the ring's face. "Dear Lamassu, wish me courage, wish me good luck in the life I have chosen."

As my little package traveled on its month's journey to Persia, I tried to imagine where it might be each day, taking my own imaginary journey around the world with it. We crossed the expanse of the Atlantic by steamer and arrived in Cherbourg the first week, and then took a train to Venice, changing trains and reaching Odessa the second week. Then across the Black Sea, hoping not to be pulled to the depths by the Whirlpool of Death or gnawed on by euxine rats. After five days at sea, we reached Poti and caught our first view of Persia, the snow-capped Alborz Mountains. We hurried to catch the train to Tiflis, where a troika was waiting to take us to Julfa. Jostling in the troika along the winding mountain roads, Mount Ararat came closer into view each day. Then, crossing the Aras River, we stepped onto Persian soil. The new railroad took us from Julfa to Tabriz, and we were home.

During my long imaginary trip with the bloodstone ring, I wrote a little book that I called "Stay at Home Journeys." In my book, the matron of an orphanage tells the children stories about her travels around the world and the missionaries she meets.

"I'll read these stories to my own children someday," I said, and I sent copies to Anna and Kitten to read to their children.

Shortly before Christmas, I received a letter from Joe. "We arrived safely in Tabriz and I was welcomed by your package," Joe wrote. "The bloodstone ring has found its way home and is returned to Persia. I'll think of you often when I wear it."

"Yes, the Lamassu has returned to Persia," I murmured. "And a piece of my heart will always be there with you."

Many are the plans in a person's heart, but it is the Lord's purpose that prevails. Proverbs 19:21.

Agnes Wilson's Relatives

Rhea Family

Grandmother Rhea (Sarah Jane Foster Rhea, 1835-1918)

Grandfather Rhea (Rev. Samuel Audley Rhea, 1827-1865)

Siblings	Spouse	Children (year born)
Annie (Agnes's Mother)	Samuel Wilson (Agnes' Father)	**Agnes (1892)**, Rose (1894), Annie (1901), Bobby (1903)
Foster	unmarried	
Sophea	William Dulles*	Dorothy (1893), Edith (1897), Rhea (1900), Winslow (1904)

*William Dulles's brother was Rev. Allen Macy Dulles, who married Edith Foster. Their children are John (b 1888), the U.S. Secretary of State under Eisenhower and for whom Dulles Airport is named, Margaret (b 1889), Allen (b 1893) Director of the CIA under Eisenhower, Eleanor (b 1895) and Nataline (b 1898).

Wilson Family

Grandmother Wilson (Anna Dick Wilson, 1833-1912)

Grandfather Wilson (Andrew Wilkins Wilson, 1826-1897)

Siblings	Spouse	Children (year born)
Harry	Margaret Patton	Lad (1886), Margaret (1889)
Robert	Ellen Howard	Howard (1890), Eleanor (1892), Sarah (1894), Anne (1896), Jane (1899), Julia (1901)

Samuel (Agnes's Father)	Annie Rhea (Agnes's Mother)	**Agnes (1892)**, Rose (1894), Annie (1901), Bobby (1903)
John	unmarried	
Andrew	Bessie Sansom	Sarah (1890), Anna (1891), Gladys (1898), Ella (1900)
Ella	George Stewart, Sr.	Andrew (1892), George Jr. (1895)
Annie	Rev. Alfred Barr	Alfred Jr. (1902), Andrew (1905)
Dick	Clara Wagner	Andrew (1913)
Jennie	Robert Mullen	
Agnes	Stacy Smith	Stacy Jr. (1906), Jane (1907)

Arthur Dana Wheeler (1861-1912) and Anna Holt Wheeler (1860-1930)–Mother's best friends

They married in 1886 and lived at "Thalfried," 565 East Deerpath Road in Lake Forest, Illinois. Arthur was a successful Chicago lawyer at Williams, Holt & Wheeler and Anna Holt's father, Devillo Robert Holt, owned the Holt & Balcom logging company, and the family had a lumber camp in northern Wisconsin. Annie Dwight Rhea went to Forest Lake College with Arthur Wheeler and Anna Holt.

NOTES

EXCEPT WHERE NOTED BELOW, THE SOURCE MATERIALS for the chapters are from journals kept by Mary Agnes Wilson from 1909 to 1920:

CHAPTER 1 – PRESBYTERIAN MISSION, TABRIZ, PERSIA, 1909

Sources for the descriptions of the Presbyterian Mission, Tabriz and Howard Baskerville, and the Persian Revolution come from a letter written by Agnes Wilson in 1906, *Persian Life and Customs* by Rev. S. G. Wilson, M.A. (1895), *My Memories* by Annie Rhea Wilson (1861-1952) and the Princeton Alumni Weekly, May 9, 2007, p. 22-25. Samuel Wilson's reference to a conversation about the wedding of Cana is also documented in *Illustrations of the Bible from Persian Life* by Annie Rhea Wilson.

CHAPTER 2 – THE PERSIAN REVOLUTION 1909

Sources for Howard Baskerville and the Persian Revolution come from a letter written by Agnes Wilson July 1,1908, "The Fight for Constitutional Liberty in Persia," by Rev. S. G. Wilson, D.D., in *The Presbyterian Banner*, June 2, 1909, p 12-14, "The Second Siege of Tabriz,

Persia," by Rev. S. G. Wilson, D.D., in *The Presbyterian Banner*, June 2, 1909, p 12-14, *My Memories* by Annie Rhea Wilson (1861-1952), *The Persian Revolution 1905-1909*, by Edward G. Browne (2006), and the *Princeton Alumni Weekly*, May 9, 2007, p. 22-25.

CHAPTER 3 – TABRIZ TO ODESSA, MAY 1909

The source for descriptions of the voyage is *Persian Life and Customs* by Rev. S. G. Wilson, M.A., (1895).

CHAPTER 10 – SOPHOMORE YEAR VASSAR, 1911

Robert Speer's views on missionary service are from *Robert E. Speer: Prophet of the American Church* by John F. Piper, Jr. (2000).

CHAPTER 12 – SENIOR YEAR VASSAR, 1912

Additional sources for the train accident are *My Memories* by Annie Rhea Wilson (1861-1952) and "Derailment at Glen Loch, PA" in *Railway Age Gazette*, vol. 53, no. 23, p. 1086-1088.

CHAPTER 19 – TEACHERS' COLLEGE, SPRING 1916

Additional sources for Samuel Wilson are "Dr. Samuel Graham Wilson," by Robert M. Labaree in *The Fourth Church*, vol. 4, p. 306-307, "Samuel Graham Wilson of Persia," by Robert E. Speer in *The Mission World*, 1917, issue 7, p. 191-195, and "Death of Dr. S.G. Wilson," in *The Princeton Seminary Bulletin*, November 1916, vol. 10, no. 3, p. 29-32.

Chapter 21 Teachers' College, Spring 1917

Robert Labaree's account of the Armenian genocide is from the article "The Jihad Rampant in Persia," by Rev. Robert M. Labaree, *The New York Times*, July 1915.

Chapter 22 – Summer 1917

The sources for contradictory information on the resignation of the Wilsons from the Presbyterian Board of Foreign Missions is *My Memories* by Annie Rhea Wilson (1861-1952), "Death of Dr. S.G. Wilson," in *The Princeton Seminary Bulletin*, November 1916, vol. 10, no. 3, p. 29-32, and *The Annual Report of the Board of Foreign Missions of the Presbyterian Church of the United States of America*, 1915, p. 321, and 1916, p. 663.

Additional background material comes from the following on-line sources:

1) **Entertainment websites**
   Internet Broadway Database (IBDB) https://www.ibdb.com/
   The New York Philharmonic Archives https://archives.nyphil.org/
   The Metropolitan Opera Archives https://www.metopera.org/discover/archives/
   Charlie Chaplin movies https://www.charliechaplin.com/en/films

2) **History websites**
   https://digital.history.pcusa.org/
   https://firstworldwar.com/
   https://americanhistory.si.edu/
   https://www.history.com/

https://www.thefamouspeople.com/
3) **College websites**
Vassar College https://newspaperarchives.vassar.edu
Williams College https://alumni.williams.edu/songbook/classic-songs/

MISSIONARY FAMILIES AND FRIENDS IN TABRIZ AND URMIA, PERSIA

The Pittmans – Tabriz Mission
Rev. Charles Read Pittman (1874-1953) and Lucille Drake Pittman (1869-1956) served as religious missionaries from 1900-1941. They retired in Southern California.

The Vanneman Family – Tabriz Mission
William Summerhill Vanneman (1863-1933) and Marguerite Amy Fox Vanneman (1866-1945) were members of the Presbyterian Mission in Tabriz as medical missionaries from 1890-1933. They had three daughters, Aimie (1892), Dorothy (1894) and Irene (1896). Aimie and Dorothy graduated from Vassar in 1914, and Irene graduated from Vassar in 1918.

The Coan Family – Urmia Mission
Rev. Frederick Gaylor Coan (1859-1943) and Ida Jane Speer Coan served as religious missionaries in Urmia from 1885 to 1924. They had four children, Elizabeth (1886), Frank (1889), Katharine (1895), and Howard (1898).

The Labaree Family – Urmia Mission
Rev. Robert M. Labaree and Mary Fleming Labaree served as religious missionaries in Urmia and Tabriz from 1904 to 1916. They moved to

Chester County, Pennsylvania, where Robert became a professor at Lincoln University.

The Cochrans – Urmia Mission
Joseph Plumb Cochran, Sr., (1855-1905) and Katherine Hale Cochran (1853-1895) had seven children, Clement (1879), Heydar (adopted, 1882), Elizabeth (1883), Suviah (1889), Harrison (1890), Joseph Jr. (1892), and Andrew (1894).

Joseph Plumb Cochran, Jr. (1892-1985)
Born in Urmia to Dr. Joseph Plumb Cochran, Sr., (1855-1905) and Katherine Hale Cochran (1853-1895), he lived at the Presbyterian mission in Urmia from 1892 to 1907. He and his younger brother, Andrew, were taken to America two years after their father's death and lived with his older siblings (Clement, Elizabeth and Harrison) and the Coan family at 1732 Clinton Place in Minneapolis. In 1910, he went to Williams College and graduated in the Class of 1914. He attended Columbia College of Physicians and Surgeons and graduated with a medical degree in 1918. In 1920, he married Bernice Gregg (1890-1983) from Storm Lake, Iowa, a teacher and high school principal. They were commissioned by the Presbyterian Board of Foreign Missions and joined the mission in Urmia in 1920, and later moved to the mission in Tabriz. Their four daughters, Dorothy, Mary, Katherine "Kitty," and Jean were born in Persia. Joe and Bernice retired in 1958, after thirty-eight years of missionary service, and settled in the Sothern California.

Friends at Vassar College
Anna Graham Wilson (1892-1983) – Agnes's cousin
Born in Saltsburg, Pennsylvania, to Bessie Gladys Sansom Wilson and Andrew Wilkins Wilson, Jr., she graduated from Kiski School in 1909 and Vassar in 1913, and that summer married John Justus Daub. They

had four children, John Jr. (1915), Elizabeth "Betsy" (1916), Craig (1919), and Marcia (1925). Jack Jr. and Craig died during WWII. Jack Jr. was aboard the USS Reuben James, the first USN ship sunk in WWII, and Craig died in an airplane accident in Panama.

Mary Alice Phillips (1892-1953)
She graduated from Vassar in 1913 and returned to Highland Park, Illinois to teach at the Roycemore School in Evanston from 1913-1915. She attended Columbia University Teachers' College in 1916-1917. In 1924, she married James Pilliod, an electrical engineer at A.T.&T.

Marcia Janet Livermore (1892-1979)
Born in New York City to Emilie Livermore and Frederick Livermore, a director at the Mount Morris Bank, she lived in Rochelle Park in New Rochelle, New York. She attended Vassar (1909-1913) and Columbia Teachers' College in 1916. She married Charles Malcolm Canedy in 1917.

Helen Elizabeth "Buzz" Howson (1891-1944)
Born in New York City to Helen Howson and Hubert Howson, she lived at 489 West End Avenue, and attended Vassar from 1909-1913. She worked in her father's patent law office, Howson & Howson, after graduation. In 1932 she married Reverend Carl Michael.

Katharine Eliza "Kitten" Scribner (1891-1983)
Born in Wallingford, Vermont, to Laura Newton Scribner and Ned Scribner, she attended Vassar from 1909-1913. After graduation she returned to Proctor, Vermont, and married Sinclair Allen in 1914. They moved to 44 Oak Street and had three children, Sinclair Jr., Anna, and James.

Friends at Columbia University

Dorothy Latou Dickinson (1892-1981)

Born in Brooklyn to Dr. Robert Latou Dickinson and Sarah Truslow Dickinson, she lived at 168 Clinton Street in Brooklyn, New York, and spent summers at the Dickinson summer house, "Kakro," in West Hampton Beach, Long Island. After graduating from Columbia University, she became the Supervisor of Religious Education. In 1920, she married George Brown Barbour (1890-1977) and moved to Peking, China, where they lived until 1931. During this time, they were professors at Yenching University, and her husband was part of the geological team that discovered Peking Man. They moved to Pasadena and lived there from 1931 to 1938, then relocated to Ohio State University in Cincinnati from 1938 to 1958, where they retired. They had three sons, Hugh, Ian, and Freeland.

Dorothy published five books: *Desired Bible: Methods for increasing the effectiveness of Christian teaching in middle schools, Sunday Schools and clubs* (1926); *Making the Bible Desired* (1928); *Christian Home Education* (1932); *Working in the Church: a third grade course* (1938); and, *Living with Other People: a Christian education unit for kindergarten* (1942).

Reverend Frank Fitt (1889-1972)

Born in Limerick, Ireland, to Francis Matthew Fitt and Harriette Ann Longbottom Fitt, he came to America and graduated from Williams in the class of 1911. He attended Union Theological Seminary from 1911-1914 and was ordained in 1915. He was a Presbyterian pastor in West Orange, New Jersey, (1915-1917), Brooklyn, New York, (1917-1918), Highland Park, Illinois, (1918-1930) and Grosse Point, Michigan, (1930-1958). He married Harriet Bradley on August 15, 1918.

Reverend Stanley Armstrong Hunter (1888-1959)

Born in Orangeville, Ontario, Canada, to Reverend William Armstrong Hunter. His stepmother was Elizabeth Chambers Hunter. He attended the University of Denver (1905-1906) and graduated with a A.B. from Princeton in 1910. He worked at a Presbyterian mission in North India from 1910-1912, then attended Columbia University and Union Theological Seminary (1913-1916) and Bryn Mawr (1914-1915). He was a pastor in Brooklyn (1916), in Pittsburgh (1916-1924), and Berkeley (1924-1954), until he retired. He married Elizabeth Pierce on March 21, 1918, and had four children, Stanley Jr., William III, Charlotte, and Converse. Stanley published five books: *With the Elephants in India* (1911), *Failing a Devil Priest* (1913), *Religious Ideals of President Wilson* (1914), *Music and Religion* (1930), and *The Music of the Gospel* (1932).

Reverend Guy Chester Converse (1888-1931)

Born in Hillsdale, Michigan, to Carrie Cox Converse and Russell Converse, he attended Hillsdale College, graduating in 1910. He attended Union Theological Seminary and received an M.A. from Columbia University in 1914. He was a missionary in Japan from 1915 to 1931 and was stationed in Tokyo (1915-1917), Sendai (1917-1918), and Osaka (1919-1931). He married Bertha Harris.

Margaret Reid Merriam (1893-1977)

Born in Newburyport, Massachusetts, to Mary Helen Reid Merriam and Frank Nixon Merriam, she attended Mount Holyoke (1911-1915) and was awarded a Bardwell Fellowship to attend Columbia University (1915-1916). From 1916 to 1919, she worked for the Recreation Association in New York City. She married Ralph Talcott Fischer in 1919. They moved to Oakland, California.

Margaret Norton Darling (1892-1924)

Born in Burlington, Vermont, to Agnes Christmas Norton and Judge Charles Hial Darling, she attended Columbia University from 1914-1915 and continued to work at Teachers' College, at the Home Service Bureau, and the American Red Cross. After she married John Randall Roberts, they moved to Ontario, Canada, then to Burlington, Vermont and had a son, John Jr.

Theodore "Ted" Day Martin (1885-1979)

Born in Manti, Utah, to Matilda Work Martin and Rev. George W. Martin, he attended Union Theological Seminary from 1912 to 1915. He served in the military in France during WWI and married Marian Edsall in Utah in 1919.

MENTORS

John Dewey (1859-1952) – American philosopher, psychologist and educational reformer

Born in Burlington, Vermont, to Lucina Rich Dewey and Archibald Sprague Dewey, he attended the University of Vermont and Johns Hopkins University. He was a professor at the University of Chicago (1894-1904) and Columbia University (1904-1930). Between 1887 and 1949, he published over 34 books and articles on education, philosophy, and psychology.

Robert Elliot Speer (1867-1947) – American Presbyterian religious leader

Born in Huntingdon, Pennsylvania, to Martha Ellen McMurtrie Speer and Robert Milton Speer, he graduated from Princeton in 1889 and studied at the Princeton Theological Seminary from 1890 to 1891. He worked as the Secretary of the Presbyterian Board of Foreign Missions from 1891 to 1937 in the Presbyterian Building at 156 Fifth Avenue in New York City. From 1896-1897, he visited the missions in Persia, India, China, Korea, and Japan, and stayed at the mission in Tabriz. He married Emma Bailey and they had five children, Elliot, Margaret, Eleanor, Constance, and William. Robert and his family lived in Englewood, New Jersey, in an area known as "Missionary Ridge," due to the number of missionaries who resided there. They attended the Presbyterian church in Englewood with the Dulles family. He has over twenty-five publications on religion and the missions.

Norman Thomas (1884-1968) – Presbyterian minister, Socialist
He graduated from Princeton in 1905 and Union Theological Seminary in 1911 and was ordained as a Presbyterian minister. He joined the Socialist Party and preached against participation in WWI. He became the president of the Fellowship for Reconciliation and ran six times for president of the United States for the Socialist Party of America.

John Raleigh Mott (1865-1955) – Evangelist, activist
He was an evangelist and activist who led the Y.M.C.A and the World Student Christian Federation. He was one of the leaders of the Student Volunteer Movement. He received the Nobel Peace Prize in 1946 for his work with Protestant student organizations to promote peace.

Harry Frederick Ward, Jr. (1873-1966) – Methodist minister, activist for social reform
He graduated with a degree in philosophy and political science from Northwestern University in 1897 and was ordained a Methodist minister in 1898. He served as pastor in churches in Chicago and was outspoken for the need for social reform. He later helped found the American Civil Liberties Union (ACLU) and became its chairman from 1920 to 1940.

Billy Sunday (1962-1935) – baseball player, Christian evangelist
Born near Ames, Iowa, to William Sonnatag "Sunday" and Mary Cory
Sunday, he became an outfielder for the Chicago White Stockings
(1883-1887), the Pittsburgh Alleghenys (1888-1890), and Philadelphia
Phillies (1890). In 1891, he refused a baseball contract to work for the
YMCA and became the assistant of J. Wilbur Chapman, the most popular evangelist of the time. In 1896, he struck out on his own to give
revival and married Nell Thompson. By 1910, his revivals were held in
large cities in tents. He was known for his colloquial sermons and fre-
netic delivery, often jumping up on tables or chairs, laughing, waving
his fists, etc. His forceful preaching against alcohol also helped support
Prohibition and the passing of the 18th Amendment.

Louise Sommer Holmquist (1879-1964) – teacher, YWCA leader
She graduated in the class of 1901 from Vassar and was a teacher at
Dr. Sach's School for Girls (1901-1904). She was the Secretary and
Executive of the Department of Method and Research at the YWCA
from 1904-1924.

CPSIA information can be obtained
at www.ICGtesting.com
Printed in the USA
LVHW040941051020
667946LV00005B/653